From Fauvism to Impressionism: Albert Marquet

An exhibition from the Centre Pompidou in Paris

French curatorial team
Didier Schlumann, MNAM/Centre Georges Pompidou, Curator
Laurent Le Bon, MNAM/Centre Georges Pompidou, Curator
Merja Laukia, MNAM/Centre Georges Pompidou, Curatorial Assistant
Hervé Ingrassia, MNAM/Centre Georges Pompidou, Registrar

American curatorial team
David Setford, ArtReach International, Curator
Cynthia Duval, ArtReach International, Registrar

Exhibition circulated by ArtReach International

With catalogue contributions from
David F. Setford, ArtReach International
Laurent le Bon, Curator, MNAM/Centre Georges Pompidou
Léon Werth (1878–1955)
Didier Ottinger, Curator, MNAM/Centre Georges Pompidou
Didier Schulmann, Curator, MNAM/Centre Georges Pompidou
Michèle Paret, Wildenstein Institute, Paris

Published by ArtReach International
0442 Toner Creek Road
Basalt, CO 81621

Published for the U.S. trade for Universe Publishing
A Division of Rizzoli International Publications, Inc.
300 Park Avenue South
New York, NY 10010

Distributed to the U.S. trade by St. Martin's Press, New York

Translated by David F. Setford, ArtReach International
Designed by Kerstin Clarke Design, London, UK
Printed by Balding and Mansell, Norwich, UK

ISBN: 0-9713268-0-0

Contents

Please note

Numbers in parentheses in texts (eg., #1) refer to catalogue numbers (see pages 23–80).

All works illustrated are by Albert Marquet from the collection of the Musée national d'art moderne/CNAC unless otherwise stated.

Acknowledgements

Jean-Jacques Aillagon, President of the Centre Pompidou

It is for an exceptionally daring artistic enterprise that ArtReach International invited our participation, in proposing to reunite for the first time in one exhibition the collection of works by Albert Marquet that are to be found in the inventories of the Musée national d'art moderne.

Originally conceived when Werner Spies was director of the Museum, and today bought to fruition by his successor Alfred Pacquement, with Didier Schulmann of the Museum acting as lead curator, this delightful project is part of an ambitious initiative that the Centre chose to take which aims at the diffusion and even greater sharing of French and European culture. In this way it joins the exhibition of masterpieces from the collection of the Centre held in Tokyo in 1997, or the Miró exhibition organized in Mexico in 1998.

It is true – and I am proud of this – that in this initiative a privileged position is given to America, or more exactly the Americas, as while the USA receives this Marquet exhibition, São Paulo, Brazil, will receive the exhibition *Parade,* which covers French creation throughout the twentieth century, as seen from the permanent collection of the Centre. But it should be noted that, to preserve the exhaustive representation of our monographic North American enterprise, the selection of masterpieces sent to South America includes no work by Marquet.

Rendezvous, a striking and spectacular confrontation of the collections of the Guggenheim and the Centre, also included no works by Marquet, our American partner never having acquired any. But the essential difference between the previous great North American manifestation of the Centre Pompidou and the Marquet exhibition goes further.

As agreed with ArtReach International, which is organizing the exhibition's tour, the choice of American venues aims to reach, at museums who have selections of modern European art, a wider public than that which has already familiarized itself with the collections of the Centre via the loans that the Centre regularly grants to the big metropolitan museums. We wish to be seen by the visitors in Columbia, Fort Lauderdale, Athens, Memphis and San Antonio, so that they may discover in their hometown museum, next to a few great masterpieces of the Fauve period, the unfolding of Marquet's entire career, right up to his last painting. With him, they will visit a pre-war European landscape, following a map of rivers and coasts where the frontiers, so hermetic, nevertheless seems so blurred as they still do today, much later.

Though they all belong to the Centre Pompidou-Musée national d'art moderne, many works brought together for this exhibition are usually on deposit and exhibition in a few instances in public buildings, but in over fifty percent of cases, with other French museums. That is why I particularly want to acknowledge the generous cooperation of these museums and the sympathetic support of their curators. In addition, for their part in reuniting all these works, I want to thank the Presidency of the French Republic, the office of the Prime Minister, and those of the French Foreign Minister. Their gracious and amiable cooperation bears witness to the enthusiasm encountered in France – up to the very highest level – for this presentation of works by Albert Marquet in the United States.

An indeed, what better way to encourage discovery and knowledge of this engaging artist whose position, at the crossroads of tradition and the birth of modern art, makes him one of the most unusual of French painters?

Alfred Pacquement, Director of the Musée national d'art moderne

A museum collection devoted to the art of its time is slow to develop. Successive generations of curators and their staff must at the same time assure the continuity and consolidation of the collection, and be attentive to the schisms that younger artists impose on their elders. Public taste changes, history itself can be rewritten according to different points of view. During the century that just ended, artists pursued an erratic course, sometimes marked by stormy and unforeseeable changes, sometimes by slowly ripening mutations. The story of the great adventure of art over the last hundred years – that a major museum like the Musée national d'art moderne offers to its visitors through the story told by its permanent exhibitions – has not known an immutable royal progress marked by untouchable icons. The continued enrichment of the patrimony of the museum, the renewal of respect for and study of the art history of the 20th century, leads infallibly to reevaluations or new perspectives the effect of which can seem, to the hurried view, as so many cases of censorship. Would it have been the same in previous years with the work of Albert Marquet? Marquet was the first artist from the historic little group of Fauves to abandon the artistic scene, before Braque, Derain, van

Dongen, Dufy, Manguin, Matisse and Vlaminck. Was the destiny of his work at the Musée national d'art moderne adversely influenced by his death that took place only four days after the inauguration of the Musée national d'art moderne at its first location (the Palais de Tokyo) in June 1947? Even today, the premature disappearance of the most moderate of the Fauves – after the explosive emergence of Fauvism and its rapid self-destruction – has left no ploughed furrow in the field of the avant-garde, and his classicism is represented by only a very few paintings on the wall of the Musée national d'art moderne. The empathy shown Marquet by a small group of curators from the Musée du Louvre whose acts of generosity enriched the collection of the Musée national d'art moderne put the finishing touch, perhaps (as the judiciously chosen title of this exhibition hints) to the relegation of Marquet to the status of a late Impressionist, at sea in the modern world.

Should not the significance and the reach of the Fauves, above and beyond the noise and infatuation instigated by the firework display of colors, be measured more by the standard of a Marquet than by the genius of a Matisse? In a few tens of works reunited for the first time, the collection of the Musée national d'art moderne permits the further pursuit of the debate on the "The Sources of the Twentieth Century," a debate first opened in 1960 by my predecessor Jean Cassou.

To all those who allowed this initiative to take place, and most of all for the benevolence and understanding of the six regional museums and four eminent national institutions which have allowed their Marquets to leave for over a year, thank you.

American Museum Directors

As directors of the American art museums hosting *From Fauvism to Impressionism: Albert Marquet at the Pompidou,* we thank the President, Director and staff of the Pompidou Center in Paris for all their hard work and commitment to this project. We are delighted to be able to show this major exhibition in our museums. It is of great importance for Marquet's reputation in the United States that an institution with the standing of the Pompidou should put its time and resources into touring this collection. Marquet is truly one of the most unsung and misunderstood artists of the French modernist era – particularly in this country – and we join the Pompidou in hoping that this exhibition begins to reestablish the artist's prominence, which was lost in the many revisions of art history during the last century. This task has already begun in Europe, where to be truthful Marquet has always been rather more revered for his painterly and single-minded blend of modernism and impressionism.

In particular we would like to thank Didier Schulmann and Laurent Le Bon, of the Centre Pompidou, who have curated this exhibition, and Merja Laukia, Hervé Ingrassia and Martine Silie, also of the Pompidou, who have spearheaded the administration and tour arrangements. We would also like to thank David Setford and ArtReach International for bringing this exhibition to this country, and affording us the opportunity of hosting it at our museums. Cynthia Duval at ArtReach also provided invaluable assistance.

Finally, our various sponsors have helped us to make this exhibition a reality, giving our diverse audiences the opportunity to judge Marquet for themselves. At the Columbia Museum of Art, we would like to thank Richland County, the City of Columbia, the Cultural Council of Richland and Lexington Counties, the South Carolina Arts Commission, and Bank of America; at the Museum of Art, Fort Lauderdale, we would like to recognize the Museum of Art Exhibition Fellows; at the Georgia Museum of Art we are particularly grateful to the W. Norton Morris Charitable Foundation, and to Mr. and Mrs. Irwin Harvey; and at the McNay Art Museum we would like to thank the Elizabeth Huth Coates Exhibition Endowment. We applaud the foresight and generosity of our sponsors, and their commitment to an artist who deserves his time in the spotlight.

William B. Bodine, JR., Interim Director and Chief Curator, the Columbia Museum of Art
Kathleen Harlemann, Director, Museum of Art, Fort Lauderdale
William Underwood Eiland, Director, the Georgia Museum of Art
William J. Chiego, Director, McNay Art Museum

Albert Marquet: from Fauvism to Impressionism?

David F. Setford

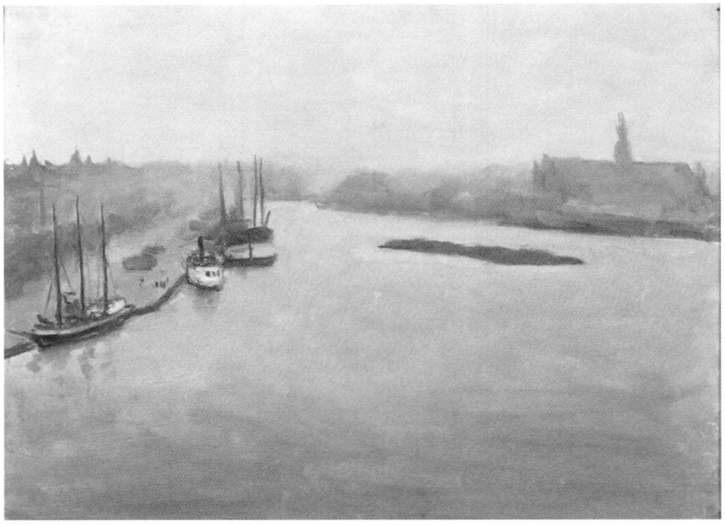

Brume à Stockholm, 1938 (#36)

Albert Marquet (1875–1947) is one of the most forgotten and neglected major artists of the twentieth century. A legend in his lifetime, he is now remembered, if at all, for his superb evocations of harbors, ports and rivers in Europe and North Africa. However, as this exhibition will demonstrate, his prints and drawings (almost Japanese in their calligraphic virtuosity), and his nudes (startling for their frankness and plasticity in an age of flat, aesthetic compositions), are also unique.

Marquet was something of an enigma. After his early years he refused to ally himself to any dominant style, preferring his own intuition, and developing a style which owed something to the compositions of Fauvism and the sensatory researches of Impressionism, but which was really and truly his own. Cubism and abstract art seem to have totally passed him by.

This exhibition begins with "Fauve" works by Marquet – but it is clear that his color schemes never reached the height of those of Braque, Derain, Vlaminck, Matisse and Dufy. Later works do indeed seem to be more "impressionistic" – yet whereas the Impressionists sought to understand the visual subtleties of atmosphere through the juxtaposition of small dabs of paint, Marquet translated light, water and land into much more solid tonal effects. For just these reasons, Marquet's is an art that from his early years seems somehow more timeless and permanent than that of his contemporaries.

The title of this exhibition is therefore simultaneously accurate, and playfully misleading in terms of traditional art historical chronology. Where it is accurate is that the exhibition does portray Marquet in a sense that is quite valid – his career did largely begin with a version of Fauvism, and it did develop into a very personal and idiosyncratic take on Impressionism.

In terms, then, of his Fauve works, Marquet's palette is more or less violent, and he was associated by bonds of friendship with some of the foremost members of the "group," in particular Matisse, Dufy, Manguin and Camoin. However, he was much less systematic in his attempt to liberate color and make it a language of its own than were, for instance, Matisse, Vlaminck and Derain. His use of color was never completely arbitrary as theirs could be. In fact, "...he chose subjects which furnished him with lively colors without the need to transpose them...This was the principal reason which led him so often to portray, like Dufy, and after Manet and Monet, streets decked out with flags."[1] Marquet seemed unable to invent violent colors which were in fact not really there, as can perhaps be sensed in is *La Plage de Fécamp*, 1906 (#10).

Marquet's color, like that of many of his contemporaries, became much more subdued after he saw the 1907 Cézanne retrospective at the *Salon d'Automne* in Paris. Under the influence of Cézanne, not only did his color

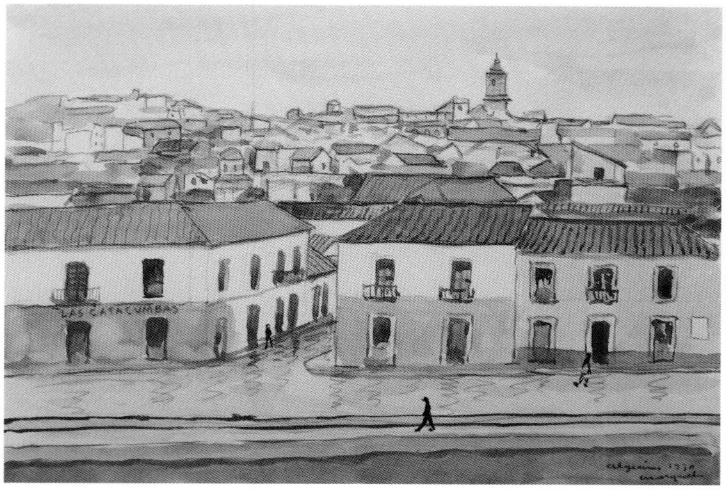

Algesiras, 1930 (#47)

become less vivid, but he also began to think more about space and the essence of the things he portrayed. Yet following the Impressionists, and in direct opposition to the Cubists, he remained concerned with reality and with effects of atmosphere. "There is no doubt," wrote Raymond Cogniat in 1972, "that Marquet, like the Impressionists, sought to understand the visual subtleties of atmosphere and to capture them on canvas."[2] But Cogniat develops the theme: "Instead of using the Impressionists' technique of an infinity of disparate brush strokes which dissolve forms, Marquet employs broad strokes which preserve the unity and larger rhythm of the landscape. In his work, sky and water are not shimmering, but have a material reality while remaining light and transparent; this space is given an almost palpable existence..."[3] Yet despite the difference in execution, which renders details to a minimum, and certainly reflects a post-Whistlerian modernist aesthetic, there is a spirit which is shared with the great Impressionist masterpieces. As one critic wrote in 1912: "...Mr. Marquet knows, with that ocular precision which characterizes him, how to condense the lesson of impressionism and to achieve in a personal conception, a work deserving to be hung next to the Cathedrals of Monet."[4]

It was in portraying landscape and water, and the human activity seen on water and land, that Marquet found the most perfect vehicle for the simultaneously realist, naturalist and modernist synthesis that was the touchstone of his art. "When the name of Marquet is pronounced one imagines water, sky and boats."[5] Indeed, scenes of ports, harbors, wharfs, jetties, seas and rivers are uppermost in our mind today when (and if) we think of Marquet. According to Jean Cassou, who speaks of Marquet's "realm of water" this predilection came from the artist's childhood. "Marquet was born near Bordeaux, which is a port, and he left it, without stopping, to paint other very diverse ports, such as Hamburg, Naples (#13), Algiers (#33), Rotterdam (#19), and Venice (#34)which is the capital of water."[6] Even when he was in Paris, it was the Seine, and its bustling quays and bridges, which attracted him, starting with the Ile St. Louis, Notre-Dame (#2) and the Quai des Grands Augustins (#7), and finishing with the Pont-Neuf (#39). Indeed, according to his biographer, for Marquet there was something special about the Seine, and it was in fact his favorite river. It appears, for instance, that Marquet would never have painted the relatively peaceful Loire, as it lacked the bustle of the Seine, and thus presented him with none of the lively interest that he craved.[7] André Dunoyer de Segonzac takes up the theme. According to him, "The Three M's were talked about incessantly at the beginning of the century, three young men noted for the independence of their art. Matisse, Marquet, Manguin...Marquet, for his extraordinary sense of observation, tied to a rare visual acuity and a love of light which he was intensely aware of, particularly the light of Paris which he expressed so admirably, all things which made him the Guardi of the River Seine." [8]

In his day, Marquet was considered at the very forefront of artistic achievement in France. Sometimes seen as "cruel" for his objectivity, or "weak" due to his seemingly delicate landscapes and seascapes, Marquet was in fact neither. Like Monet, he was the "eye," and like Cézanne he sensed the hidden basis of things. According to his wife, "The dream of Marquet was to be the invisible but ever-present witness, a witness who missed nothing and who knew, without a system or an apparent plan, how to disencumber things from that which weighed them down and deformed them, so as to arrive at their essential truth."[9]

Today, with the publication of the forthcoming Wildenstein catalogue raisonné in the near future, and with recent and forthcoming exhibitions at Lodève, São Paulo, Bilbao, St. Tropez, and Québec (as well as the five US museums on this exhibition tour), it seems timely for the first major reevaluation of Marquet's works since the 1976 retrospective at the Orangerie des Tuileries in Paris. Marquet, however, was a retiring man and would not have clamored for major shows and top art-historical billing. His hopes were simple, and unassuming. As he once said, "I know not how to write, nor to speak, only to paint and draw. Look at my work. Either I have expressed myself or I have failed. Whichever, if you do not comprehend me, by your own fault or by mine, I can do no more."[10]

---

1 Hélène Adhémar and Gilberte Martin-Méry, editors, *Le Petit Journal des Grands Expositions*, for the exhibition *Albert Marquet* (Paris: Réunion des Musées Nationaux, 1976), 1

2 Raymond Cogniat, in *Albert Marquet*, 1875–1947, catalogue for an exhibition of the same name (London: Wildenstein, 1972), 5

3 Ibid, 6

4 J.C. Holl, quoted in Adhémar et al., 3

5 Marcelle Marquet, *Albert Marquet* (Paris: Fernand Hazan, 1955), no page numbers

6 Jean Cassou quoted in Adhémar et al., 3

7 Marcelle Marquet, no page numbers

8 André Dunoyer de Segonzac in Pierre Cabane, *Henri Manguin*. Hommages de André Dunoyer de Segonzac et Charles Terasse. Souvenirs de Madame Albert Marquet et Hans R. Hahnloser (Neuchatel: Editions Ides et Calendes, 1964), 53

9 Marcelle Marquet, no page numbers

10 Ibid

French Kiss

Laurent Le Bon

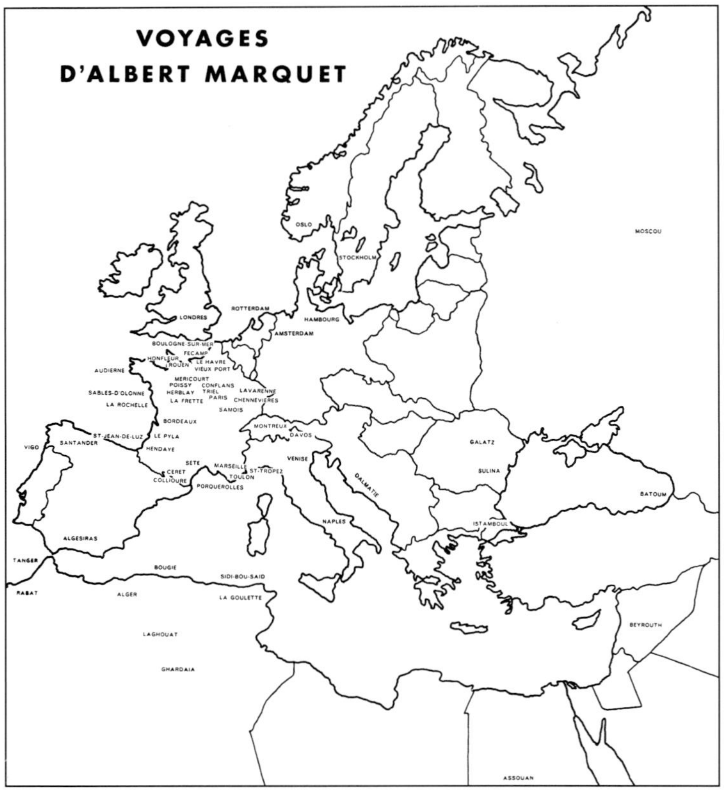

Map showing Marquet's travel destinations during his lifetime.[1]

It is definitely not by chance that this exhibition of works by Albert Marquet is being held at the same time as the exhibition in France dedicated to the *Très Singulier Vallotton* (highly singular Vallotton). As with Félix Vallotton, there is not doubt that Marquet deserves to be rediscovered and seen anew in the context of the history of art of the twentieth century. Both were mysterious and discreet men, who made nudes and landscapes, which suffered by being relegated too hastily to the classical scheme of things (an overly simplistic interpretation?). Thus as the Impressionist movement has undergone wave after wave of reevaluations and new analyses during the last twenty years, it seems a good bet that the reexamination of the painting of the early twentieth century in Europe will give rise to some surprises. Let us therefore get down to Marquet, that "anachronistic painter probably destined not to interest many, but for whom we will once again be able to affirm our love," to use the words of Didier Semin.[2]

This process can be achieved only on certain terms. Marquet's paintings are to be found mainly in storage in the great modern art museums of the world (such is the case at the Centre Pompidou). With some reticence, curators deign to exhibit a few Fauve works. "And so?" the curators would ask, "It's rather sober Fauvism." After 1908, there is no question of them showing any painting by the artist though the career of Marquet goes on for another 40 years. But it seems to be impossible to exhibit those ports and rivers that on the surface seem to ignore contemporary trends. "The painter traveled, but did not see. Yet he was the friend of Matisse! Our condolences." No space for him on the picture-rails of Paris, therein lies the terrible sanction: relegation under fire to brilliantly and flamboyantly converted French provincial museums where Marquet's paintings give great joy to visitors who see in them the paragon of modernity (Oh the beautiful sunset on the beach!); and they become the flower of the collections, unable to be lent. The worse fate: the work is sent as an ambassador for national creativity within France or abroad. Nothing like a view of Notre-Dame in the snow, for an aseptic office at the UN! In such a way, Marquet has for a long time graced the picture gallery of the Elysée Palace, a gallery created for Président Pompidou by Pierre Paulin. The danger of being sent to the ornaments of the Republic is oblivion, confusion, as nothing resembles one Marquet more than another. In the realm of palace decoration, there are also changes of taste (which lead directly to the cellars) as long as works continue to represent landscapes and flowers.

Marquet is therefore the archetype of the GAF: the *Grand Artiste Français* (Great French Artist), the prototypical artist, landscapist, the perfect subject for a monographic retrospective of the type that delights the RMN (Réunion des Musées Nationaux). Marquet was the subject of just such an enterprise in 1975 at the Orangerie; the recent Signac exhibition at the Grand Palais is an avatar of this inexhaustible torrent. Before that, many artists who were references for Marquet have been the subject of shows at the Grand Palais (Poussin, Claude, Watteau, Corot, Manet, etc.). Marquet's themes perhaps do not give themselves to a brilliant division of subjects: trees, rocks, and jetties; but in looking hard one could concentrate on river banks, beaches, ports, other rivers, with an erotic section where certain nudes could be shown. Jacques Chaban-Delmas, a consummate politician, well understood the unique place of Marquet when he brought together the collection that is featured today at the musée des Beaux-Arts in Bordeaux. He said at the time, "It was necessary for the twentieth century to come to terms with the century of light, in this town which is a little out of touch with the capital. The people of Bordeaux should be interested in more than just the quotidian. You must now come to Bordeaux to appreciate what Marquet bought to French painting."[3]

Often mistaken at the beginning of his career with the sculptor Albert Marque,[4] Albert Marquet was seen at first as a classic, the quietest in that "national tradition which found its measure in lyricism and simplicity of expression," according to Elie Faure.[5] The spirit of works by Marquet can be seen reduced in quotes from anthologies of more or less contemporary poets. Some chosen morsels:

Port de Boulogne, 1934
Ceramic tiles painted by Marquet
for his bathroom in Paris.
Musée des Beaux-Arts, Bordeaux

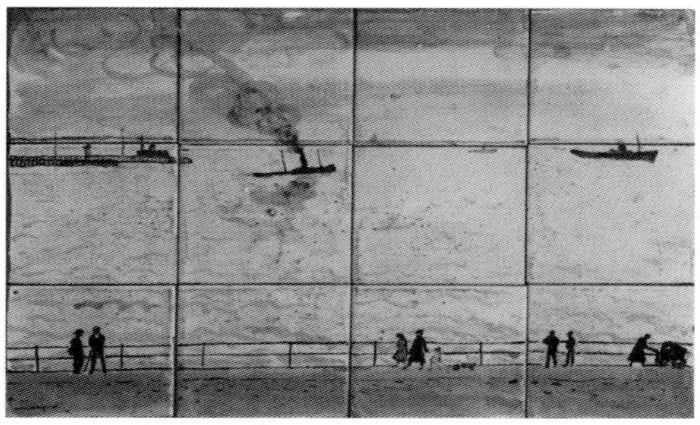

Homme libre, toujours tu chériras la mer !
La mer est ton miroir ; tu contemples ton âme
Dans le déroulement infini de sa lame,
Et ton esprit n'est pas un gouffre moins amer.[6]

Free man, always you love the sea!
The sea is your mirror; it reflects your soul
In the infinite unfolding of its roll,
Your spirit's gulf tastes just as bitterly.

Elle est retrouvée.
Quoi ? – L'Eternité.
C'est la mer allée
Avec le soleil.[7]

I have recovered it.
What? Eternity
It is the sea
Matched with the sun.

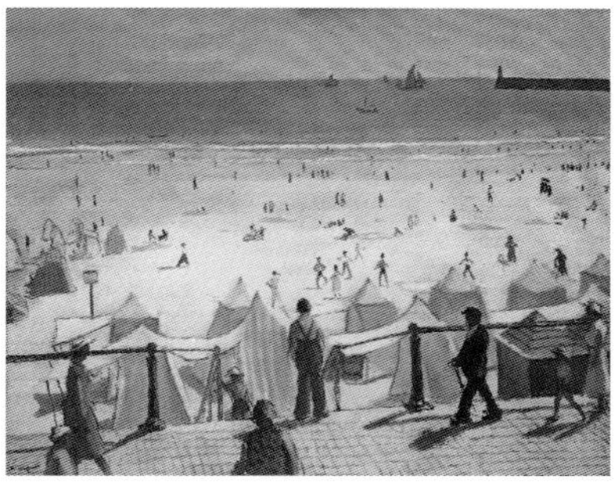

Plage des Sables-d'Olonne, 1933 (#31)

Le Pont Saint-Michel et le Quai des Grands Augustins, 1912 (#14)

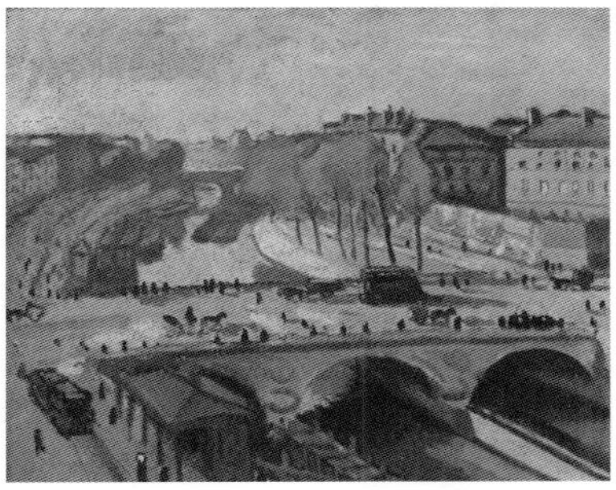

Passent les jours et passent les semaines
Ni temps passé
Ni les amours reviennent
Sous le pont Mirabeau coule la Seine[8]

The days the weeks pass beyond our ken
Neither times past
Nor loves come back again
Under the Mirabeau Bridge flows the Seine

Midi le juste y compose de feux
La mer, la mer, toujours recommencée !
Ô recompense après une pensée
Qu'un long regard sur le calme des dieux ![9]

Precise midday the sea from fire composes
The sea, the sea, forever re-begun!
What recompense after a thought is one
Look on the calm of gods the sea disposes!

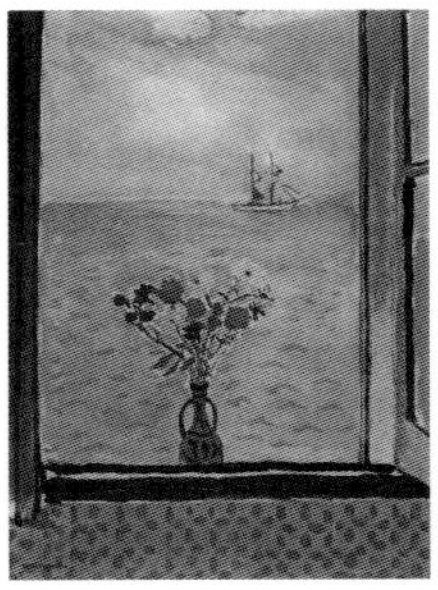

La Fenêtre à La Goulette, 1926
Musée des Beaux-Arts, Bordeaux

Le Pyla, 1935
Musée des Beaux-Arts, Bordeaux

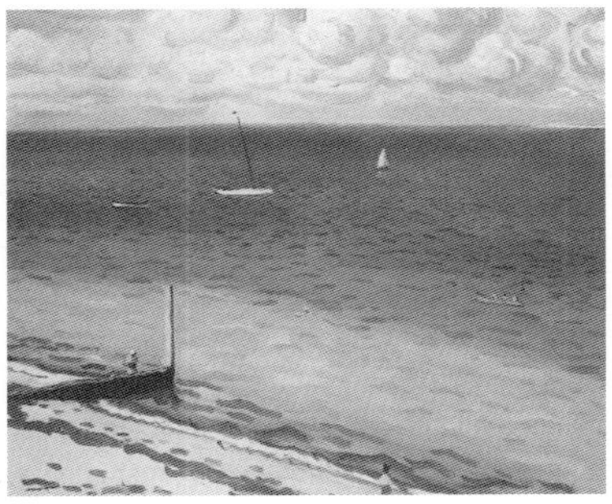

« Mer de Baal, Mer de Mammon – Mer de tout âge et de tout nom,
« Ô Mer sans âge ni raison, ô Mer sans hâte ni saison,

« Mer de Baal et de Dagon – face première de nos songes,
« Ô Mer promesse de toujours et Celle qui passe toute promesse,[10]

"Sea of Baal, Sea of Mammon – Sea of all ages and all names
"Oh Sea without age or reason, oh Sea without haste or season,

"Sea of Baal and Dagon – first side of our dreams
"Oh Sea of everlasting promise and She who permits all promise,

Marquet, the classical, can be associated with a whole series of French creative artists beginning with the film-maker Jean Renoir and the murmured message of all his films: the music of the river that does not know where it is headed, but which keeps going nonetheless. You immerse yourself in the seduction of that river. "Down with the intellect, long live the senses!" Like Robert Doisneau, the photographer, Marquet's work is a long stroll without emphasis or insistence, of a remarkable transparency with no zone of shadow or cruelty, with the "taste of eternity in the instantaneous." One can also compare his paintings and drawings with the creations of Henri Cartier-Bresson who also had a taste for travel, for *Vive la France!* and for that way of giving permanence to that which is fugitive.

Born the same year that Corot died, and dying himself the same year as Bonnard, with a pronounced taste for Balzac and Stendhal, Marquet showed an unconquerable attachment to the local, enlarged in his views of the Seine, "the only French river." His paintings evoke the work of a whole generation of French writers, starting of course with Charles-Louis Philippe (1874–1909), who sought the direct expression of feelings along with a sense of equilibrium. Satisfied with his small-time job, Philippe transposed into his novels his quotidian life in a measured and sober style. But above all, it is the generation born in the 1870s – Rolland, Gide, Claudel, Suarès, Colette, and later on Simenon and Martin du Gard – who can be interpreted by Marquet's standards. Is it by accident that the sulphury Jacques Chardonne – with his classic prose in the tradition of French moralism, nostalgic for an elegiac universe in sync with the seasons – lived until his death at La Frette, where Marquet is buried, a stone's throw from Argenteuil, the birth-place of impressionism?

Like all good classic artists, Marquet's wife Marcelle was his hagiographer, and she tells us of his difficult childhood (plain boiled lentils, eaten without bread). "He knew how to go as far as his talent would allow, and he was who he was because that was how he was."[11] Unhealthy, "...he was tied only to the essential and with such strength of purpose that nothing risked deviating him."[12] He spoke little, and rarely showed any emotion. When she asked him if he had not had enough of her constant presence, without hesitating he replied: "No, with you I can be alone."[13] A premature death opened once again for him the gilded doors of immortality, to use the words of Marc Sandoz.

His life is a long tranquil river that has allowed several art historians to concentrate on his work. "His peacefulness never descended into softness, according to one." "The pictorial matter gives an appearance of spontaneity," he continued. The virtue of his original composition is extolled, as well as the feeling of flat color with interior modulations. "The alternate stability and suppleness found in his outline is also found in his use of color." There are a few criticisms: "Efforts of interpretative imagination or chromatic invention are rare in the *oeuvre* which does not appreciably evolve. Nudes are falsely cruel and stripped of their real sensuality." But eulogies easily surpass criticism: "Without theoretical research, his painting is new, modern, and offers us a very original vision." "Nothing less than a seeker and portrayer of new plastic expressions, his originality was to show himself less imaginative, more of a subtle observer, capable of associating in his calm paintings the reality of the forms he portrayed alongside the shimmering atmosphere in which they were poeticized. He gave in less and less to the temptation of heightening his tone by adding too much of himself to the simple perfection of tangible reality, and disdained the effects of impasto and virtuosity. He used colors as they came out of the tube adding to them sometimes a little turps or oil. He took perception to a very high degree, along with the science of emphasis."[14] The final words go to Marc Sandoz - he was an "architect of space on whom were stamped the rhythms of the universe," – and to Hector Obalk – "the more the artist is personal, the less so is his style, and the more his subjects are anecdotal, the more is he metaphysical."

It is difficult to confront work at the same time so slick and so delicate. The artist traversed half the century, like the countries he visited, on automatic pilot, but towards what end? 1907, the year of the death of his mother, his first one-man show, and the Cézanne retrospective, fixed the next forty years of his career. In 1908, he set up on the banks of the Seine where soon he was communicating with Matisse through knocking on the ceiling with a broomstick, symbolizing the enormous gulf that separates Marquet's *La Fenêtre à La Goulette*, 1926,[15] from Matisse's *Porte-Fenêtre à Collioure*, 1914.[16] In 1934, he crossed the USSR curious to be acquainted with a new way of living and comforted by the welcome he was given... During the Second World War, he painted the allied flotilla in Algeria as if it was the arrival of a luxury liner...

And what if the artist of one hundred voyages revealed himself as a conceptual artist, an apostle of Land art, before its time? There is something of Richard Long in Marquet in that multiplication of voyages and experiences ending in the same type of location and thus in similar works. One could bet that the artist would have loved this American exhibition tour in towns with urban landscape so close. Naïvely put, the map of his travels bears witness to a colonial France in a bruised Europe. It seems destined for a geography textbook where in a quest without end, Marquet visits at the same time holiday resorts born of the discovery of leisure, and towns where the adventures of modern man unfold. That dichotomy is not found in his paintings. In the manner of a Niele Toroni, Marquet always uses the same technique, often the same composition. There is a lack of constraint in Marquet's method. Those visits may be long: but he always draws and paints like a man in a hurry. The paintings are often brilliant exercises in *fa presto* but always with the majestic detail of an invigorating touch of red or his signature in high color. "The means is always so simple that it is not apparent."[17] The format is always sober and even the paintings that in illustration seem atypical like the imposing portrait of *André Rouveyre*, 1904 (#5) are in fact in the same key.

As a good minimal artist, Marquet is an artist who paints in series. He is therefore in the tradition of Monet and even more of Boudin, and anticipates the steps taken by Bernd and Hilla Becher, with his marked attention for the industrial world. Each work is like a painting of Roman Opalka. We ought to have the courage to un-frame Marquet's paintings (though they would be totally at home spiritually in our little white boxes, they are often surrounded by horrible and inept wainscoting which permit a hypocritical transition with the interiors that surround them in collectors' houses) and insert them in the wall so as to create a continuity of pictorial surface (made up of flat and fluid colors) and the wall. With close hanging, it would be possible to magnify the invariable flood of the artist's production over forty years. The exception would be the ten or so fantastic nudes of the years after 1910, a parenthesis closed quickly, an impossible escape, which showed at its height Marquet's sense of seclusion. The nudes against backgrounds are like targets for a savage psychoanalyst to decode. Marcelle soon arrived in the artist's life, so the nudes disappeared.

There is a paradox in Marquet, who is rather in the tradition of the Venetian vedutists, with those diverse voyages that always took him to the same place. Those paintings with their precarious equilibrium are like so many symbols of an insatiable hunt for happiness. The passion for the sea does not refer to a "relaxed epicurism but to a serene tragedy." In these non-heroic landscapes, Marquet paints so many brief black ellipses that are as many people with indefinable destinies. A large part of his work could be dedicated to the passers-by. Marquet is the artist of the *passeggiata*. He is painting himself when he paints those people leaning outwards, as he leans out at his window. Most of all, one must not mix with that crowd, so the artist always gives himself some altitude, a mixture of disdain and timidity which led to all those plunging perspectives showered with praise by the critics. He steps back to better admire the water, the river, the sea. Descending towards the ocean then the waters muster, there is a return to undifferentiating. The river inspires both veneration and fear. It symbolizes human existence and the variety of detours (rather sober with Marquet). The water, the undifferentiated mass like Marquet's people, represents the infinity of the possible. There one draws on a new force as in an IKB of Yves Klein. The water effaces history to leave on its banks only little stories. To quote the motto of the City of Paris, *Fluctuat nec mergitur*. The precise limits (those famous edges) of each work by the artist are so many images of resolve.

Marquet was the prisoner of an aquatic microcosm, magnified in his Parisian bathroom, an incredible abyss representing all his voyages: the walls were decorated with ceramics designed by the artist representing all his destinations by the water. He no longer needed to travel. His principal path consisted of the one between bathroom and window, and back again. The silence of his life is explained. Marquet became some sort of ascetic truth-seeker, contemplating the water in all its tones, the symbol of a vanished ideal, of another France of carefree happiness, headed for tragedy. His works are sometimes like children's games, other times like derisive naval battles. His ports, beaches and other water's edges are like reductions of the world made so as to better conquer it. They are the meandering of a soul in search of itself, the philosophy of an insouciant France, a quest divided between bitterness and confidence, a gentle, nostalgic matinee about a lost world. They are a place of despair for so many. The seasons pass by. To *L'Amandier*[18] (The Almond Tree) by Bonnard, Marquet replied with the last few snowy Parisian landscapes, ultimate invitations to get back on the road. According to Bachelard, "At first there is nothing, then there is a really deep nothing, then there is a profound blue".

> « A port is a charming stop for a soul tired of the struggles of life ... there is a sort of aristocratic and mysterious pleasure for the person who no longer has curiosity or ambition, in the contemplation, high on a terrace or on elbows on the pier, of all the movements of those leaving and those returning, of those who still have the strength to want, the desire to travel, or enrich themselves. »[19]

1 *Marquet* in *La Bibliothèque des Arts:* (Lausanne: Editions Spes, 1953)

2 Didier Semin, *Postface*, in *L'Eau* (Paris: ENSBA, number 3, September 2000)

3 Jacques Chaban-Delmas, *Avant-propos*, in exhibition catalogue *Hommage à Marcelle et Albert Marquet* (Bordeaux: Galerie des Beaux-Arts, 1983)

4 Marque exhibited a sculpture in the *quattrocento* style at the *Salon d'Automne* of 1905, allowing Louis Vauxcelles to voice the criticism "Donatello among the wild beasts (*fauves*)."

5 Elie Faure, *l'Art moderne* in *Histoire de l'art* (Paris: 1921)

6 Charles Baudelaire, *L'Homme et la mer*, 1857

7 Arthur Rimbaud, *L'Eternité*, 1872

8 Guillaume Apollinaire, *Le Pont Mirabeau*, 1913

9 Paul Valéry, *Le Cimetière marin*, 1920

10 Saint-John Perse, *Amers*, 1960

11 Marcelle Marquet, *Marquet* (Paris: 1951)

12 Ibid

13 Ibid

14 Maximilien Gauthier, in *Larousse de la Peinture*

15 Musée des Beaux-Arts, Bordeaux

16 Musée national d'art moderne, Centre Georges Pompidou, Paris

17 Elie Faure, *Histoire de l'art*

18 Musée national d'art moderne, Centre Georges Pompidou, Paris

19 Charles Baudelaire, *Le Port*, 1869

Marquet

Léon Werth (1878–1955)
Originally published in Léon Werth, *Quelques Peintres* (Paris: Les Editions G. Crès et Cie, 1923), 133–139

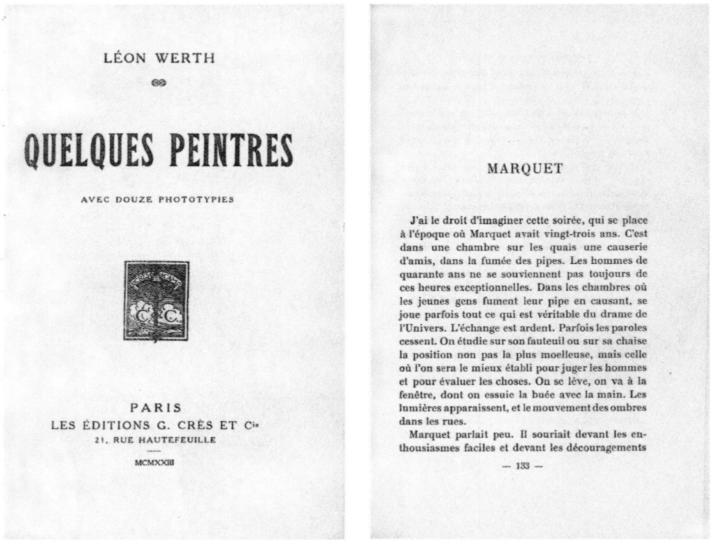
LÉON WERTH

QUELQUES PEINTRES

AVEC DOUZE PHOTOTYPIES

PARIS
LES ÉDITIONS G. CRÈS ET Cie
21, RUE HAUTEFEUILLE
MCMXXIII

MARQUET

J'ai le droit d'imaginer cette soirée, qui se place à l'époque où Marquet avait vingt-trois ans. C'est dans une chambre sur les quais une causerie d'amis, dans la fumée des pipes. Les hommes de quarante ans ne se souviennent pas toujours de ces heures exceptionnelles. Dans les chambres où les jeunes gens fument leur pipe en causant, se joue parfois tout ce qui est véritable du drame de l'Univers. L'échange est ardent. Parfois les paroles cessent. On étudie sur son fauteuil ou sur sa chaise la position non pas la plus moelleuse, mais celle où l'on sera le mieux établi pour juger les hommes et pour évaluer les choses. On se lève, on va à la fenêtre, dont on essuie la buée avec la main. Les lumières apparaissent, et le mouvement des ombres dans les rues.

Marquet parlait peu. Il souriait devant les enthousiasmes faciles et devant les découragements

— 133 —

Frontispiece and first page of Marquet essay, Léon Werth, published in *Quelques Peintres*, 1923

« I allow myself the liberty of imagining an evening gathering which may have taken place when Marquet was twenty-three years old. A discussion among friends in a room full of pipe smoke on the *quais de Paris*. Men of forty don't always remember these exceptional moments. In rooms where youngsters smoke their pipes while they chat, the real drama of the universe sometimes unrolls. The exchange becomes heated. Sometimes the words abruptly stop. From your armchair you examine not necessarily the pithiest argument, but the one that best enables you to judge men and evaluate things. You get up, go to the window, and wipe the condensation from the pane. Lights and the movement of shadows appear outside.

Marquet said little. He smiled at facile enthusiasms and hasty judgments. He silently listened to the lines of battle being established. He went to the window, and stared out. Tomorrow he would paint.

Marquet, like everyone else, has heard it said that truth exists in classicism, or with the Japanese, or with Corot. Marquet only smiles. He paints.

Firstly he painted landscapes and towns. To begin with, nature for him was Paris. He was not misled by the bustle of the town or the convulsions of its inhabitants. His first paintings were often tragic or sad, and we think of walks at dusk on the *quais*, at glances at the Seine and the town, when the *bouquinistes* shacks are a prop to take a breather rather than an opportunity to rummage through old books. But the backdrop to the drama is atmosphere and the actors are the perspective of the *quais*, the parapets, the facades of houses, the trees, and the silhouettes of passing things – omnibuses, cars and people. The apocalyptic mass of an omnibus, the exhausted effort of a horse pulling a delivery van, the businessman going to work – all are equally inhabitants of this town. Marquet gave to each one the place he deserved. Trees are sickly and puny rather than sumptuous. Marquet assigns them their place with no sense of pity. Facades have faces which perspective indefinitely elongates. But Marquet's feeling knows equally well the line of a parapet or the cruel enslavement of the Seine between its banks. The Seine was clearly a part of it, it is there in the faces of men, and it is not its dignity as a river that must be painted, rather its actual passing. The atmosphere of Paris, which Marquet shows sad or happy, neither is that his favorite. Marquet is not here to amuse us with tricks of light.

The quai Saint-Michel in the fog is a game of mists and smokes, but a precise game in which Marquet neither looses nor disperses himself. The same quai Saint-Michel in the rain, Notre-Dame, those passers-by under their umbrellas who go who knows where, the youngster going to school, the grocers van pulled by a donkey, these are only elements of a grand view which Marquet made his own. "Seine with yellowish mud, *bateaux-lavoirs*, I have you, you are mine. As for you, donkey, I am not St. Francis of Assisi, I am Albert Marquet." Nothing is touching in Marquet's paintings, like the double state that they express: an appetite for seizing the essence of things, rapid and decisive, a perfect equilibrium after victory.

In many earlier paintings (roofs and greenery, paintings of Notre-Dame), Marquet is less avid to seize the essential and to fix it with a melancholic precision. He waits a little more. He enjoys the charm of matter both heavy and transparent. He coolly indulges himself. His more recent paintings show an encroaching certainty of execution. There are those who reproach Marquet and complain that the paintings do not vibrate more perceptibly. I think on the contrary that Marquet wants to take to its very limit this certainty. Then maybe he will return uneasy and indecisive when he confronts new emotions.

I would like to speak for a long time about Marquet's drawings. With one single stroke, he raises the sail of a boat. That raised sail speaks volumes about his strength. His palms and his ferns seem, by the grace of their execution, to be related to the plants drawn by the Japanese. But never have I sensed better than in front of a Marquet drawing the grandeur of our European tradition. The line of a Japanese artist, describing a subtle and charming play of nuances, nevertheless remains abstract and quotidian. It does not reveal to us that emotion of victory that accompanies an act of thought. The most audacious Japanese innovations retain the coldness of a repeated rite, the poverty of a cold chased line. With the great Europeans, the style is the man. Marquet's style is Marquet himself.

I am imagining the gallery in a museum where visitors will pass in front of his paintings. They will go up to a painting and say, "Ah! It's a Marquet..." Sometimes a quiet visitor will push himself to understand and appreciate. He will discover the man who was Marquet. He will be able to sense him in front of the townscapes and the female nudes. He will compare himself to Marquet, he will have found a friend. Maybe he will keep quiet about the whole experience, so as not to be teased.

Critics will write: "This art, it represents a whole *époque*, the *époque* of towns where industrial society was just beginning, where docks, factories and bridges were being built. A painter could therefore paint the barges of the Seine. For the spectacle was a picturesque one. It was a question of showing the battle between the old and the new. So close to Notre-Dame stood mechanical cranes. There was the mist of the Ile-de-France, and the smoke of the factories. Nothing could have given greater inspiration to an artist. Today, smoke-consuming machines have devoured the heavy floating clouds of smoke, the pretty plumes from boats and factories. The world is no longer a spectacle. Today's life is without beauty. That is why we should indulge our artists, even if they are not equal to Marquet..." And, commentating on Marquet's nudes, critics will find good reason to show that men of the 24th century can no longer be moved by the female form.

When I look at a landscape by Marquet, I am seized by an astonishing hesitation. Is it the agile sign of a little hunchback who suffered throughout his life? Is it the unmistakable mark of a giant who speaks firmly and marches straight ahead? Marquet's force is so certain that he seems sometimes to renounce it. Or maybe he chooses just not to show it. He does not leap up with outstretched arms, he does not cry "From strength to strength..." Many painters are boastful in their paintings and self-consciously require us to indulge in a commentary. A painting by Marquet, on the other hand, imposes silence upon us.

Marquet paints the essential, and does not pretend to paint the essence. He chooses, and does not attempt to abstract things. He knows that the certainties of painting are no more those of geometry than those of photography. He has simply taken his vocation to be a painter. He does not paint in categories of color.

How lovely is that force that does not strain to bound ahead, that force which works quietly and which is not purely for show. Marquet's landscapes are dramatic, because he is never a tragedian. Our hero never seeks drama, which is grotesque, but is a surgeon, who is caring. Precision and real need suffice. No effusion, no sentimentalism, no theories, which are for the spirit what sentimentalism is for the heart.

Marquet's nudes are like unimpeachable witness accounts. Marquet is not distrustful, but neither is he a dupe. Those who found him ferocious did not understand that he distrusted facile drunkenness. His sensuality is not mysticism. Is there other homage than attention?

For what obscure reasons does he make us think of Corot? And spiritually he is closer to Cézanne than many pupils of Cézanne who make variations on the theme of the master like so many pianists. It is by his attentiveness and his religion of the real that Marquet escapes a mundane vision. That escape constitutes a true dream.

I know a master about whom, in centuries to come, men will make stupid statements. And I can, if I so desire, sit down with him on the terrace of a *café* and absorb with him the reality of a Paris street. »

Léon Werth was born in Remiremont in 1878. What independence of spirit is manifest in his writings? A virulent antimilitarism can be seen in *Clavel soldat* (The Soldier Clavel) published in 1919. *Cochinchine* (Cochin China) published in 1926 promotes an anti colonialism that even today engenders lively polemics. Very early on Werth denounced Stalin even though he is considered left wing. He frightened publishers who feared that "this fierce independent" would not be supported by the press. In 1931, visiting friends, he met Antoine de Saint-Exupéry. The two men who seemed divided by everything became very great friends, and in 1943 "Tonio" dedicated *Le Petit Prince* to Werth. Léon Werth died in Paris on December 13, 1955.

Albert Marquet – Wharfs and Whores

Didier Ottinger

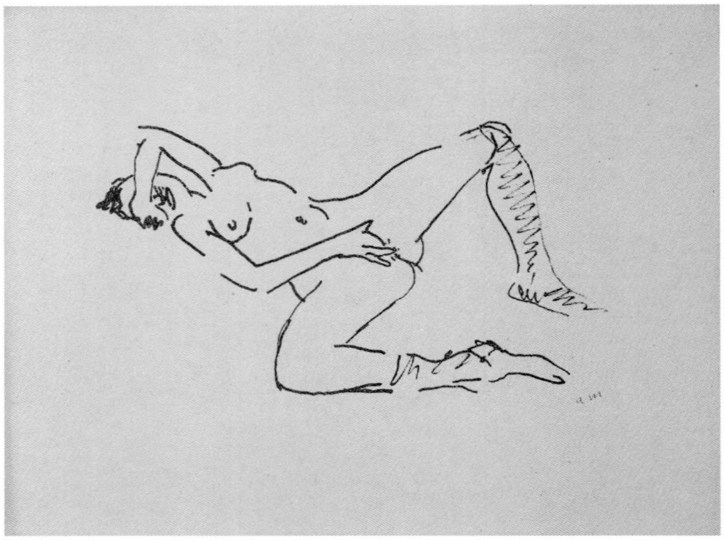

L'Académie des Dames, Musée Fabre, Montpellier

That the first painting in the chronicle of modern art is the image of a prostitute cannot pass for mere chance. *Olympia*, 1863, by Edouard Manet (Musée d'Orsay, Paris), is the perfect emblem for an aesthetic open to fantasy and desire, the standard of an art dedicated to the presentation of the plain truth. Speaking of another work, André Malraux described the nature of modernity that he associated with the sovereign affirmation of subjectivity: "For Manet to paint the portrait of Clemenceau, he had to resolve to dare to be everything, leaving Clemenceau as practically nothing."[1]

With Malraux's formula as a point of departure, let us retain the fact that modernity instills a new relationship between the painter and the world, one that is passionate and compulsive. Modern painting turns the canvas into an area where the real and the subjective clash; it opens on the world the floodgates of fantasy and irrationality. This modernity had its "primitives": Cézanne and Van Gogh. The former defined himself for a while as an artist in terms of being *couillard*, or "ballsy."[2] He made paintings in which he expressed his erotic fantasies. He portrayed rapes, abductions and immodest Venuses. He covered the real with a thick and muddy crust. Van Gogh (on the other hand) transposed onto his canvases a psychology which Hollywood has judiciously labeled "passionate" – twisted, deforming motifs, giving them the colors of his own madness. Expressionism is really a modern phenomenon. Fauvism, in which Marquet participated, is from that point of view a new episode in this subjectivisation of the real.

After its "primitivism," modernity began its classic phase. Cézanne once again showed the way. For a whole generation of painters (including Marquet), the visit to the Cézanne retrospective at the *Salon d'Automne* in 1907 was a road to Damascus. All remained fascinated by the titanic effort made by the master of Aix to supersede the obsessions of his youth, and to found instead an art based on a new equilibrium. Bowled over by the revelation, Braque, Dufy and Derain took the road to Estaque, renounced the incandescence of Fauvism, and adopted the greens and ochres of Cézanne. Almost immediately, Cubism appeared, of which Carl Einstein said, "...the motif is no longer an objective thing, separated from the viewer, but is now a thing which participates fully with the viewer."[3]

Marquet was born of this mutation. Everything prepared him for the lessons of Cézanne – his Fauvism was circumstantial. In reply to the exaltation given to paintings by Dufy, with whom he worked in Le Havre in 1906, and to heighten the colors in his paintings, he hit upon the pretext of flag bedecked streets on the occasion of the French national holiday, the 14th of July. His Fauvism literally resembles marquetry; whether showing posters at Trouville, or tri-colored flags at Le Havre, his work remained bound by an

L'Académie des Dames,
Musée Fabre,
Montpellier

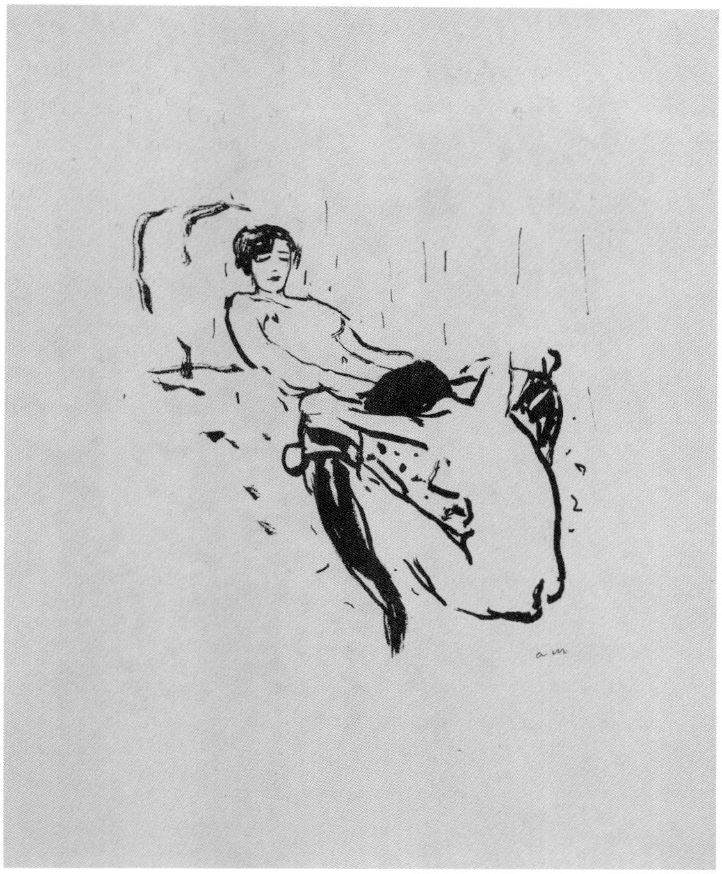

almost crystalline sense of geometry. Like Cézanne, Marquet learned from Poussin his sense of volumes, and of skillfully arranged compositional hierarchies. As was the case for the Fauves and the future Cubists, the retrospective of 1907 delineated the direction he was to travel.

On the example of the Cubists (whose speculations on the representation of space accompanied a reduction in colors used until brown was dominant), for a while Marquet painted works with somber gray-brown harmonies (see *Notre-Dame en Hiver*, 1908, Pushkin Museum, Moscow). For him also the central question became that of evoking space in new and simplified ways.

What remained of the bellowing of the Fauve years in his post-1908 works? Exquisite nudes, which with Marquet are the most visible side of a fever that is hidden behind a mask of respectability. From 1909 to 1913, Marquet painted a series of nudes that are striking in their realist leanings and their plasticity. They reveal a vigor and a force that the contemporary and dangerous liaison between Louis XV commodes and Marquet paintings tends to deny. His nudes exert an almost animal presence and energy. They exude the full memory of *Olympia*. The *Nu au divan*, 1912 (#17) startles with its frank insolence, the very same insolence which revolted the first viewers of Manet's masterpiece. The model wears around her neck the black ribbon, proof for her detractors of her scandalous profession. *Les deux amies*, 1912 (#15), painted the same year, brings us precise details of the nature of the work of the models. They have escaped from the *Académie des Dames*, the collection of lithographs by Marquet that concentrated on Sapphic love. Who remembers today that Marquet became such a specialist in the world of these 'girls of pleasure?'

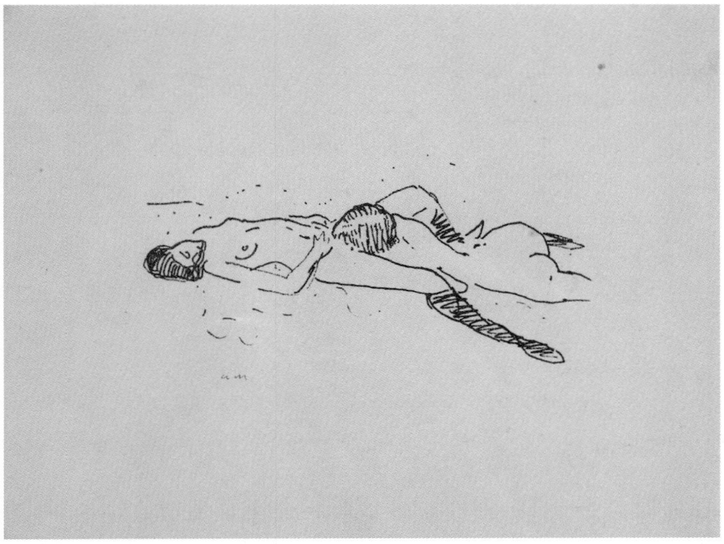

L'Académie des Dames, Musée Fabre, Montpellier

In 1903, the writer Charles-Louis Philippe who Marquet "...frequented with fair assiduity"[4] according to his biographer, was looking for an artist capable of conceiving drawings for an illustrated edition of his *Bubu de Montparnasse*. The work aimed to be a "documentary novel" where, the author tells us, "...one would see the process by which a young worker became a prostitute." Philippe, who was close to anarchist circles, wanted his novel to constitute a charge against society. "(Bubu) had worked at first, then had understood that workers who spend their lives worrying and suffering are dupes.[5] A convinced Nietzschean, Philippe described the world of "girls" and gigolos, without bringing even a suspicion of moral judgment. He decided that Marquet was, for his novel *Bubu*, the perfect illustrator – an image of Marquet that does not exactly gel with the gentle image of the painter left to us by posterity.

Nevertheless, after the war the painter manifested traces of a personal anarchism. Several times he rejected the Légion d'honneur. When the Institut Français proposed to elect him to their midst, he exploded: "The Ecole des Beaux-Arts... if I had any power, I would close it down without the least hesitation... What a peculiar idea of theirs to want me to get togged up as a messenger-boy!"[6] In her biography of the painter, Marcelle Marquet reported that the anarchist and amoral Philippe remembered Marquet's "cruelty." An anecdote, reported by Matisse, gives us an idea of this facet of Marquet's character. At a certain moment, Matisse was overwhelmed by the death of a certain Evenpöel. Marquet arrived. "What is the matter," he asked. "Evenpöel is dead, old chap." "Well," replied Marquet, "If people did not die, they would have to be killed."[7]

In Marquet's nudes there is a lingering suspicion of his "cruelty." With their realism, pushed close to absolute truth – see *La femme blonde*, 1919

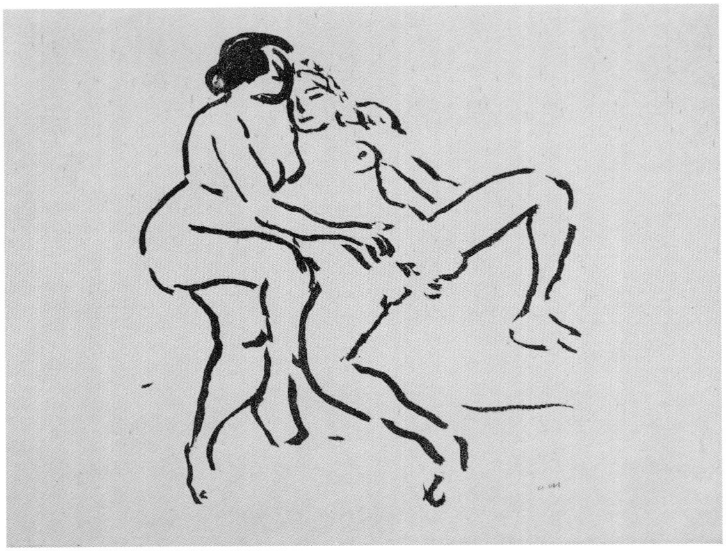

L'Académie des Dames,
Musée Fabre,
Montpellier

(#23) – and their dry and precise drawing, they are precursors of the artists of the German New Objectivity – artists such as George Grosz, Otto Dix, and Christian Schad, for whom realism was the most effective of political weapons.

These works are striking first of all for their plasticity. Marquet does not use any effects to exalt the plain forms and the salient volumes. He uses raking light, and poses models against flat backgrounds the better to outline their forms. Matisse at the same time was painting figures denuded of all modeling; his nudes for *La Danse*, 1910 (Hermitage, St. Petersburg), for example, are as flat as the figures on playing cards. The plasticity to which Marquet adhered has a history. Adolf von Hildebrand (1847–1921) published in 1839 *The problem of form in plastic art*, in which he contrasted the "tactile vision" (close-up and fragmentary) with the "artistic vision" (from a distance and synthetic), which is defined as purely artistic. Right up until Clement Greenberg, the condemnation of the "tactile vision" (seen often in Marquet, and opposed for instance with that of Matisse) only grew stronger. This "tactile vision" became equated with sensual vice, an eroticism that renders it suspect to all thoughts of purification of art. It was only when Marxism and its consubstantial materialism took the gloss off aestheticism, that the tactile vision was finally re-evaluated. For Henri Focillon, form is not "a thing in itself" but engenders "both the tactile and the visual."[8]

What remains of the "ballsy" and "cruel" Marquet in his apparently delicate landscapes? Their very plasticity is "ballsy", its frankness distancing them from aesthetically purified flat works, the works of his contemporaries. No less "ballsy" is his attachment to the real and the banal, to the most stereotyped of motifs, and their reference to Monet[9], that "pure eye", voluntarily immersed in the confusion of the senses. Cruel is their realism without concession, their authority, their insolence, and their apparent freedom of execution.

Matisse saw in Marquet a French Hokusai. He was fascinated by the speed of his brush, by his ability to seize a gesture, a movement, the psychology of a distant silhouette. That dazzling vision, that cavalier handling of the brush prevalent in his landscapes, where there never seems to be any doubts or second thoughts: that precision, that rapidity, links Marquet with Manet. The painter of *Olympia* once declared to Antonin Proust, "There is only one truth. Do at the first attempt what you see. When it works, it works. When it does not, start again. All the rest is bluff."[10] The sovereign authority of Manet's painting haunts the work of Marquet. Each of his fishermen on the bay of Naples, each of his barges on the Seine, imply the memory of Manet's *Départ du vapeur de Folkestone*, 1868 (Philadelphia Museum of Art). Each portrait – that of *André Rouveyre*, 1904 (#5), and that of the *Sergent de la coloniale*, 1906 (Musée des Beaux-Arts, Bordeaux) – are reminiscent of *Le Fifre*, 1866 (Musée d'Orsay, Paris) or the *Portrait de Clemenceau*, 1879 (Musée d'Orsay, Paris) painted by Manet.

Marquet, the one-time Fauve, the secret *couillard*, never forgot the seventeenth century painters that Gustave Moreau (his teacher) told him to copy in the Louvre. Son of the Impressionists, contemporary of the Cubists, witness to the re-reading of Cézanne, he balanced in his work rigor and naivety. Order and sensation are in equilibrium, as in Cézanne, in a continual dialogue. "When I begin a painting, I do not know how I will finish it."[11] "To paint like a child without forgetting Poussin: that is the ambition of Marquet. (Children) are lost in the day where they know that a house has a roof, a door, a window. That is what one must progress past so as to continue."[12]

Under the provocative gaze of *Olympia*, modern artists tackled this impossible dialectic between knowing and forgetting. Marquet managed this by re-creating Lorrain from nature.

1 Quoted by Georges Bataille, *Manet* in *Oeuvres complètes* (Paris: Gallimard, 1979), Tome IX, 161
2 The French phrase that Cézanne used about his early works was "*une couillarde*." *Couillard* is even today a slightly *risqué* word in French, and encompasses the testicular reference, along with overtones of a coarse and "ostentatious virility". See Lawrence Gowing, *The Early Works of Cézanne*, in the exhibition catalogue Lawrence Gowing, *Cézanne: The Early Years* (Washington DC, and New York: National Gallery of Art in association with Harry N. Abrams, 1988), 10
3 Carl Einstein, *Notes sur le cubisme* (Documents, no. 3, June 1929), 153
4 Marcelle Marquet, *Marquet* (Paris: Robert Laffont, 1951), 22
5 Charles-Louis Philippe, *Bubu de Montparnasse* (Paris: Albin Michel, 1958), 49–50 (first edition 1905)
6 Quoted in Marcelle Marquet, 183
7 Reported in Marcelle Marquet, 37
8 Henri Focillon, *La Vie des formes* (Paris: Editions Maspero, 1920), 72
9 See *Jour de soleil à Paris*, *Le Quai du Louvre* (Pushkin Museum, Moscow), in which the misty evocation of the sun evokes irresistibly Monet's *Impression, soleil couchant*.
10 Quoted by Georges Bataille, *Manet* in *Oeuvres complètes* (Paris: Gallimard, 1979), Tome IX, 116
11 Albert Marquet, cited in Marcelle Marquet, 105
12 Ibid

The Marquet Affair

Didier Schulmann

« Only details returned to the commissioner's mind, as he watched the traffic from the Pont Saint-Michel. A string of barges passed under the bridge, pulled by a tug-boat with an enormous clover-leaf painted on its smoke-stack. The pink sky was tinged with blue, the leaves on the trees were of a still-tender green, and the birds sang to beat the band. » Georges Simenon, *La folle de Maigret*

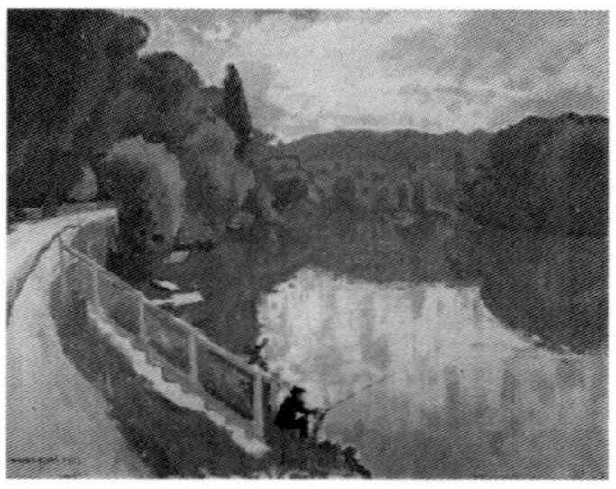

Bords de rivière, 1913 (#18)
Purchased, 1913

One is always best served by oneself. How one earth, by what feat of intuition, did Albert Marquet realize so readily that the best supplier to a museum of the works of any artist is...the artist himself? But, particularly early in an artist's career, not every method seems right. No question of any donations, for example! On the contrary, so as to take true stock of how the collection will gain, and appreciate, and so the artist can be sure that the work will be hung, the institution should be made to pay. A good price as for a friend, of course: "I take the liberty," it seems likely that Jean Cassou[1] wrote to the Director General of Fine Arts on April 23, 1940, "to tell you of this very fine painting[2] the museum price for which will be only 20,000 francs,[3] Mr. Marquet is the seller of this painting and has consented to a reduction of 10,000 francs on the asking price. They both ask only that this reduction remains our secret: it is given to us as a personal mark of friendship." And thus, between 1913, the date of the first purchase (from Marquet himself) and 1947, the date of Marquet's death, of the 16 paintings by the artist which gradually entered the collection of the Musée du Luxembourg and then the Musée national d'art moderne, ten were purchased directly from the artist.

In 1913, the museum acquired its first Marquet. As if to anticipate the title of the of this exhibition, the state, which purchased nothing from Marquet's Fauve period, chose for this first piece a resolutely Impressionist painting of the year: *Bords de rivière*, 1913 (#18). Was it the exemplary character of this first purchase that gave the painting such a remarkable destiny? For nearly forty years, under the watchful eye of the Permanent French Mission at the United Nations, it has been in the office of the Secretary-General of the UN.

Only a few days after the first purchase, *Le quai de Rouen à Paris*, 1912 (#16) shook off the dust of the studio to enter the museum. Eleven years went by and, in 1924, *Femmes de Laghouat*, ca. 1921 (#25) was purchased from the artist. It was not until 1930 that the first painting contemporary with historic Fauvism – *Bassin au Havre*, 1906 (#12) – was purchased from Marquet. As the ten years that preceded the Second World War went by, the museum reaffirmed its commitment to Marquet, to his gain, in purchasing six paintings of which five were contemporary: in 1934, *Eté, la plage des Sables-d'Olonne*, 1933 (#30), *La lagune à Venise*, 1936 (#35) and *Venise. La voile jaune*, 1936 (#34); in 1939, two more paintings, *Brume à Stockholm* of 1938 (#36), and surely the first really Fauve work to enter the collections, *Le Quai des Grands Augustins*, 1905 (#7). In the letter of the following year already cited, and in justifying the purchase of *Rotterdam*, 1914 (#19), Jean Cassou stated, "...if we possess a Marquet from the Fauve period, recently purchased, and another from slightly later, we are poor as far as his series of ports is concerned..." He concluded "(we)...have little after that but for much more recent works,"[4] as if to put

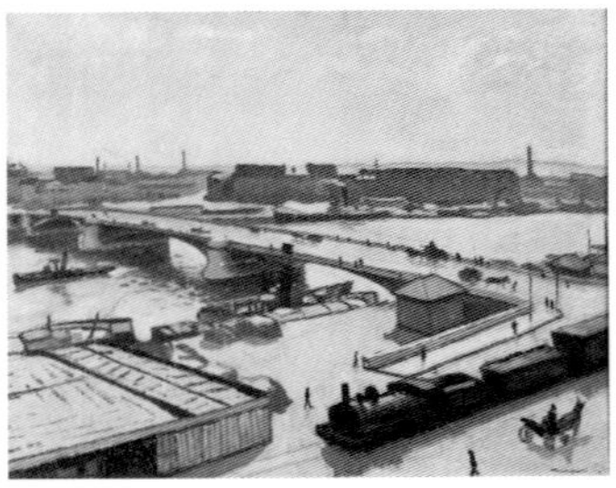

Le quai de Rouen à Paris, 1912 (#16)
Purchased, 1913

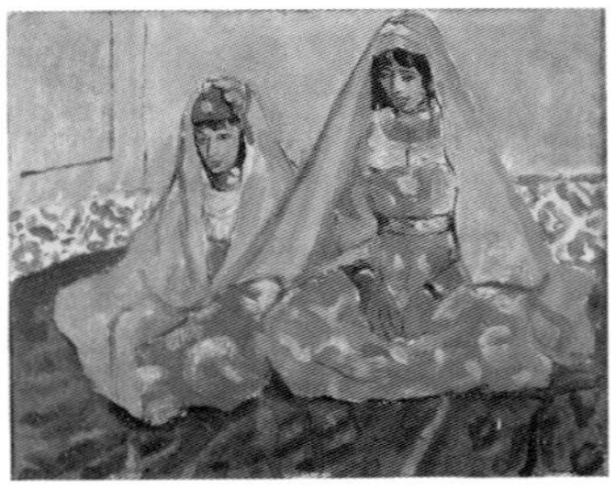

Femmes de Laghouat, ca. 1921 (#25)
Purchased, 1924

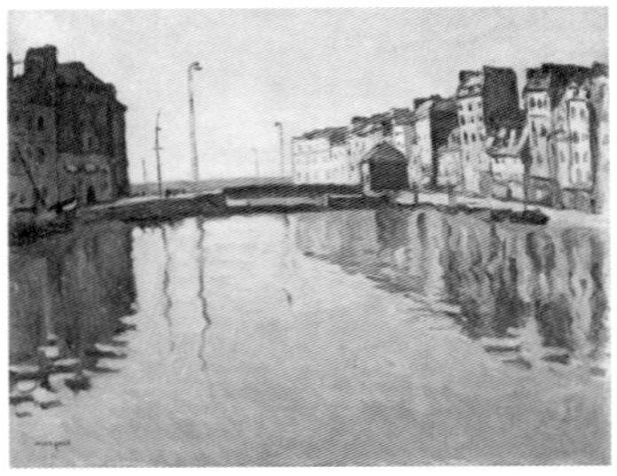

Bassin au Havre, 1906 (#12)
Purchased, 1930

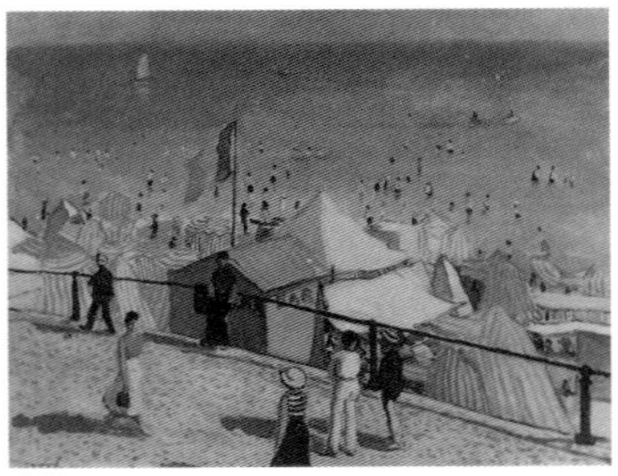

Eté, la plage des Sables-d'Olonne, 1933 (#30)
Purchased, 1934

into perspective the gains made by his predecessors (and at last) credibility to Gustave Coquiot who in 1914 had already written: "Mr. Marquet...always gives (his public) water; bridges; he and they are made for each other; and it is to be hoped that this happy collaboration will last as long as bridges and water exist: Mr. Marquet to paint them, and connoisseurs to celebrate his paintings."[5]

On the eve of the declaration of the Second World War, the portrait of *André Rouveyre*, 1904 (#5) was purchased from André Rouveyre himself![6] Rouveyre had conscientiously hung on to the painting, making it the only purchase during Marquet's lifetime that was not concluded with the artist. The five other paintings added to the inventory arrived thanks to gifts. From the 1929 gift of Madame Druet[7] came *Nu au divan*, 1912 (#17). Such a painting could never have come direct from the artist's studio (as is pointed out by Didier Ottinger's article) any more than *La femme blonde*, 1919 (#23) which came a year later from the 1939 gift of collector Olivier Senn.[8] Next came the bequest of museum curator Gaston Migeon,[9] which brought the polite *Vue d'Agay*, ca. 1905 (#6). Then, just before the arrival in the collection of the smallest and most touching of Marquet's works, the Fauve *La plage de Fécamp*, 1906, (#10) which came in the bequest of Paul Jamot (another curator),[10] Marquet actually gave a painting himself! Persuaded perhaps by the delightful collection of his work that had developed at the museum over thirty years, in 1940 he gave one of his most original, nocturnal and rain-soaked urban landscapes – indeed, one of the most successful twentieth century paintings of that genre – *Le Pont-Neuf, la nuit*, 1935–39 (#32). So concluded the seventeen Marquet acquisitions made by the museum during his lifetime: seven years later, he was dead. By what ironic twist of fate did his bequest bring the museum the precocious *La cafetière*, 1902 (#4), no less unusual for its Chardinesque qualities than for being a coffee pot!

An interesting coincidence from the point of view of the support that Marquet was given by the museum world: the last two Marquet works given to the Musée national d'art moderne during the artist's lifetime came from bequests of curators at the Louvre, who were only slightly older than Marquet (The Migeon Bequest came in 1931, that of Paul Jamot in 1943). The next to arrive after the gift of the artist was *L'Île aux cygnes*, 1919 (#24), which entered the collection in 1953 thanks to the bequest of Carle Dreyfus (1875–1952), pre-war curator of the Louvre department of objets d'art. Three bequests, from three curators; in this way began the twenty-one additions to come – nine works from bequests, one gift, seven donations, one work appropriated following the peace treaty with Japan, one state-mandated gift in lieu of tax, and only two purchases.

It appears notwithstanding, on examination of the circumstances that brought works by Marquet to the national collection after 1947, that a shift in taste which had already made itself apparent before his death, mercilessly relegated the artist's work to the sphere of faithful, erudite but aging collectors, and to a widow, Marcelle Marquet. The latter was fully aware that in such a climate the perpetuation of her husband's life's work would be achieved principally by the opening of the Marquet rooms of the museum in his hometown of Bordeaux. To achieve this, at the end of the 1950s, she took to Bordeaux, as donations, tens of paintings by Marquet, and adroitly pressured the heads of the Musée national d'art moderne, Jean Cassou and Bernard Dorival, so that the verbal bequest she had made to the museum which included nine Matisses she had kept as an investment, would be housed at the Musée de Bordeaux, along with *La Cafetière*. This game between Paris and Bordeaux did not influence either the first or the final generosity of Madame Marquet to the Musée national d'art moderne: in 1948, she gave the *Portrait d'Albert Marquet*, 1904, by Camoin (#40), and in 1955, long before the

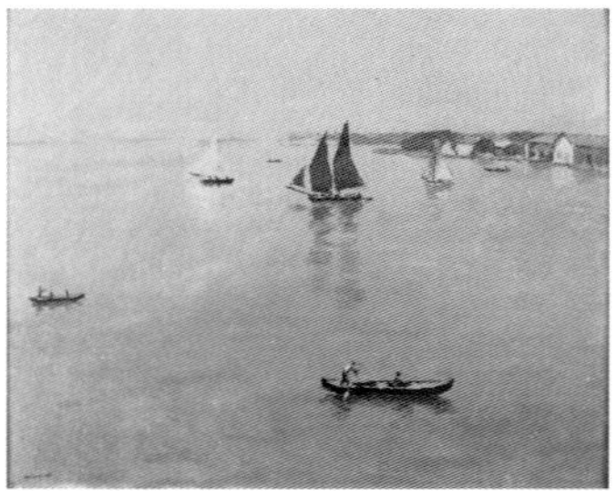

La lagune à Venise, 1936 (#35)
Purchased, 1937

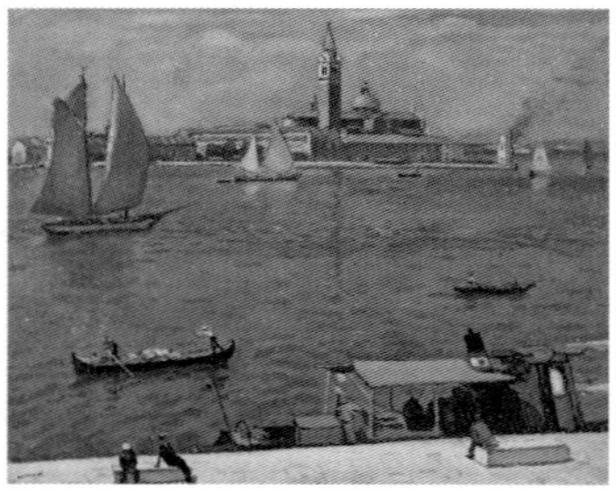

Venise. La voile jaune, 1936 (#34)
Purchased, 1937

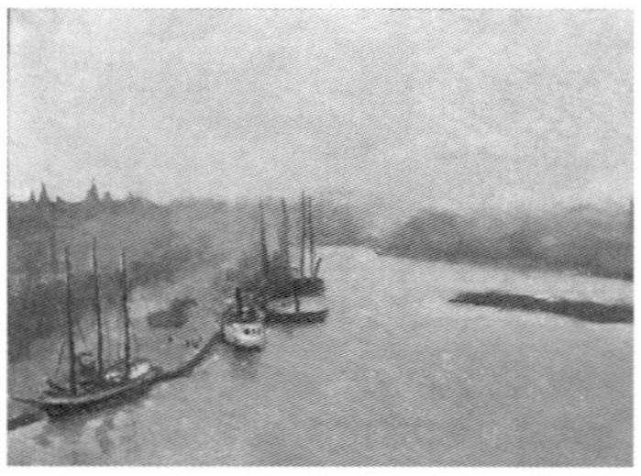

Brume à Stockholm 1938 (#36)
Purchased, 1939

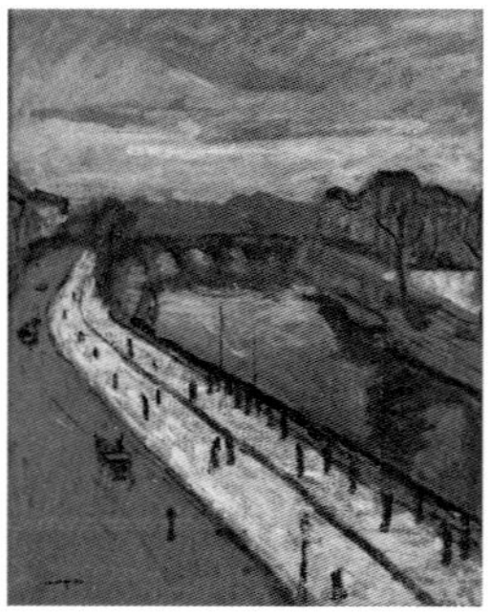

Le Quai des Grands Augustins, 1905 (#7)
Purchased, 1939

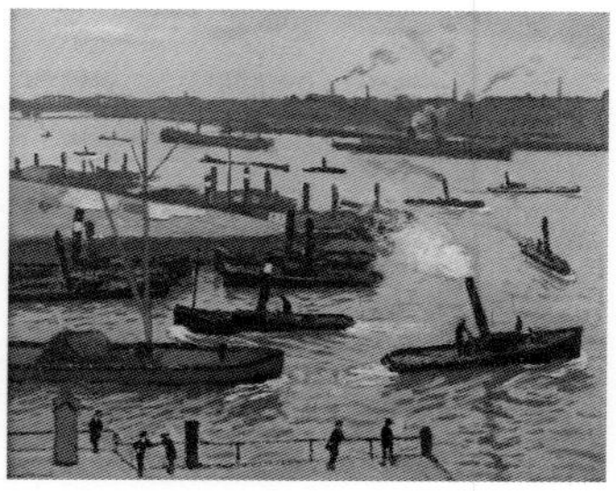

Rotterdam, 1914 (#19)
Purchased, 1940

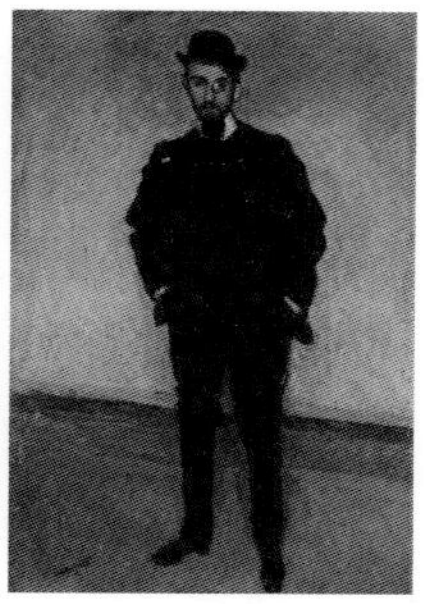

André Rouveyre, 1904 (#5)
Purchased, 1939

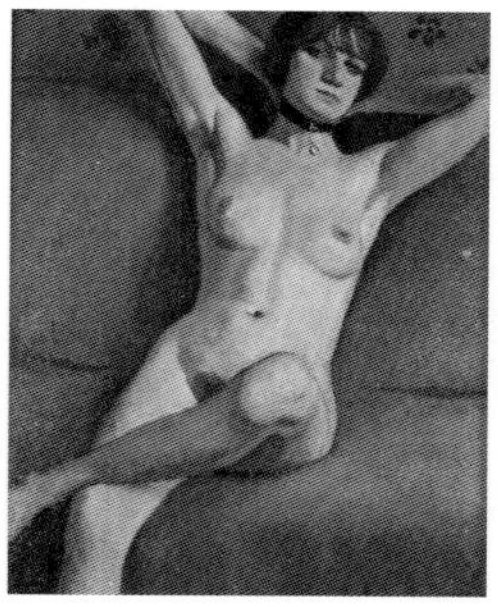

Nu au divan, 1912 (#17)
Gift, 1929

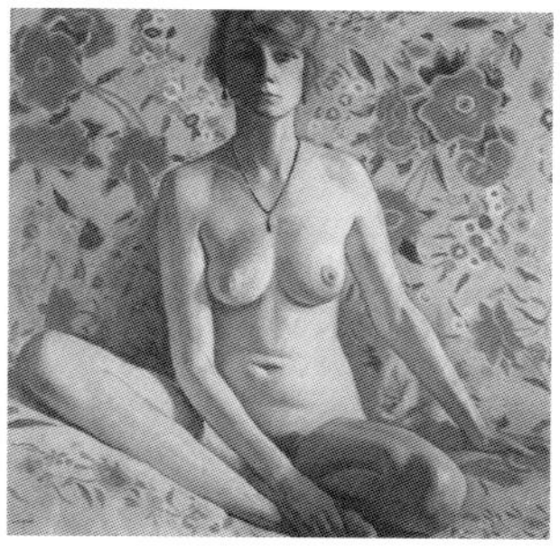

La femme blonde, 1919 (#23)
Gift, 1939

Bordeaux project was signed, sealed and delivered, it was solely to the national collection that she gave the last (or among the last) of Marquet's paintings: the ghostly *Pont-Neuf sous la neige*, 1947 (#39), that she followed the year later with a collection of sixteen drawings.

The year 1957 was rich in acquisitions of works by Marquet: five paintings entered the collections from different sources. A financial group bought the national museums together with the society of friends of the Musées de Poitiers, to buy *Plage des Sables-d'Olonne*, 1933 (#31), which the year later went off to be housed at the musée de Poitiers, for whom it was intended. The same year, an exceptional budgetary device was required, also necessitating an outside partner, to enable the purchase of three paintings of great historical interest. For the sum of 20,000,000 old francs,[11] three paintings were purchased which represent the same model in Manguin's studio, painted by three different artists during the winter of 1904–1905. They are Matisse's *Marquet peignant un nu dans l'atelier de Manguin*, 1904–1905 (#42); Manguin's *Nu dans l'atelier*, 1904–1905 (#41), originally attributed to Matisse; and Marquet's *Matisse dans l'atelier de Manguin*, 1904–1905 (#8). Pierre David-Weill contributed half the funds for this purchase, one of the most onerous financially of the period. The stakes, to judge by the acquisition file for these three works, were high: on February 14, 1957, Jean Cassou, purse-string for Georges Salles, Director of the Musées de France, the comptroller of the operation, wrote, "For several years it has not been possible to buy at sales at Drouot's or even at the Galerie Charpentier, paintings by the great masters of contemporary art. You can only get things by second rate artists, works by Matisse, Braque, Rouault, Bonnard, are hardly ever to be found. This absence is explained by the fact that works by these masters pass directly from the artists' studios, or from some French collection that still contains them, into private or public collections in the United States that will buy them at any price. The proof of this comes each week with export licenses."

The counterpoint to this economic battle was a difference in historical order and interpretation, which also pitted the Musée national d'art moderne against the Museum of Modern Art, New York. Writing the next day to the collector who had sold the three works, Jean Cassou confided in him, "(The documents that you gave me) allowed me to embellish the presentation I made to the Committee of Curators and the Conseil des Musées (Museum Council), and to fix upon a historical point of order on which we are in direct opposition to my eminent colleague Alfred Barr, who, in his very lovely book on Matisse, cites this painting as dating from Matisse's arrival in Paris, 1899, after his first neo-Impressionist period. On the contrary, it is from the second neo-Iimpressionist period, that of Saint-Tropez, in 1905, and just at the beginning of the Fauve period, and it is thanks to the precious testimony of Madame Manguin that we can now situate this prodigious painting. It dates precisely from the period when the two friends and their whole group were deliberately about to accomplish the Fauve revolution. Therein lies the enormous interest of this acquisition, a historical interest tied to the splendid beauty of the works."[12]

Amid a donation of considerable generosity (fifty-seven works by fourteen artists) from the collection of Frédéric Lung came the three other Marquets of 1957, opening up, in a manner of speaking, the way for two further large collections to follow: the Grammont bequest (1959), and the Besson bequest (1963), both confirming the extinction of a generation of collectors the same age as Marquet, who had no successors. Frédéric Lung was born in Saint-Dié in 1863, moved to Bordeaux, then in 1885 to Algiers, where he ran an important wine shipper. His collection included works by Bonnard, Matisse, La Fresnaye, Marquet, Dunoyer de Segonzac, and a Magreb collection from Charles Dufresne and Jean Launois. Despite the facts that the painter and the collector both lived in Algiers, and the fact that it was land-

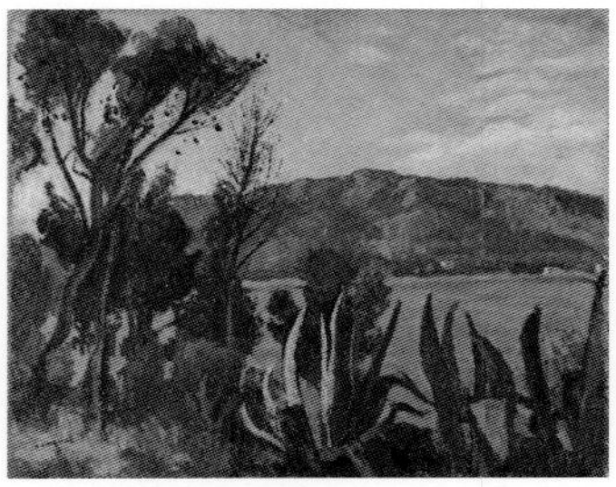

Vue d'Agay, ca. 1905 (#6)
Bequest, 1931

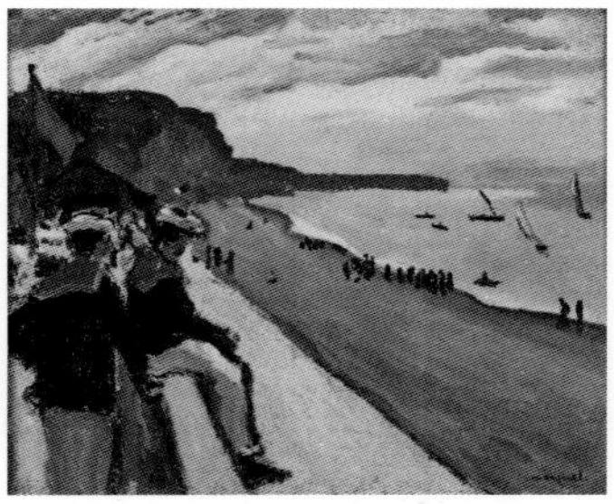

La plage de Fécamp, 1906, (#10)
Bequest, 1943

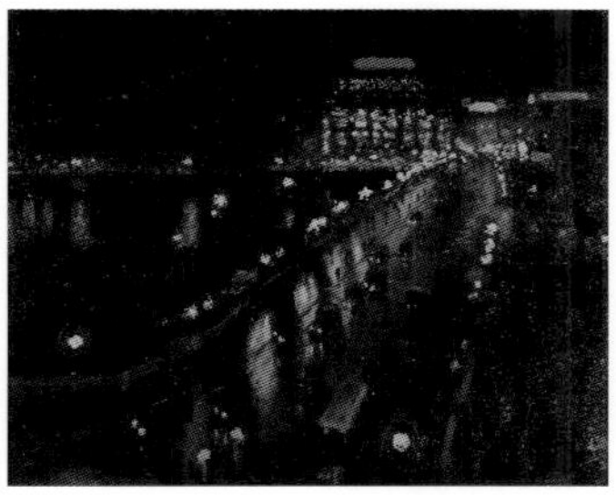

Le Pont-Neuf, la nuit, 1935–39 (#32)
Gift, 1940

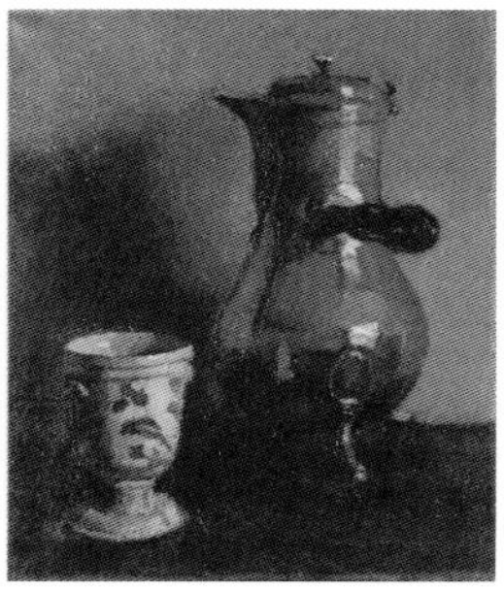

La cafetière, 1902 (#4)
Bequest, 1948

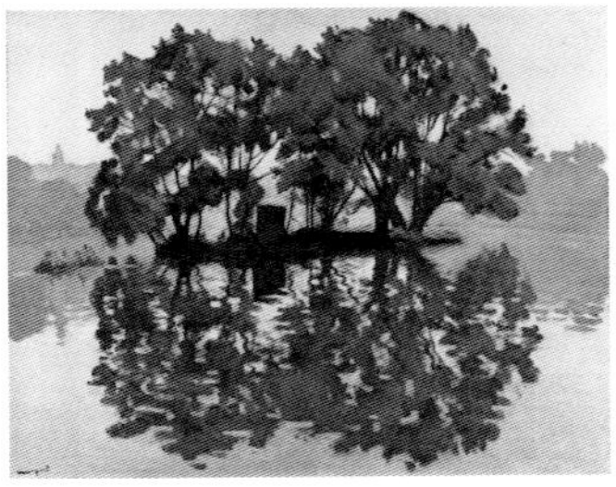

L'Île aux cygnes, 1919 (#24)
Bequest, 1953

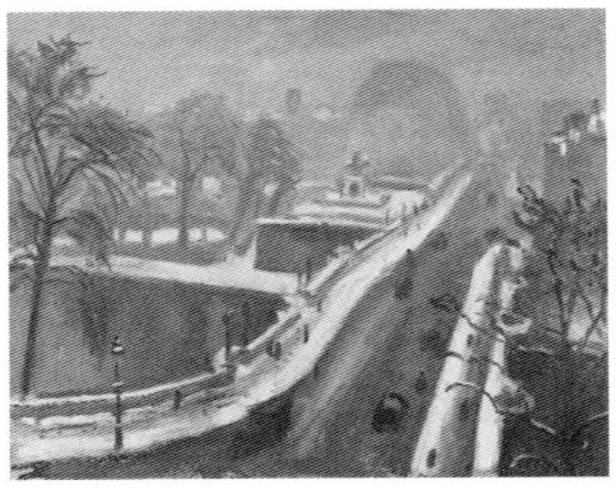

Pont-Neuf sous la neige, 1947 (#39)
Gift, 1955

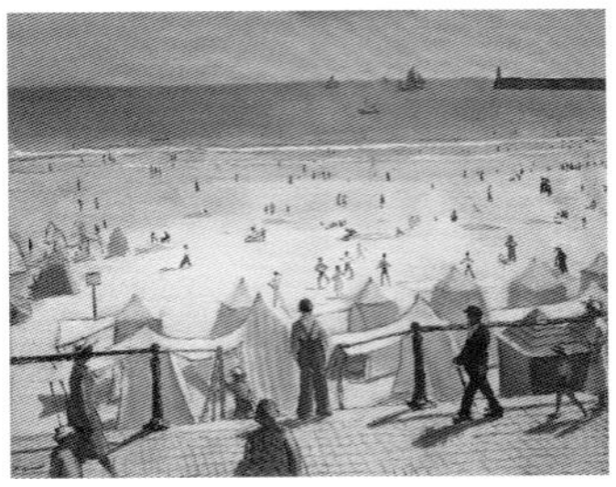

Plage des Sables-d'Olonne, 1933 (#31)
Purchased, 1957

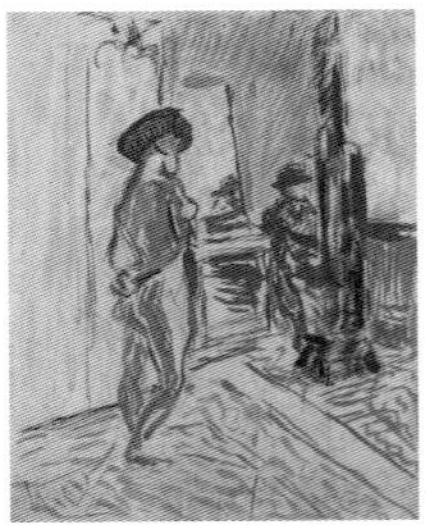

Marquet peignant un nu dans l'atelier de Manguin, 1904–1905, by Henri Matisse (#42)
Purchased, 1957

scapes of the far-flung *département* that Lung purchased, two of them were not acquired from the painter. *Le port de Bougie par temps gris,* 1925 (#27) was purchased by Lung from the galerie Bernheim-Jeune on May 19, 1925 a few days after Marquet left it there; *La place du gouvernement à Alger,* 1927 (#28) was purchased from Marquet by Bernheim-Jeune on May 23, 1927, and sold to Lung on June 7! In contradistinction, *Le port d'Alger,* 1939 (#37) was given by the artist to the collector, in Algeria, at the time of his absence from France during the occupation, which allowed him to prolong one of his favorite visits much longer than usual. For the Musée national d'art moderne, these paintings – at long last! – were the first views of Algeria to enter the collection. Lung's personal and family ties with Bordeaux opportunely took *Le port d'Alger,* with other works from the bequest, to the musée de Bordeaux.

In March 1959, a group of fifty-four masterpieces from twenty-six artists (including Bonnard, Braque, Camoin, Dufy, Derain, Signac, Vlaminck and Vuillard) were bequeathed to the national museums by the collector Georges Grammont (1898–1956) to constitute the core of the Musée de l'Annonciade of Saint-Tropez. Their entry into the inventory of the Musée national d'art moderne was only a matter of form: the six Marquets included in this formidably generous act – *Port de Saint-Tropez,* 1905 (#9), *Port de Marseille,* 1918 (#22), *Sète, le Canal de Beaucaire,* 1924 (#26), *Port de Boulogne,* 1930 (#29), *Paris, quai d'Orléans vu du quai de Béthune,* ca. 1914–1915 (#20), and *Port d'Alger,* 1935 (#33) – have never appeared on the walls of the Musée nationale d'art moderne.

Two months later, in May 1959, the settlement of the articles of the peace treaty with Japan allowed France to appropriate seventeen works from the old collection of Baron Kojiro Matsukata. Sequestrated as enemy goods during the Second World War, the greater part of the collection was returned to Japan and now forms the core of the National Museum of Occidental Art in Tokyo. Amid the great masterpieces that stayed in French museums, and apart from *La Chambre à Arles* by Van Gogh, *La Serveuse de Bocks* by Manet, *Vaïrumati* by Gauguin, and *Montagne Sainte-Victoire* by Cézanne, the Musée national d'art moderne was to receive *La Liseuse* by Picasso, *Le Groom* and *La Volaille* by Soutine, and *Le Pont Saint-Michel et le Quai des Grands-Augustins,* 1912 (#14), by Marquet.

In a similar spirit to that which animated Georges Grammont, in 1963 Georges Besson (1882–1971) – art critic, collector, organizer of exhibitions and producer of reviews – made an immense donation of works that he had collected, intended for the museums of Besançon and Bagnols-sur-Cèze. At a time when the reliability of provincial museums was still rather feeble, the everlasting nature of his generosity was such that it had to be guaranteed under the auspices of the national museum system. In such a manner tens of works by Bonnard, Signac, Matisse, Jean Puy, Valadon, Lhote and Valtat were brought to the inventory of the Musée national d'art moderne without ever gracing its picture rails. Among them were six older works by Marquet which were integral to the collection and which in everyday terms are the basis of the renown of the two museums of Besançon and Bagnols-sur-Cèze: *Banlieue parisienne,* 1897 (#1), *Abside de Notre Dame de Paris,* 1901 (#2), *Le 14 juillet au Havre,* 1906 (#11), *Le port de Naples,* 1909 (#13), *Les deux amies,* 1912 (#15), and *Le Vieux Port à Marseille,* 1917 (#21).

Two more paintings still had to come to the Musée national d'art moderne before its representation of works by Marquet took on its present (final?) form. In 1968, among a large body of eighteenth and nineteenth century drawings, the gift of Jean-Pierre and Louise Hugot brought *Paysage au remorqueur,* 1939 (#38) to the museum, a luminous Marquet painting of the

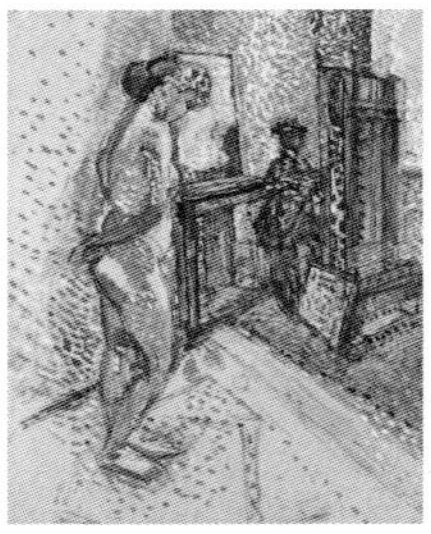

Nu dans l'atelier, 1904–1905, by Henri Manguin (#41)
Purchased, 1957

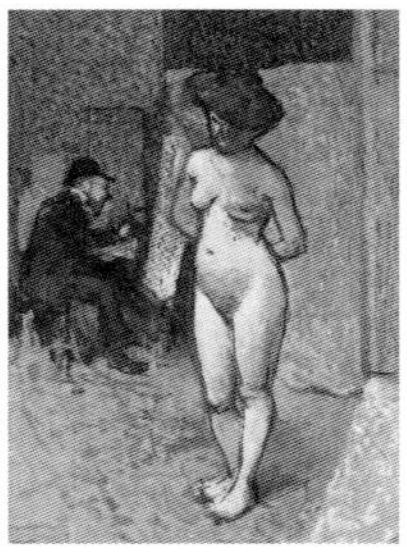

Matisse dans l'atelier de Manguin, 1904–1905 (#8)
Purchased, 1957

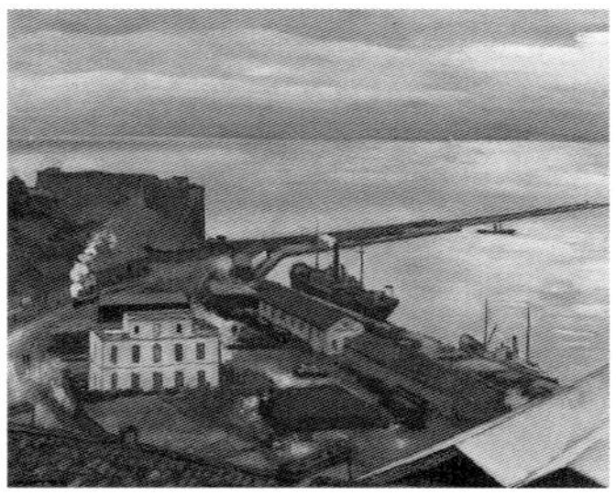

Le port de Bougie par temps gris, 1925 (#27)
Bequest, 1957

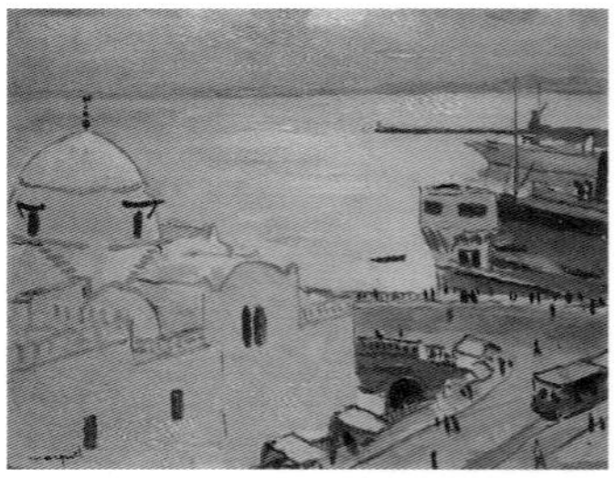

La place du gouvernement à Alger, 1927 (#28)
Bequest, 1957

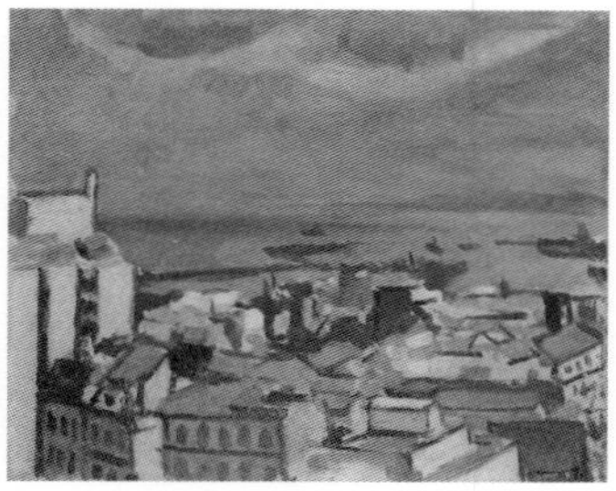

Le port d'Alger, 1939 (#37)
Bequest, 1957

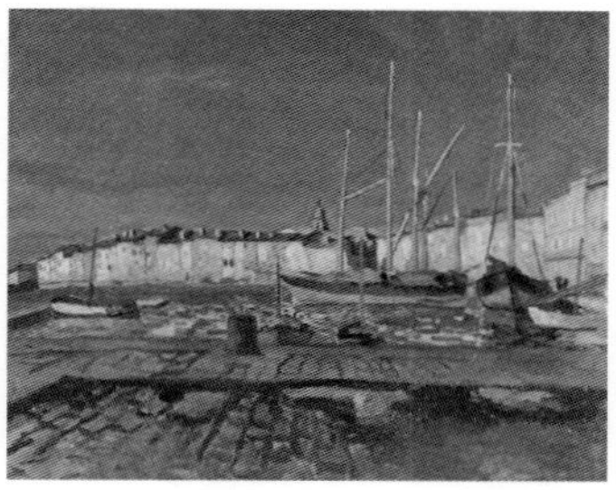

Port de Saint-Tropez, 1905 (#9)
Bequest, 1959

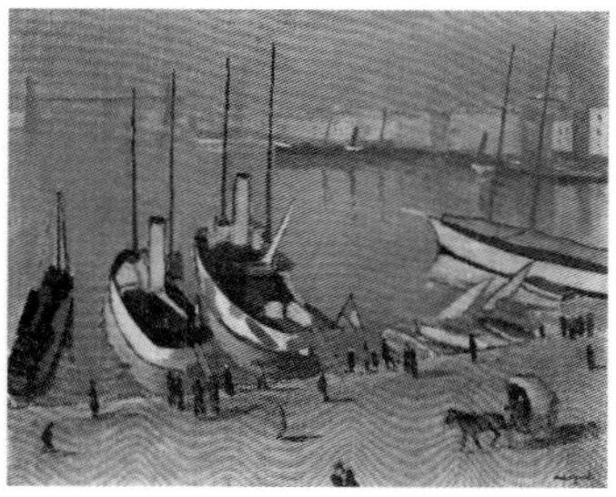

Port de Marseille, 1918 (#22)
Bequest, 1959

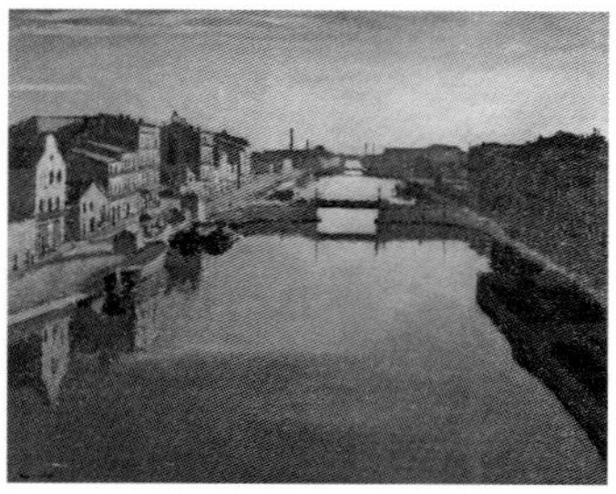

Sète, le Canal de Beaucaire, 1924 (#26)
Bequest, 1959

Port of Algiers. Twenty years later, in 1988, a state-sanctioned transfer of property in lieu of estate tax permitted a Marquet painting from the collection of Pierre Lévy, *La Seine et l'abside de Notre-Dame*, 1902 (#3), to re-enter its usual environment. It returned to the musée de Troyes, which also bears witness to an *époque* and the sensibility of great French collectors (shared by Albert Marquet) who in the links of friendship and culture that bound them to museums, liked to build, explain and transmit.

At the end of this reckoning, it will be understood that there is in fact no 'Marquet affair,' no mystery deviously hidden somewhere within the history and development of our fine group of paintings. Would the Maigrets at the Pompidou wear themselves out in vain hunting for a whiff of rottenness, or vanished tempests, under these calm waters of the ports of France and its Empire? It has to be said that it would not be the first time that the temptation has seized our museums to tear from our artist the elegance of tone and the distinction of his reflections, the tranquility of the aqueous universes which seem to speak French, so much are these banks and shores bathed by civilization and culture. How else if not by such a perverse desire to read more into the story can we explain a violent and worrying 'Marquet before Marquet,' a depiction of tempest and shipwreck, one of the works of art that in 1949 the national museums kept in order to satisfy demands of restitution, after it had been found in Germany in a trove of works spoliated from Jews? Hundreds of other mediocre paintings, seldom identifiable, were finally sold by the Administration des Domaines (administration of lands and properties) after having been exhibited for three years at the Château de Compiègne. The painting in question, though signed MARQUET is not by Marquet. Perhaps it was kept out of a perverse willfulness simply because it was so extraordinarily unlike him.

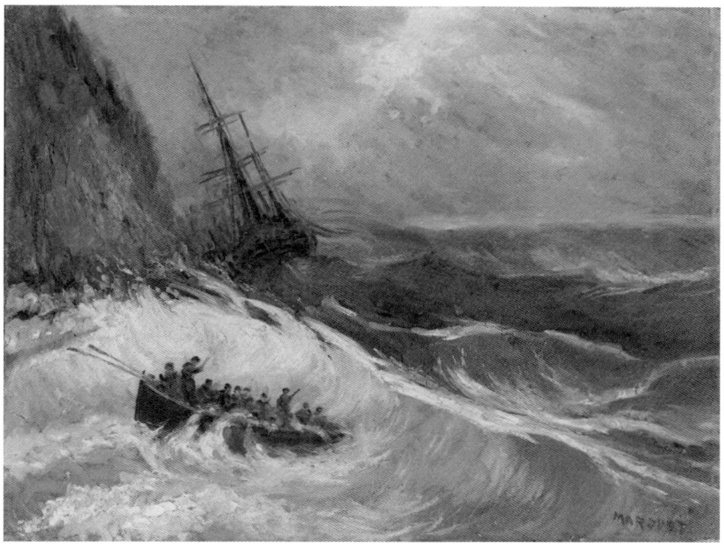

The real 'Marquet affair' is there, in that bad painting of a furious sea and men in peril. It bears witness today to many torments; those of persecution clearly; but also those of Albert Marquet in his perpetual interior exile that the war only aggravated; and those of the art world, finally, and its attempt to subvert a refuge from worry and strangeness.

1 The carbon copy of this letter, which is at the department of documentation of the Musée national d'art moderne, is not signed. However, his style (see also note #4) indicates the author, whose nomination as head of the museum was not officially recognized until September 26, 1940. "But the very same day while twiddling the dial of his radio, Jean Cassou heard the following: "The communist jew red spanish popular front freemason anarchist Jean Cassou, cabinet member of a Jewish minister of the ministry of the Jew Blum, the Jew Jean Zay fomenter of war, etc., has been named as head curator of the Musée national

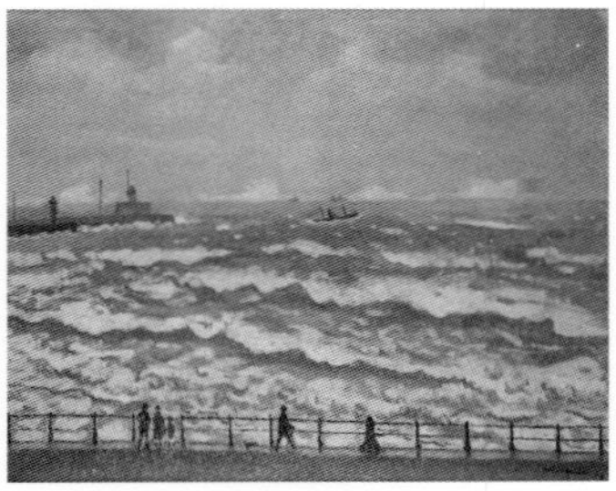

Port de Boulogne, 1930 (#29)
Bequest, 1959

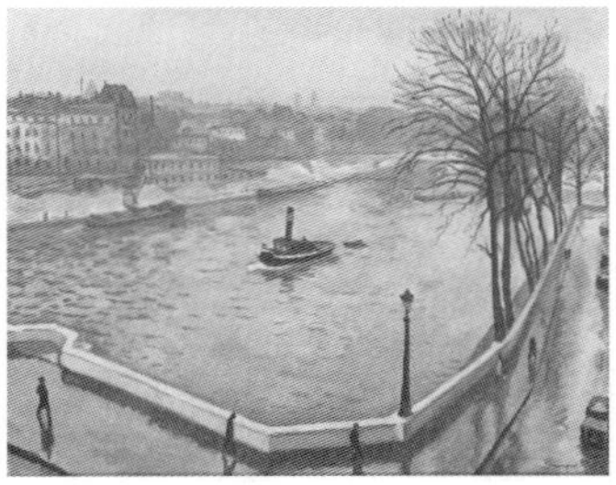

La Seine à Paris or
Paris, quai d'Orléans vu du quai de Béthune, 1914–1915 (#20)
Bequest, 1959

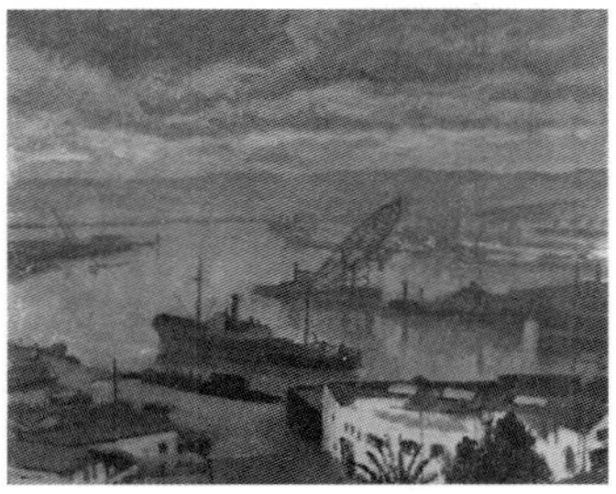

Port d'Alger, 1935 (#33)
Bequest, 1959

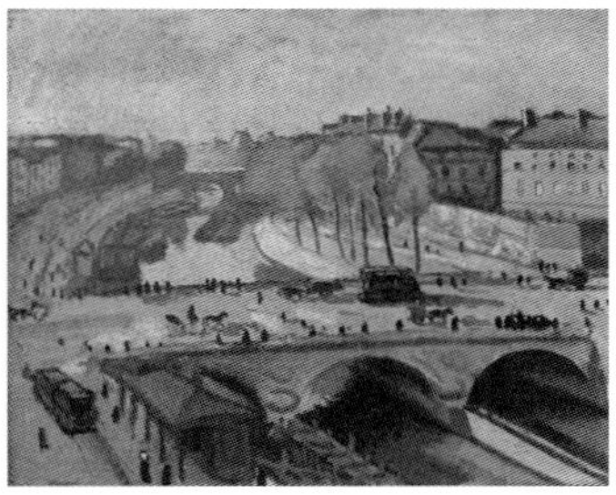

Le Pont Saint-Michel et le Quai des Grands-Augustins, 1912 (#14)
Ceded, 1959

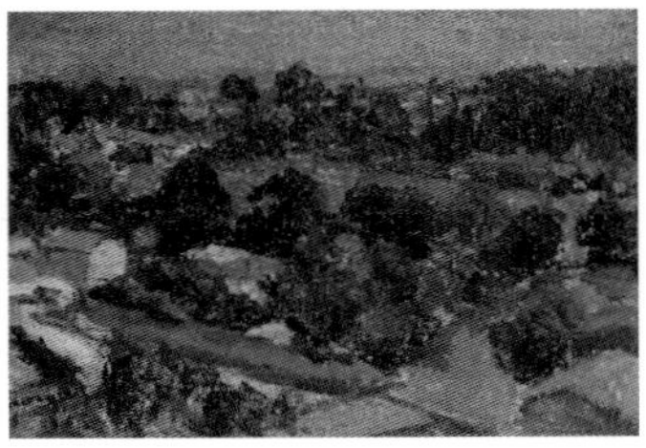

Banlieue parisienne, 1897 (#1)
Donation, 1963

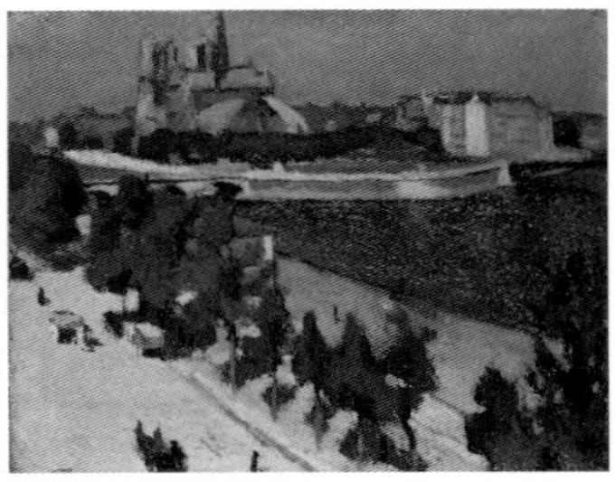

Abside de Notre Dame de Paris, 1901 (#2)
Donation, 1963

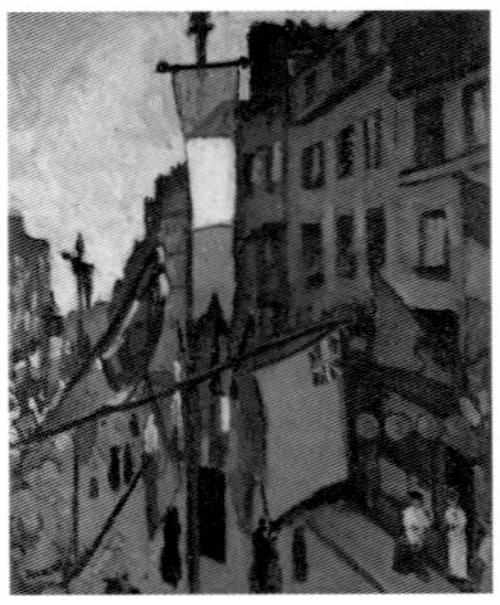

Le 14 juillet au Havre, 1906 (#11)
Donation, 1963

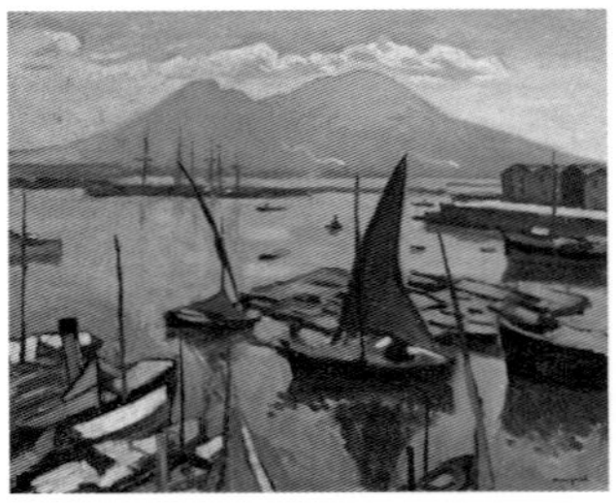

Le port de Naples, 1909 (#13)
Donation, 1963

d'art moderne [see Jean Cassou, *Une vie pour la Liberté* (Paris: Robert Laffont, 1981), 142]. The next day, Jean Cassou was "retired" and replaced in the position by Pierre Ladoué…" (see Luc Alary, *De l' "Art Vivant" à l' "Art Moderne": genèse du Musée national d'art moderne* (Paris: University of Paris non-published thesis, January 1997) 260

2 The work concerned is *Rotterdam*, 1914, AM 2353P (#19)

3 In the region of 41,000 francs ($5,520, or 6311€) in 2001

4 Letter cited in note #1

5 Gustave Coquiot, *Cubistes, futuristes, passéistes* (Paris: Ollendorf, 1914) Tome VI, 14

6 6,000 francs were paid to this very well known Montparnasse celebrity, an habitué of the *Closerie des Lilas* at the turn of the century, an intimate of Apollinaire, a caricaturist and headline writer for the *Mercure de France* to whom Matisse and Marquet were tied with bonds of friendship since the days of the studio of Gustave Moreau in 1898. Matisse drew his portrait in charcoal (now at the Cabinet d'art Graphique of the Musée national d'art moderne); Rouveyre and George Besson published (in 1943) a small book on Marquet's drawings; and Marquet, in addition to the painting at the Musée national d'art moderne, made in 1903 a portrait of Rouveyre at work, which appeared (lent by Mr. & Mrs. Leon A. Mnuchin, New York) in the Marquet retrospective in San Francisco in 1958. See catalogue, *André Rouveyre, 1879–1862, entre Apollinaire et Matisse* (Paris: Bibliothèque historique de la Ville de Paris, 1995)

7 With regard to the Druet Gallery, see Marcelle Marquet, *Marquet* (Paris: Robert Laffont, 1951)

8 The personality of the collector Olivier Senn is difficult to trace. A letter of 1976 from his son to the Director of the Musées de France, with regard to the transfer of this painting from the Palais de Tokyo to the Beaubourg, carried the following statements: "My father bought from Marquet a nude on the edge of a shawl embroidered with flowers. Some time later, before the war, he found himself asked by the painter to sell the painting back. My father, who maintained a very sympathetic relationship with Marquet, replied: "*I will not sell it back to you, but would be happy to see it hung at the Musée du Luxembourg, and will do the necessary…*" I think moreover that that museum (the Palais de Tokyo) will continue to keep the majority of works by Marquet. I will add that, for my part, I deplored seeing this painting disappear from the Musée national d'art moderne…when the second story was entirely polluted by that which goes by the name "contemporary art," notably two intertwined department store mannequins, for whom it had been judged fitting to create a plastic and velvet setting, and that at the time when the Musée national d'art moderne was not hung at Beaubourg…"

9 Gaston Migeon (1861–1930), entered the Louvre in 1889 as a librarian and crowned his career, after retiring in 1923, as the Honorary Director of the National Museums. For over twenty years he was chief curator of the department of objets d'art at the Louvre, where his erudition and knowledge of the field, as much in Islamic art (architecture and textiles) as in Japanese art, contributed to the opening of the French national collections to material from the far east.

10 Paul Jamot (1863–1939) was more of an antiquarian. He began his career at the Louvre in 1902 as adjunct curator in the department of Greco-Roman antiquities, before becoming curator of the department of paintings in 1934. With Charles Sterling, he was one of the "inventors" of Georges de la Tour, whom they introduced to the public in the memorable exhibition *Les peintres de la Réalité*, which they curated, and which was held at the Orangerie in 1934.

11 Or 2,200,000 francs (approximately $294,000 or 335,400€) in 2001

12 On the current state surrounding the questions regarding these three works, see in particular Isabelle Monod-Fontaine in *Matisse*, the catalogue raisonné of the collection at the Musée national d'art moderne (Paris: Editions du Centre Pompidou, 1989), 30

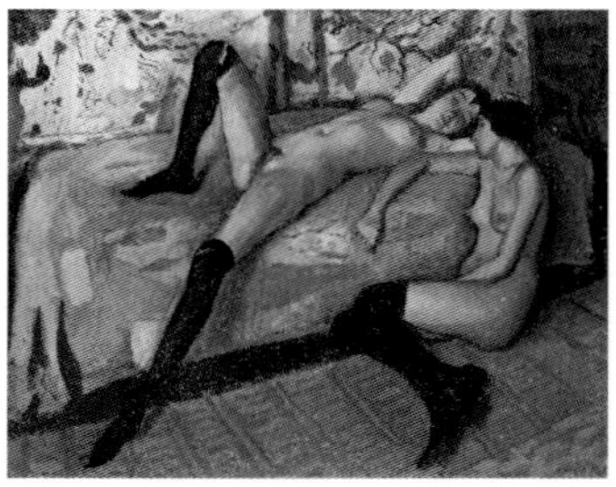

Les deux amies, 1912 (#15)
Donation, 1963

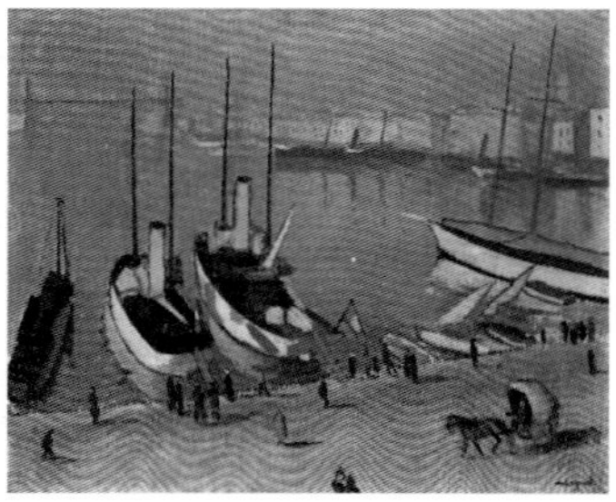

Le Vieux-Port à Marseille, 1917 (#21)
Donation, 1963

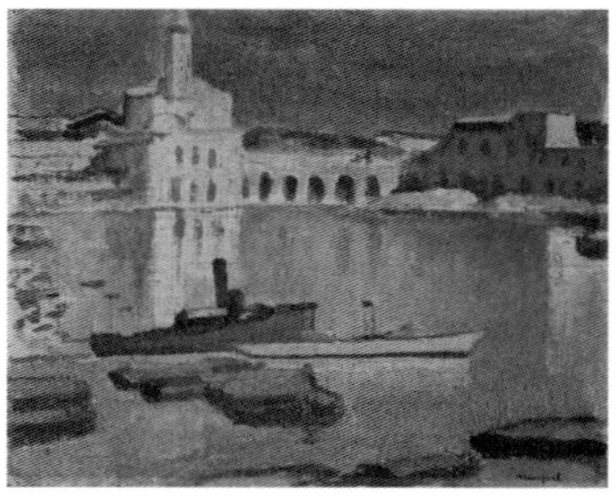

Paysage au remorqueur, 1939 (#38)
Donation, 1968

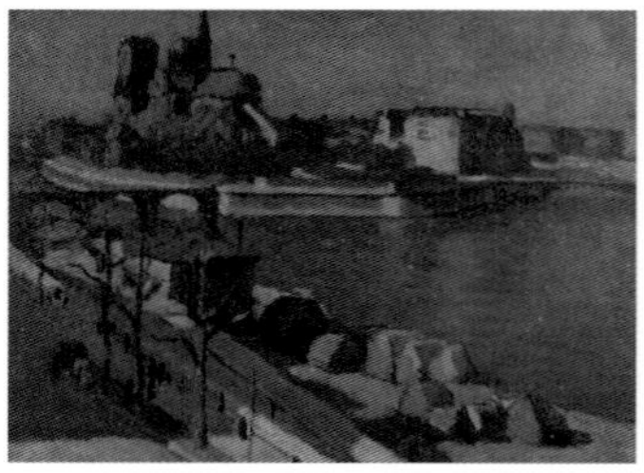

La Seine et l'abside de Notre-Dame, 1902 (#3)
Ceded, 1988

Catalogue of works

Please note

All works illustrated are by Albert Marquet from the collection of the Musée national d'art moderne/CNAC unless otherwise stated.

Catalogue #42, *Marquet peignant un nu dans l'atelier de Mauguin,* 1904–1905 by Henri Matisse will be shown at the first venue only (Columbia Museum of Art).

For reasons of conservation, only a selection of works on paper will be shown at each venue.

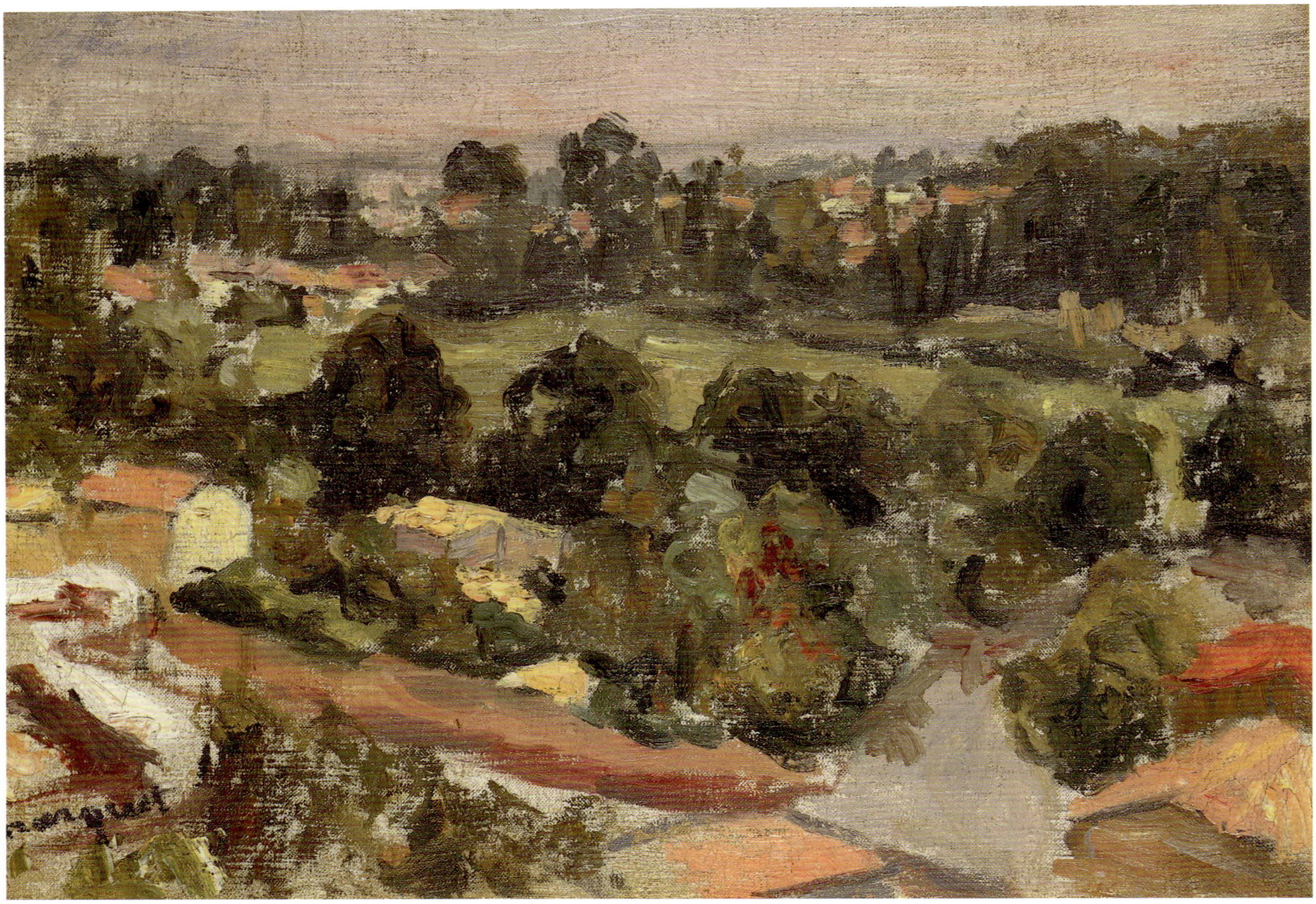

1 *Banlieue parisienne,* 1897

Oil on canvas

32 x 45 cms

Donation of Adèle and Georges Besson in 1963

On deposit at the Musée des Beaux-Arts et

d'Archéologie de Besançon

AM 4224 P(96)

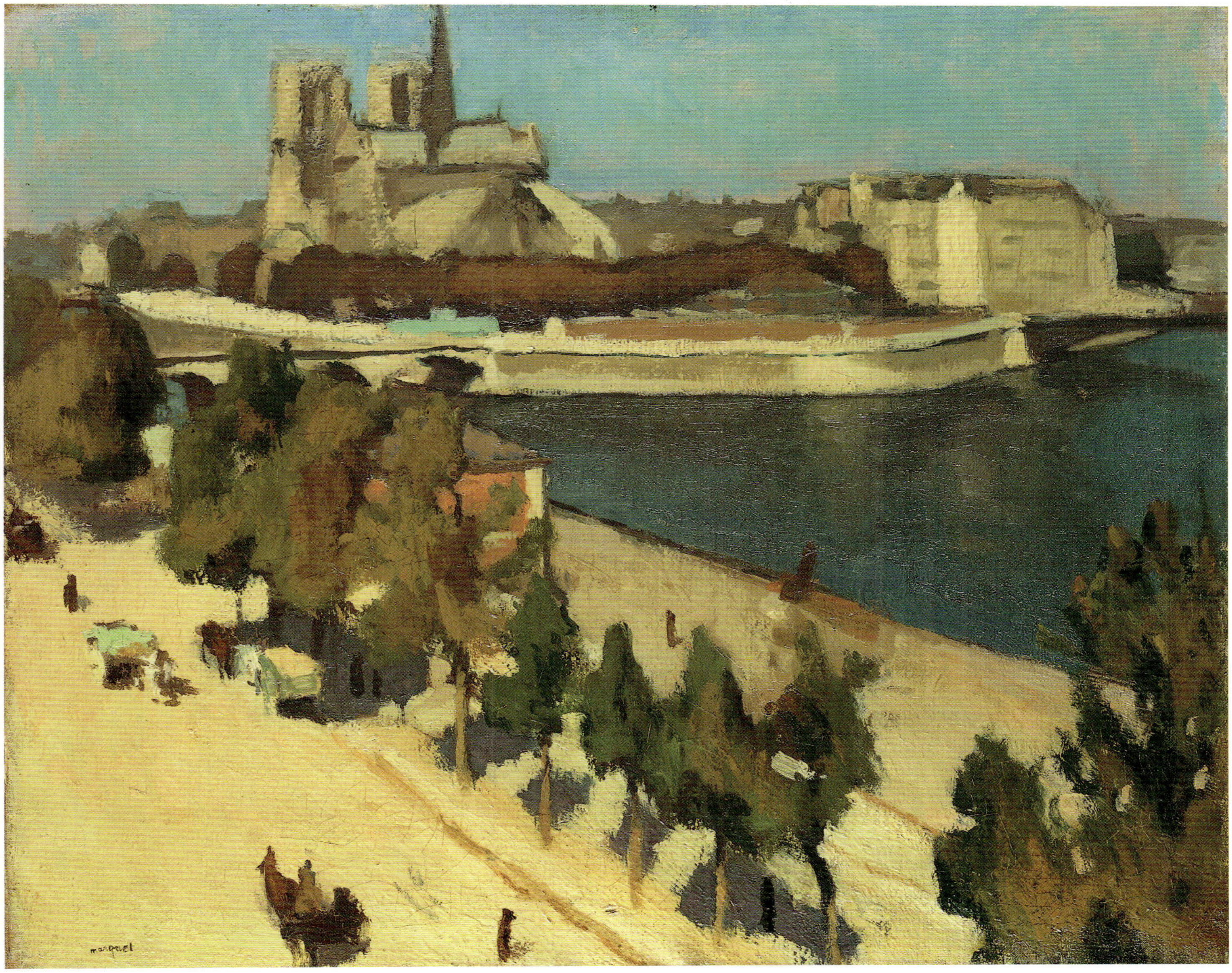

2 *Abside de Notre-Dame de Paris*, 1901

Oil on canvas

50 x 61 cms

Donation of Adèle and Georges Besson in 1963

On deposit at the Musée des Beaux-Arts et

d'Archéologie de Besançon

AM 4224 P(52)

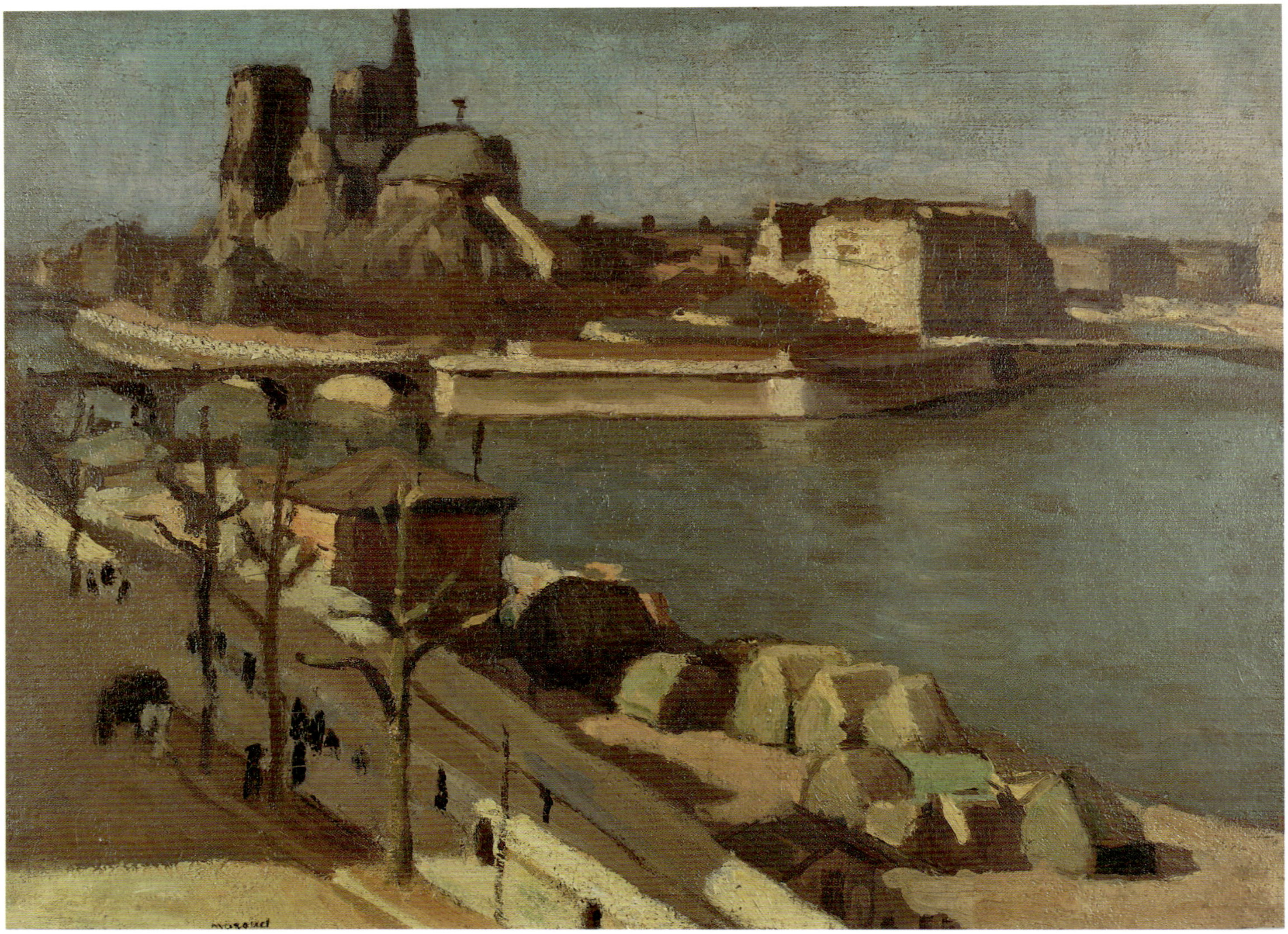

3 *La Seine et l'abside de Notre-Dame,* 1902

Oil on canvas

54 x 72.5 cms

Ceded in lieu of estate tax, 1988

On deposit at the Musée d'art moderne de Troyes

AM 1988-755

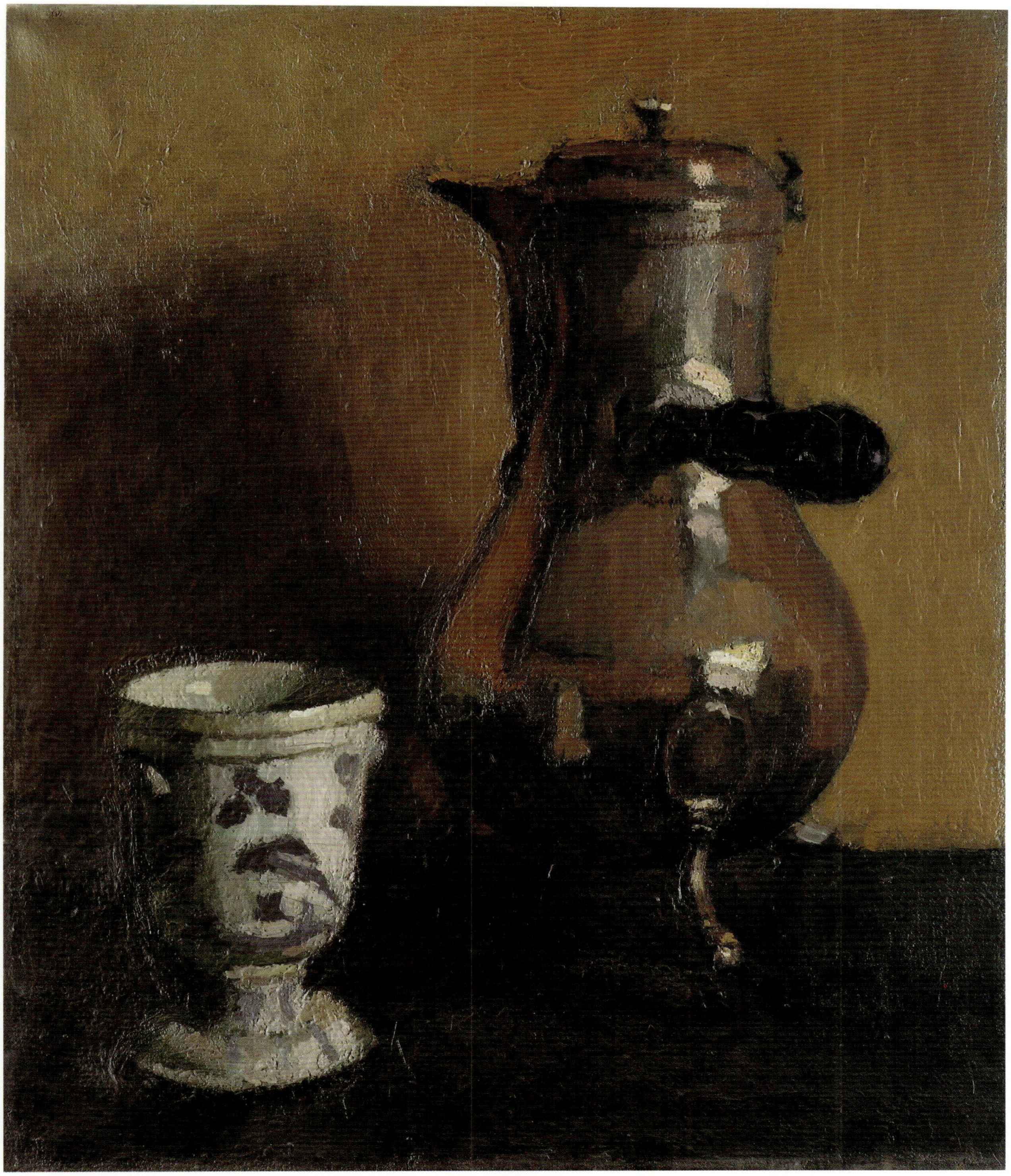

4 *La cafetière*, 1902

Oil on canvas

55 x 46 cms

Bequest of the artist, 1948

On deposit at the Musée des Beaux-Arts de Bordeaux

AM 3276 P

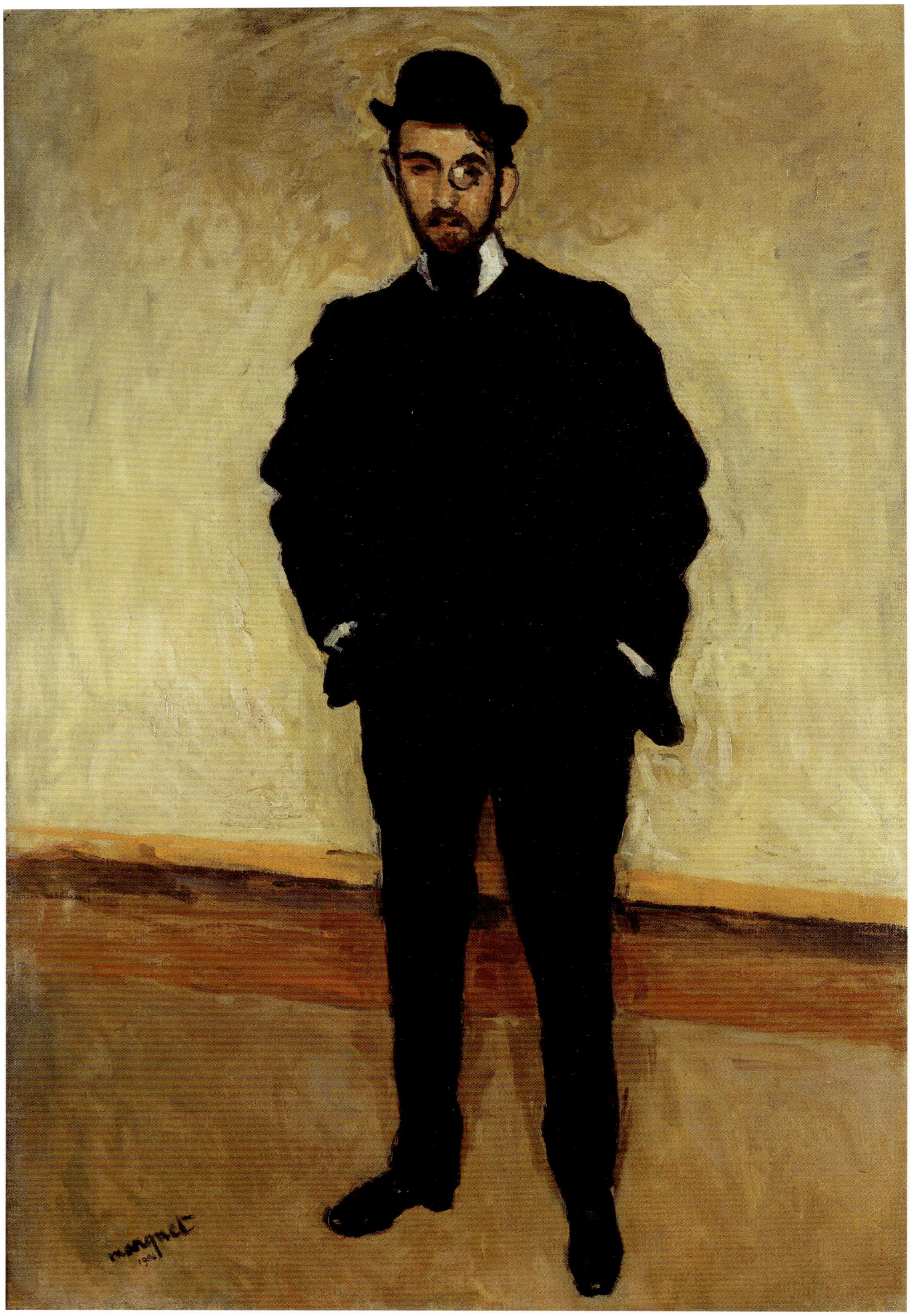

5 *André Rouveyre,* 1904

Oil on canvas

92 x 61 cms

Purchased from André Rouveyre, 1939

AM 2227 P

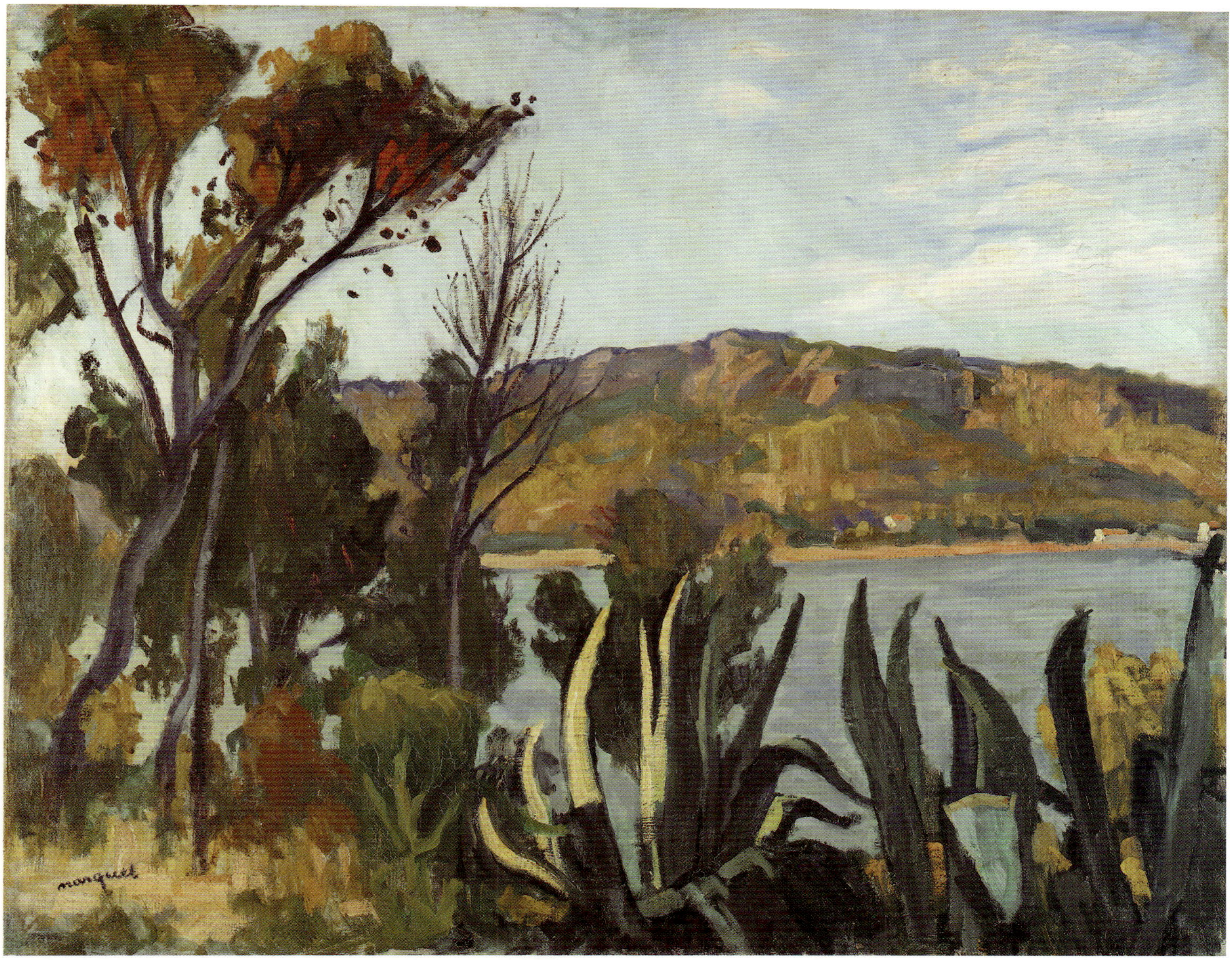

6 *Vue d'Agay*, ca. 1905

Oil on canvas

64.5 x 80.7 cms

Bequest of Gaston Migeon, 1931

AM 1826 P

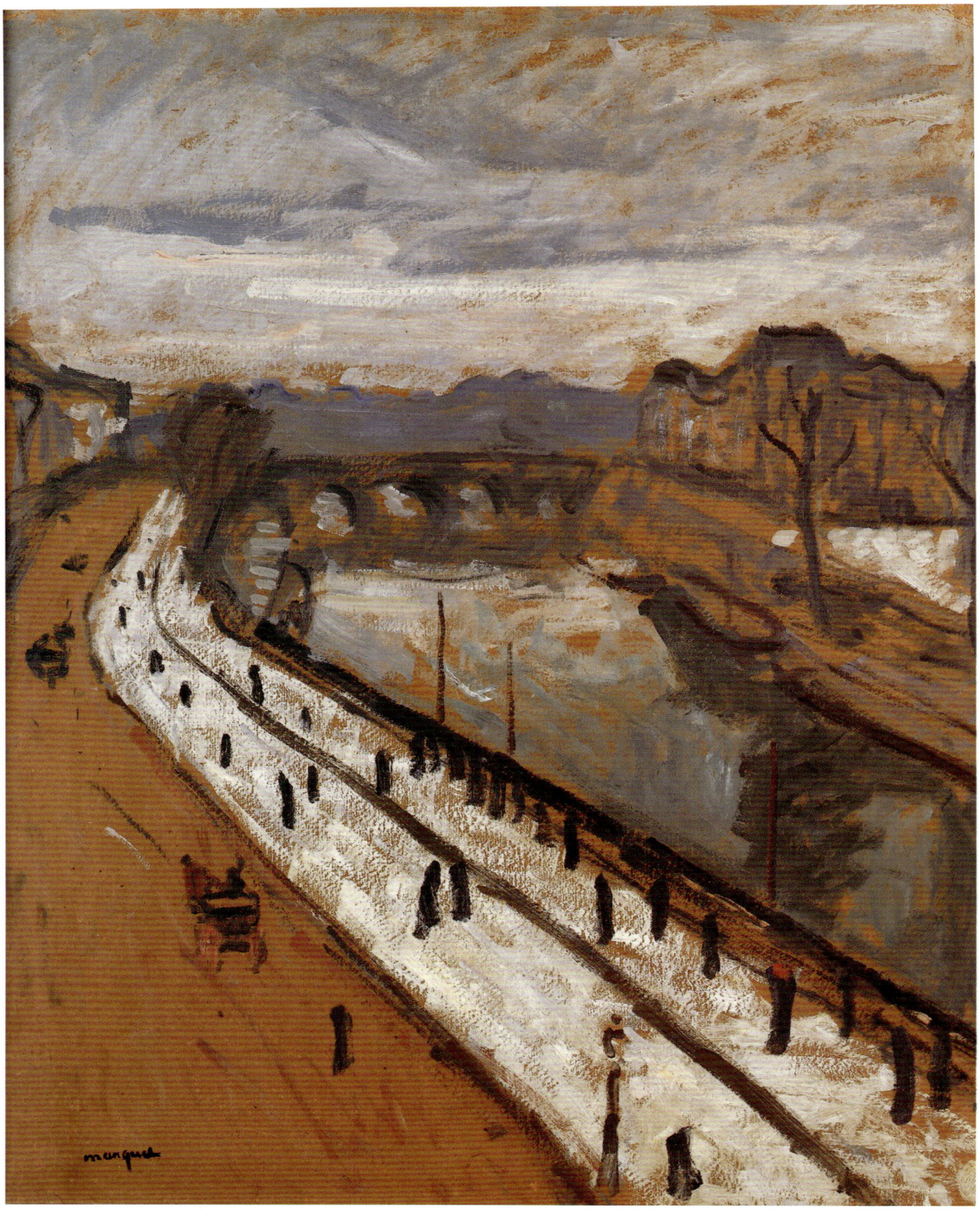

7 *Le Quai des Grands Augustins*, 1905

Oil on cardboard

80 x 65 cms

Purchased from the artist, 1939

AM 2230 P

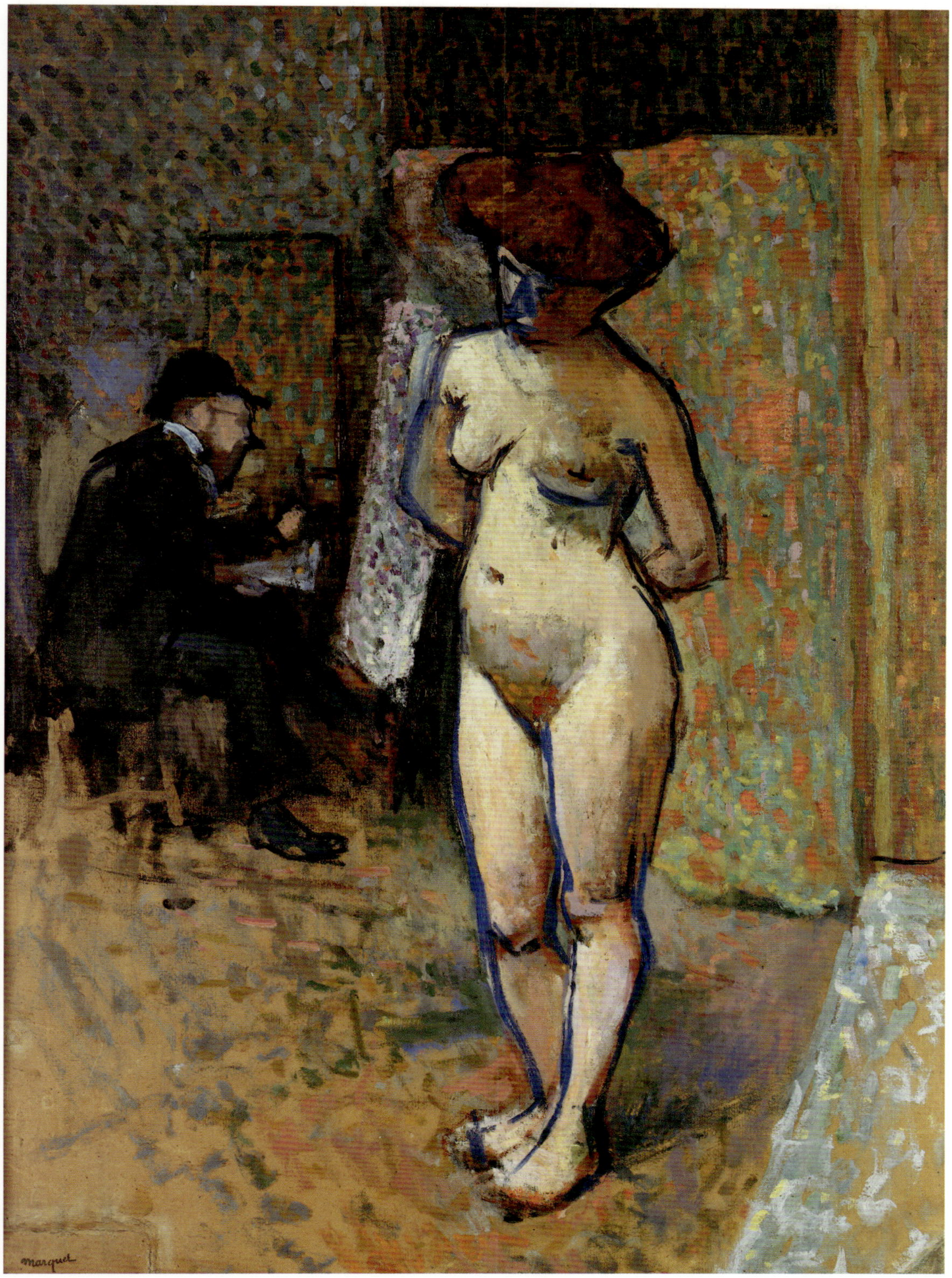

8 *Matisse dans l'atelier de Manguin*, 1905

Oil on cardboard

100 x 73 cms

Purchased from M. Martinet with the participation of

M. Pierre David-Weill, 1957

AM 3488 P

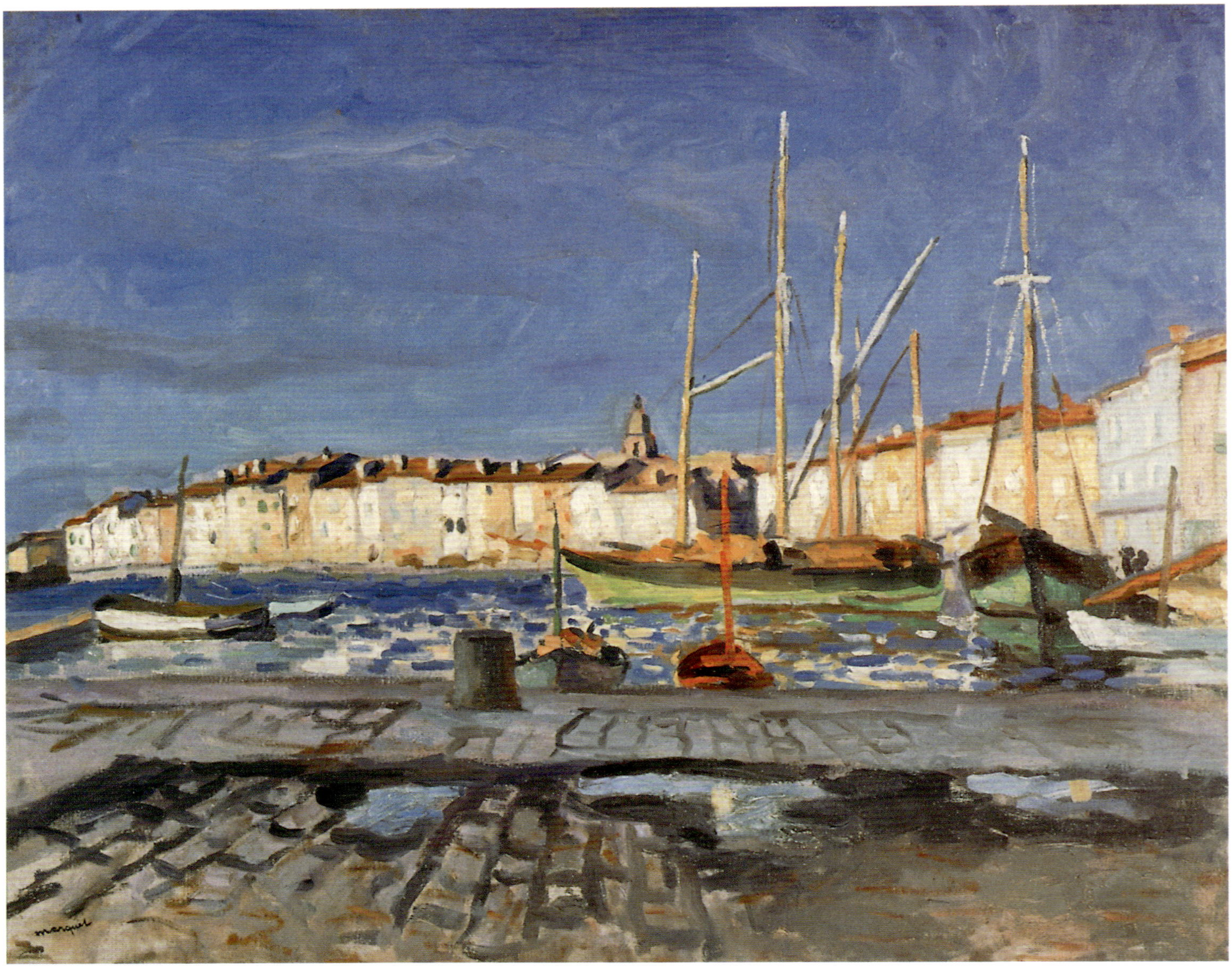

9 Port de Saint-Tropez, 1905

Oil on canvas

49.5 x 61 cms

Georges Grammont bequest to the national museums, exclusively for the Musée de l'Annonciade de Saint-Tropez, 1959

On deposit at the Musée de l'Annonciade de Saint-Tropez

AM 3856 P

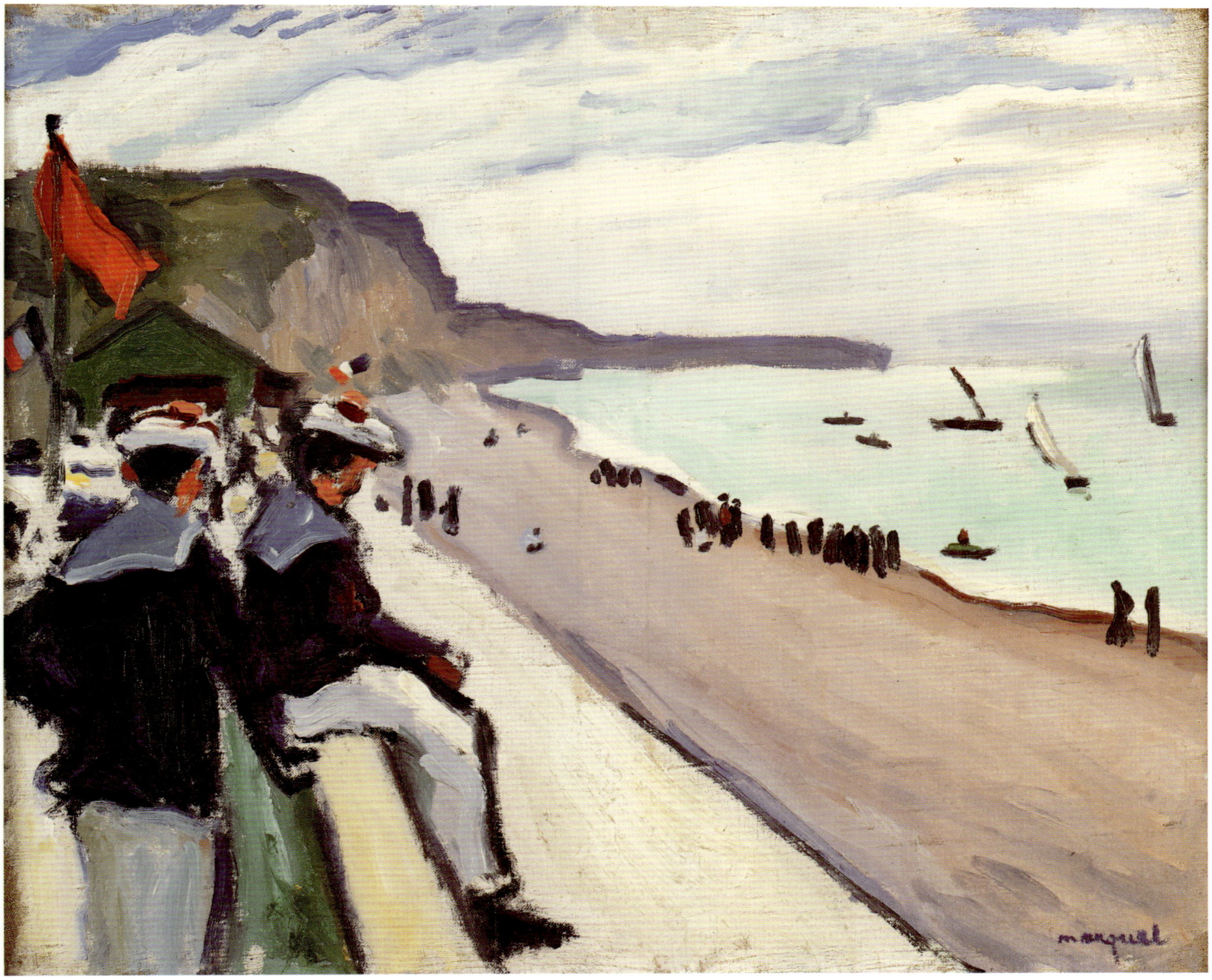

10 *La plage de Fécamp*, 1906

Oil on canvas

50 x 60.8 cms

Bequest of Paul Jamot, 1943

AM 2429 P

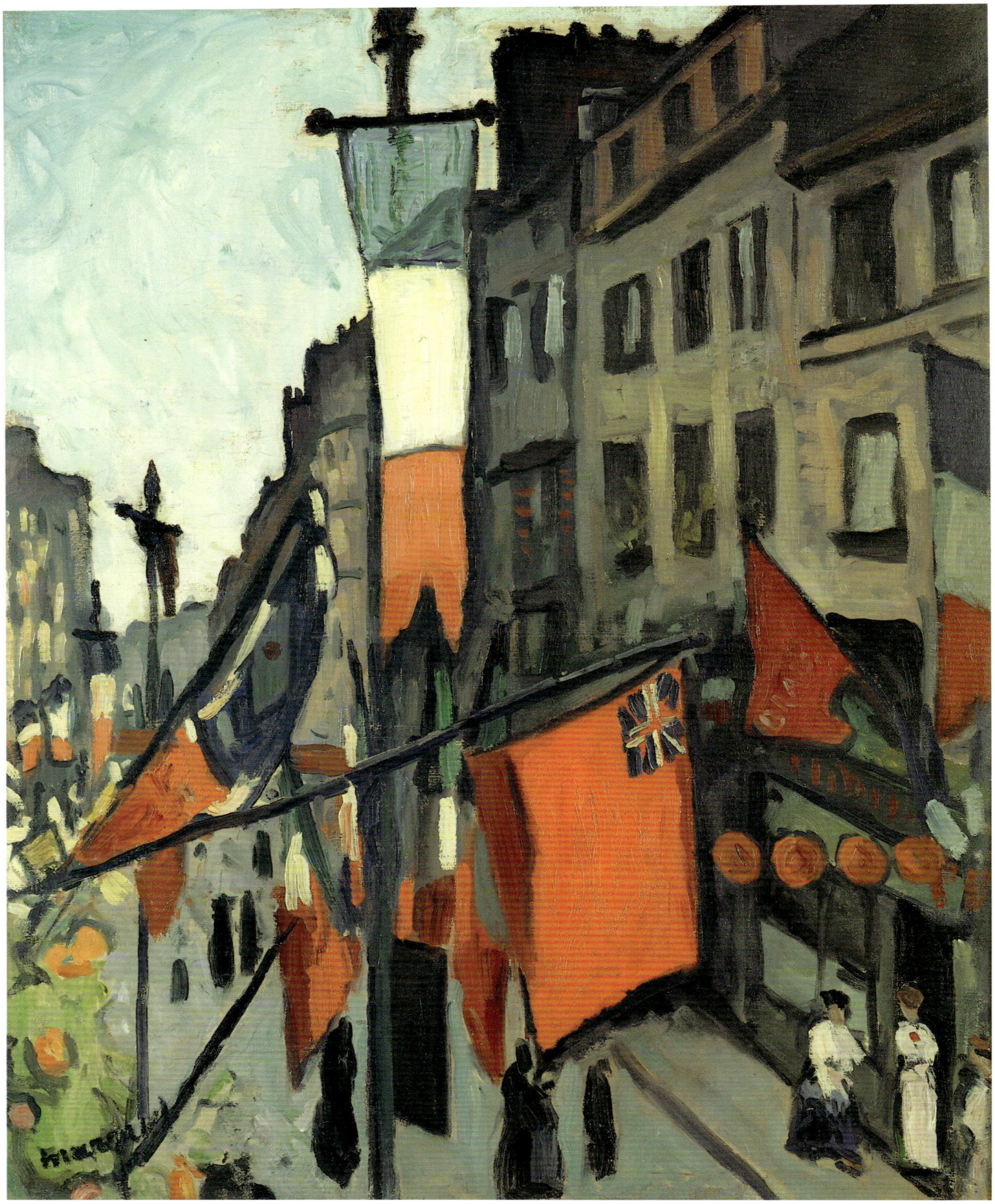

11 *Le 14 juillet au Havre*, 1906

Oil on canvas

81 x 65 cms

Donation of Adèle and Georges Besson, 1963

On deposit at the Musée Albert-André, Bagnols-sur-Cèze

AM 4224 P(20)

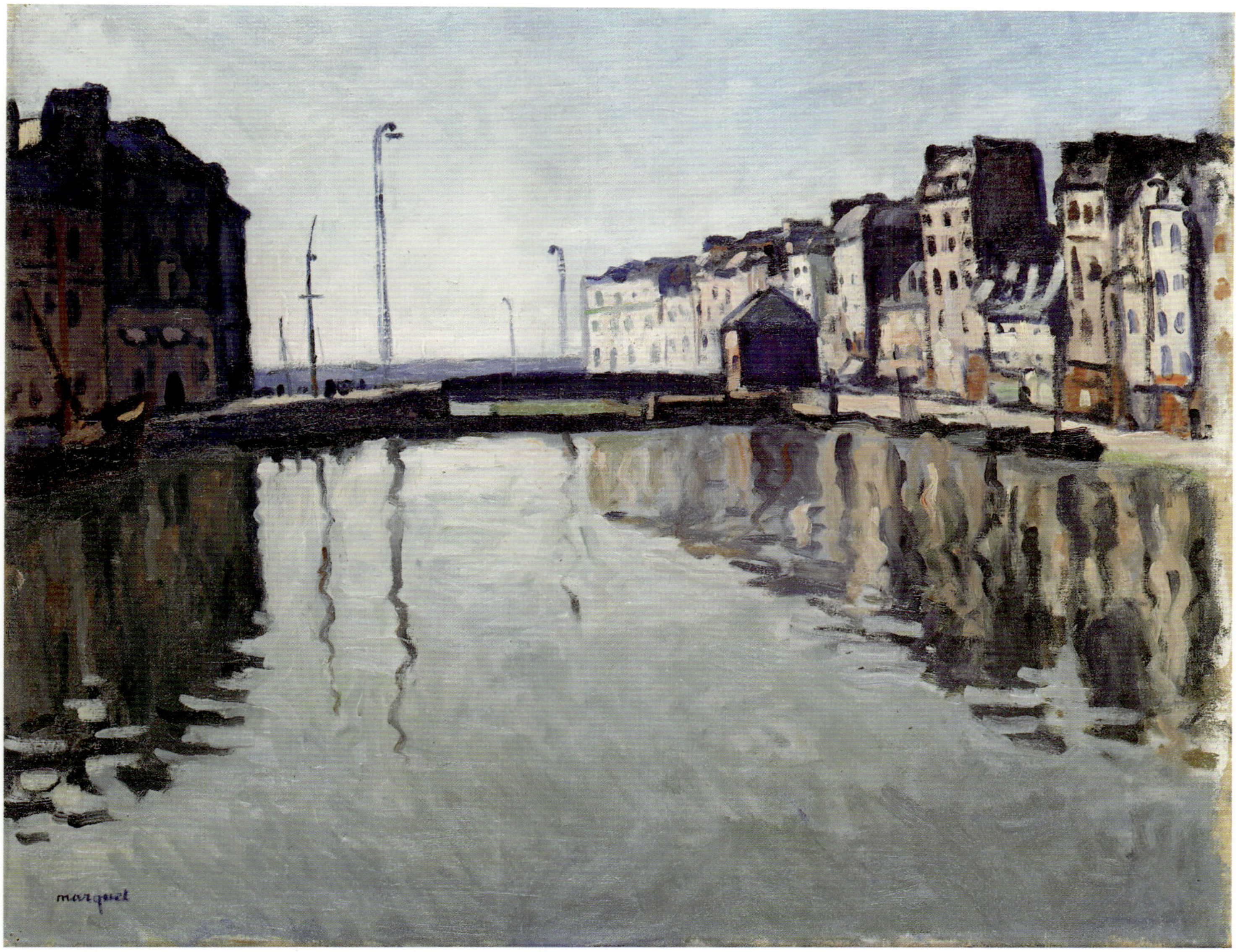

12 *Bassin au Havre,* 1906

Oil on canvas

65 x 80.5 cms

Purchased from the artist and assigned to the Musée national d'art moderne in 1930

LUX.1805 P

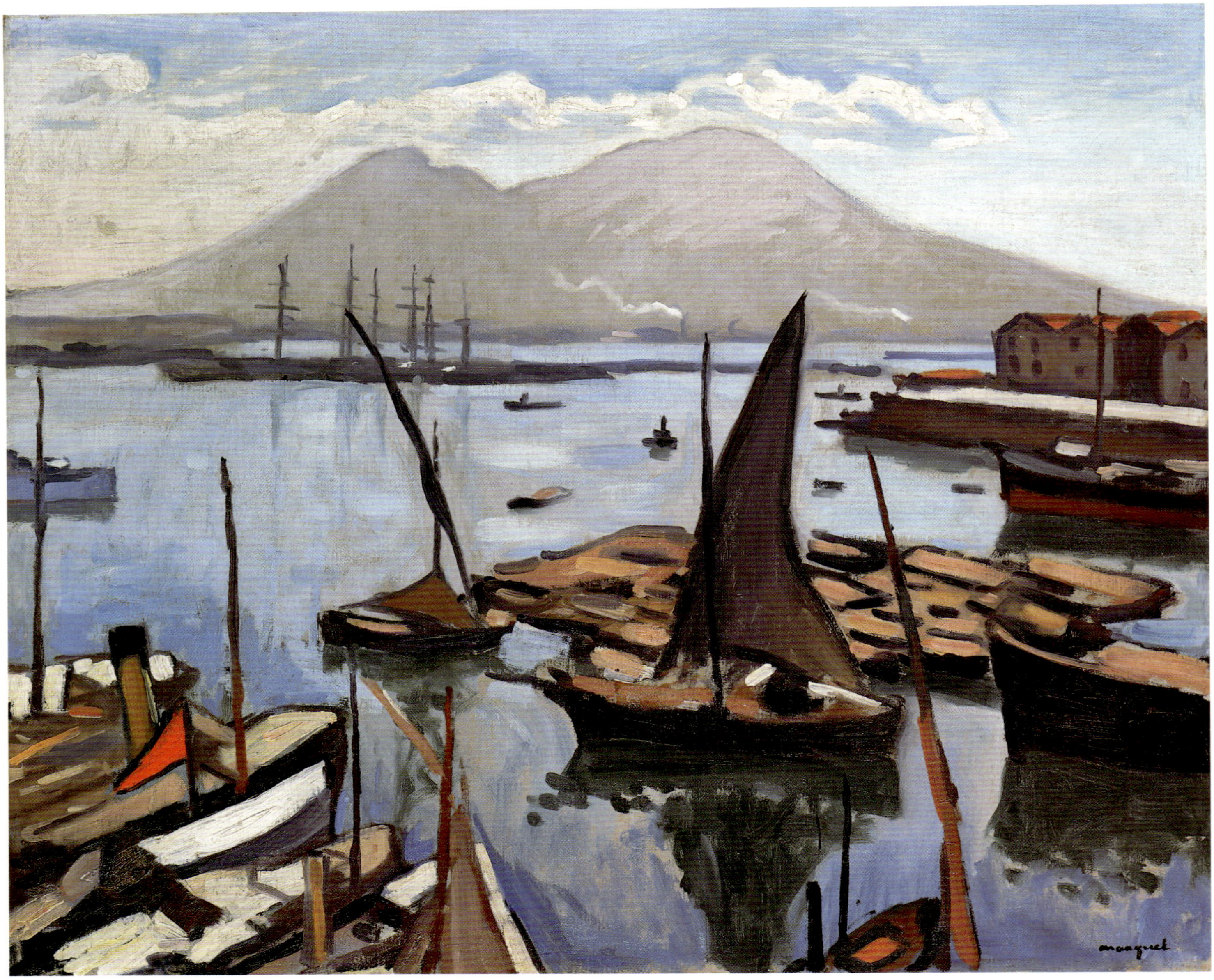

13 *Le port de Naples*, 1909

Oil on canvas

63.5 x 76.5 cms

Donation of Adèle and Georges Besson, 1963

On deposit at the Musée des Beaux-Arts et

d'Archéologie de Besançon

AM 4224 P

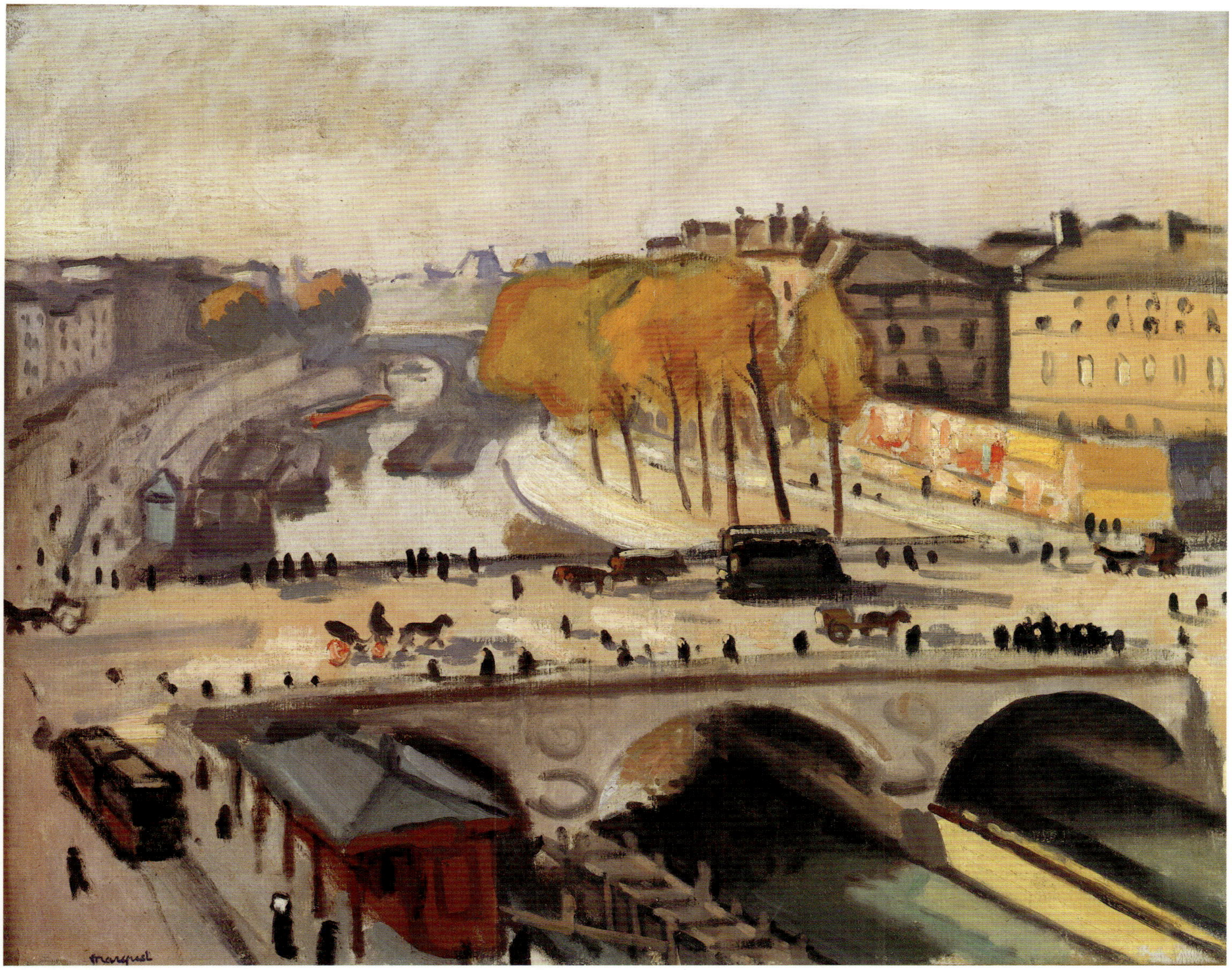

14 *Le Pont Saint-Michel et le Quai des Grands Augustins*, 1912

Oil on canvas

66 x 82 cms

Formerly collection of Baron Kojiro Matsukata, ceded to the Musée national d'art moderne by the peace treaty with Japan, 1959

AM 3614 P

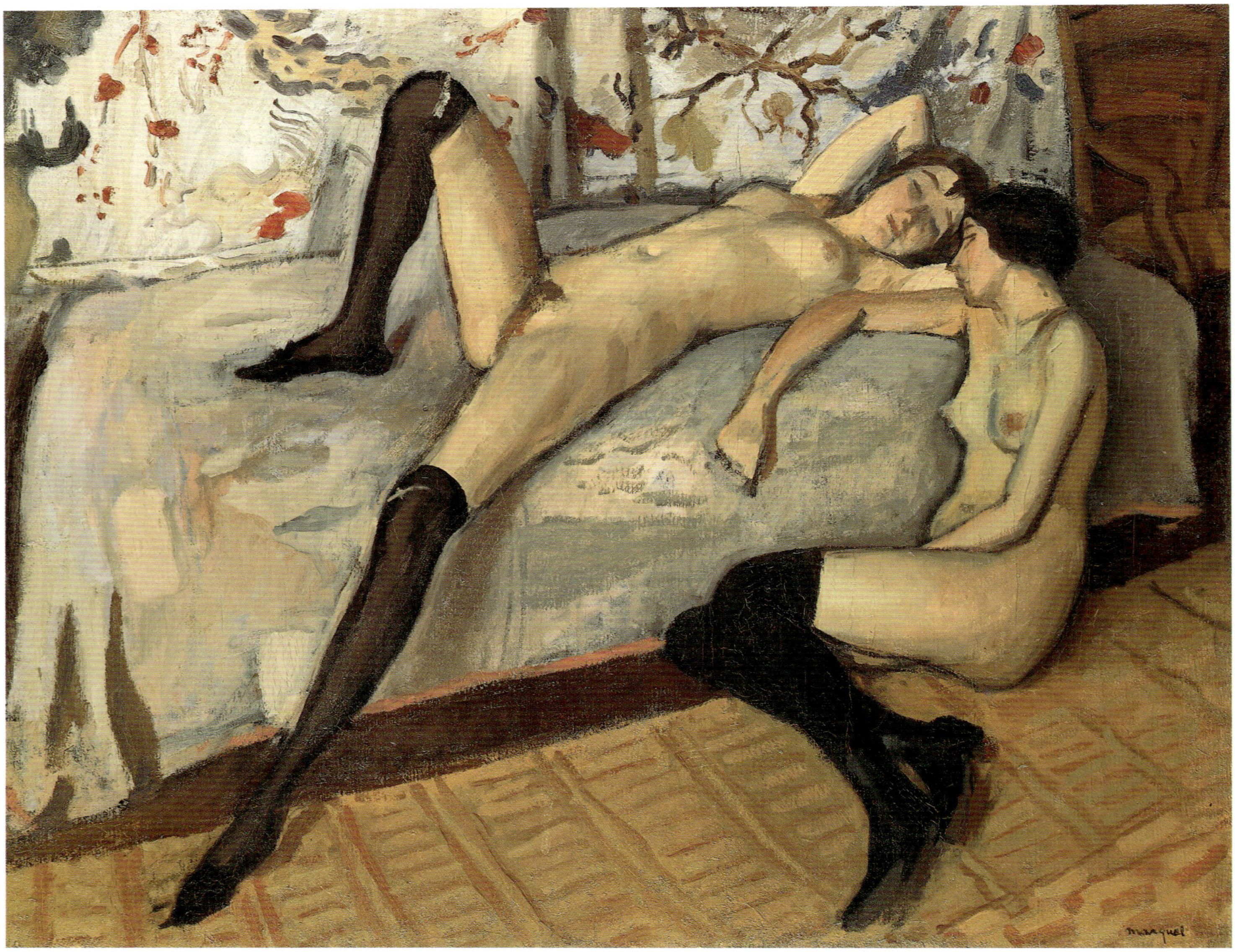

15 *Les deux amies*, 1912

Oil on canvas

60 x 92 cms

Donation of Adèle and Georges Besson, 1963

On deposit at the Musée des Beaux-Arts et

d'Archéologie de Besançon

AM 4224 P(55)

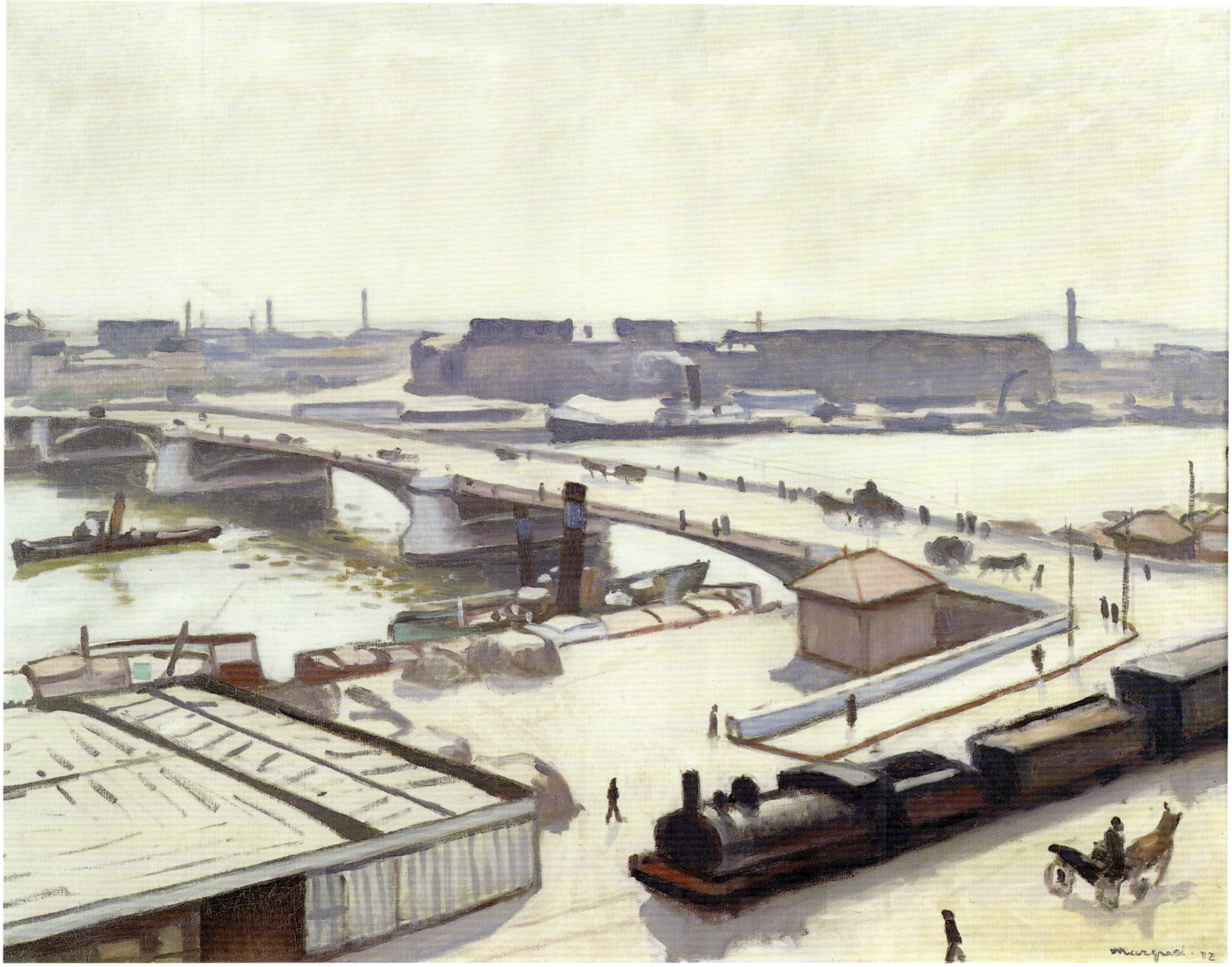

16 *Le quai de Paris à Rouen*, 1912

Oil on canvas

65 x 82 cms

Purchased from the artist and assigned to the

Musée national d'art moderne in 1913

LUX.1019 P

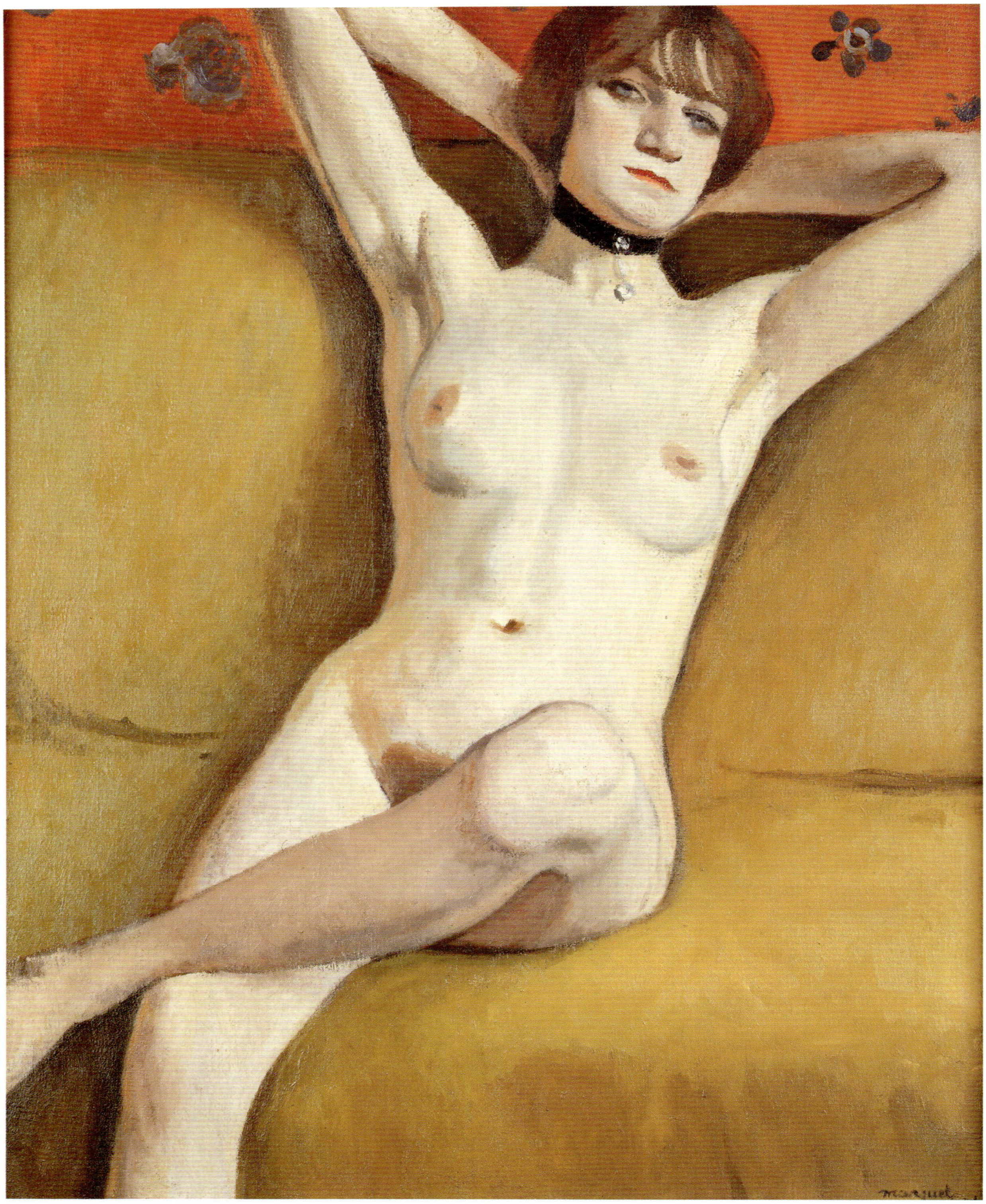

17 *Nu au divan*, 1912

Oil on canvas

100 x 81 cms

Gift of Mme Druet, 1929

LUX.1643 P

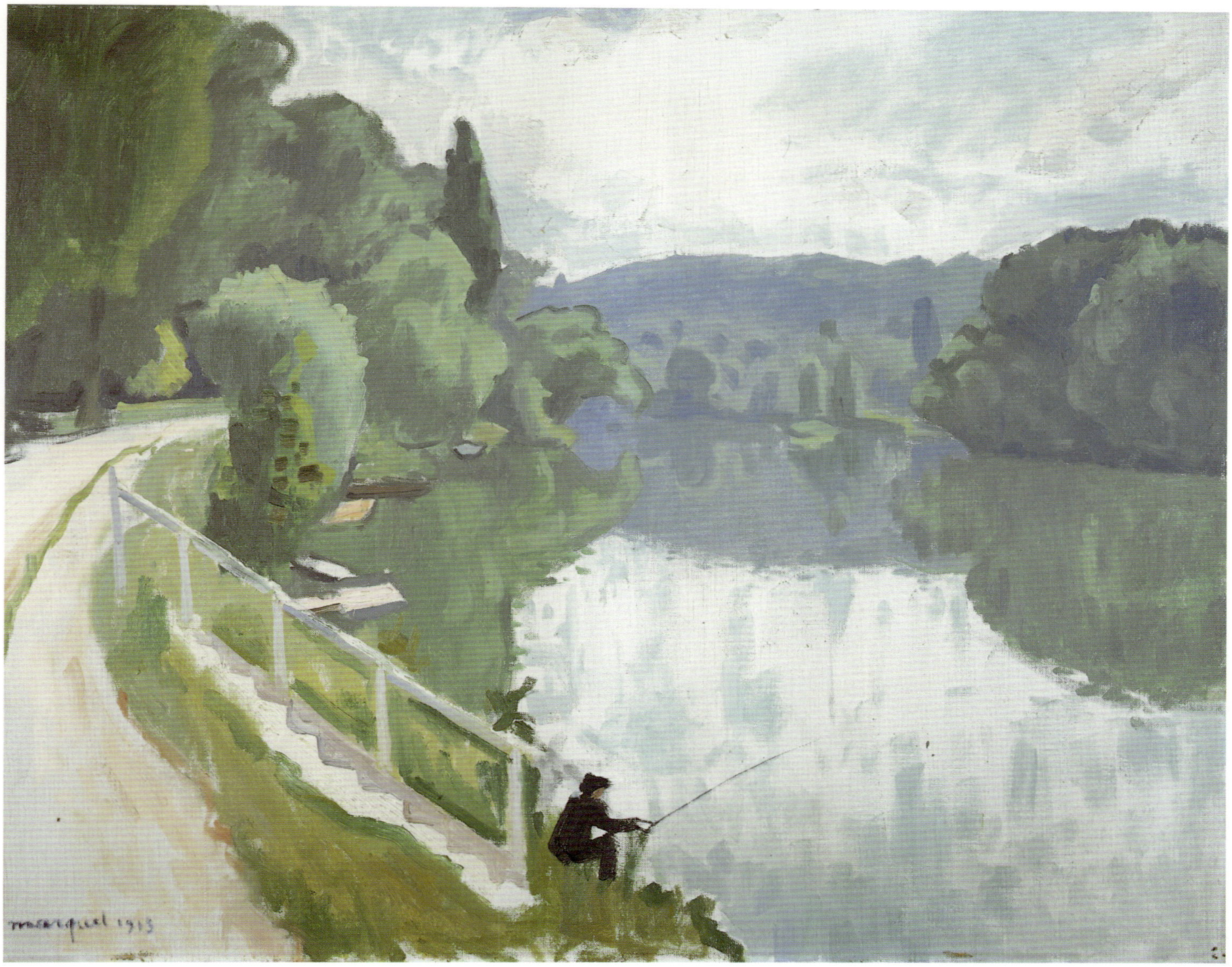

18 Bords de rivière, 1913

Oil on canvas

46 x 81 cms

Purchased from the artist in 1913 and assigned to the Musée national d'art moderne in 1958

LUX.1030 P

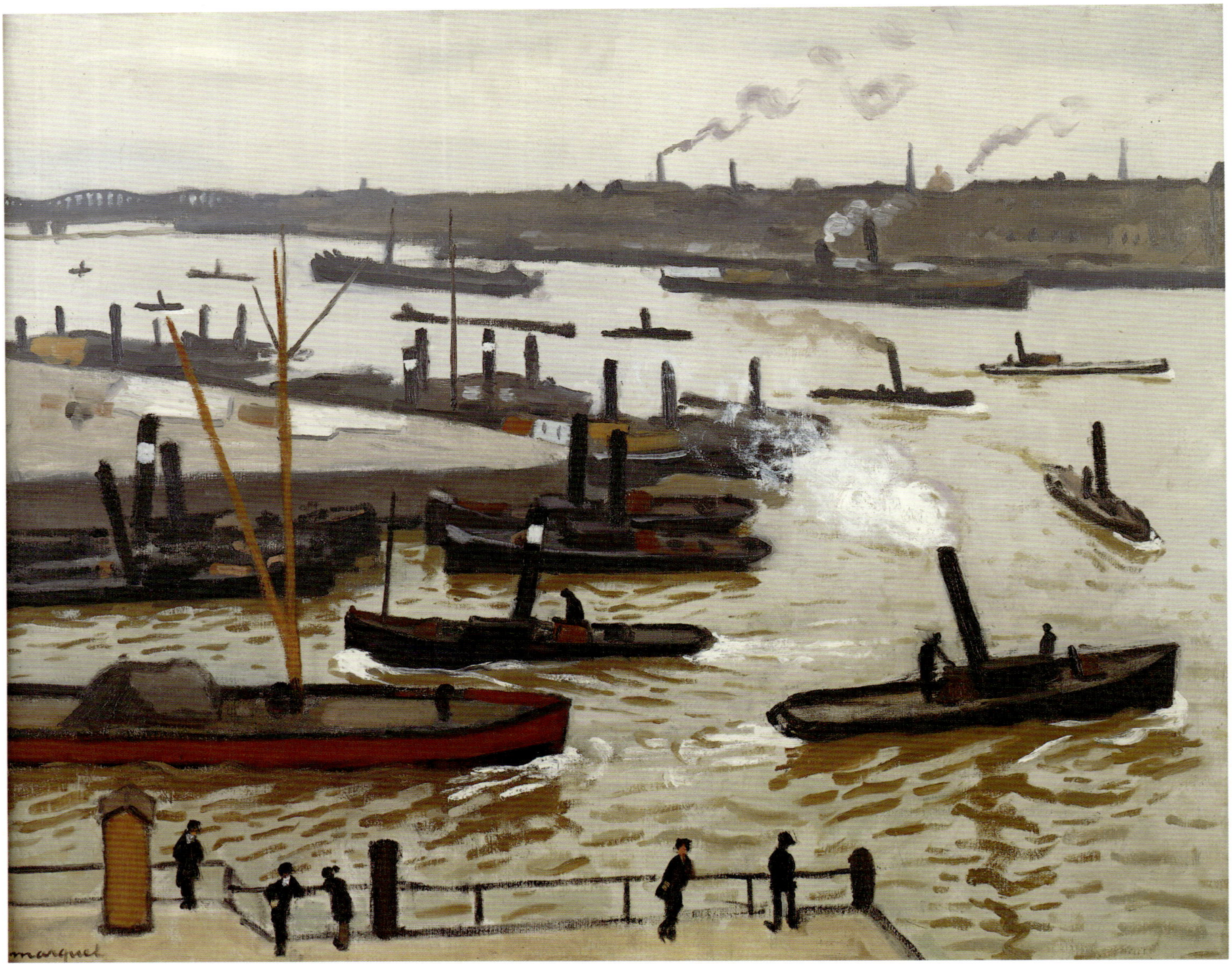

19 Rotterdam, 1914

Oil on canvas

65.2 x 81.2 cms

Purchased from the artist in 1940 and assigned to the

Musée national d'art moderne in 1942

AM 2353 P

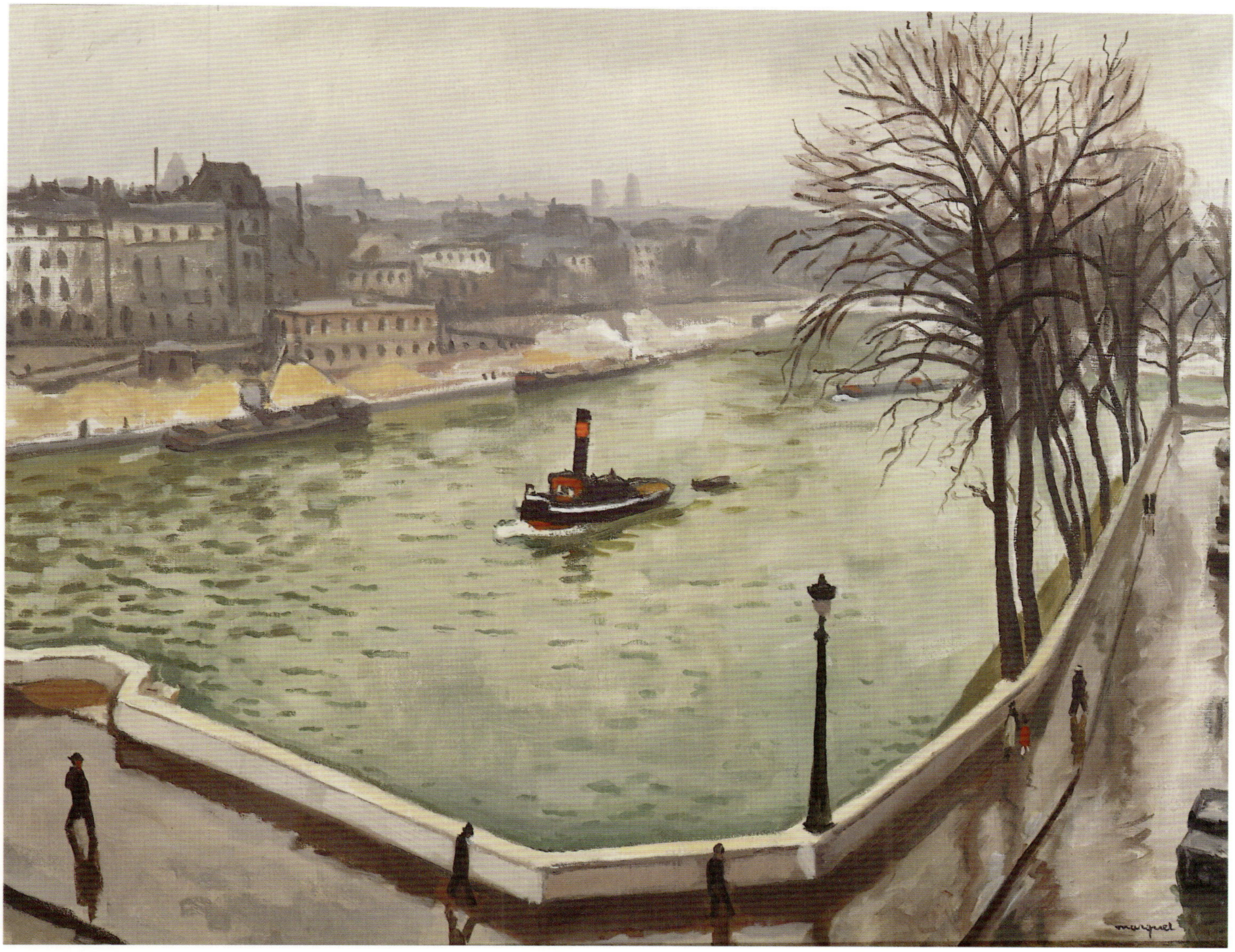

20 *La Seine à Paris* or *Paris, quai d'Orléans vu du quai de Béthune*, ca. 1914–1915

Oil on canvas

63 x 80 cms

Georges Grammont bequest to the national museums, exclusively for the Musée de l'Annonciade de Saint-Tropez, 1959

On deposit at the Musée de l'Annonciade de Saint-Tropez

AM 3838 P

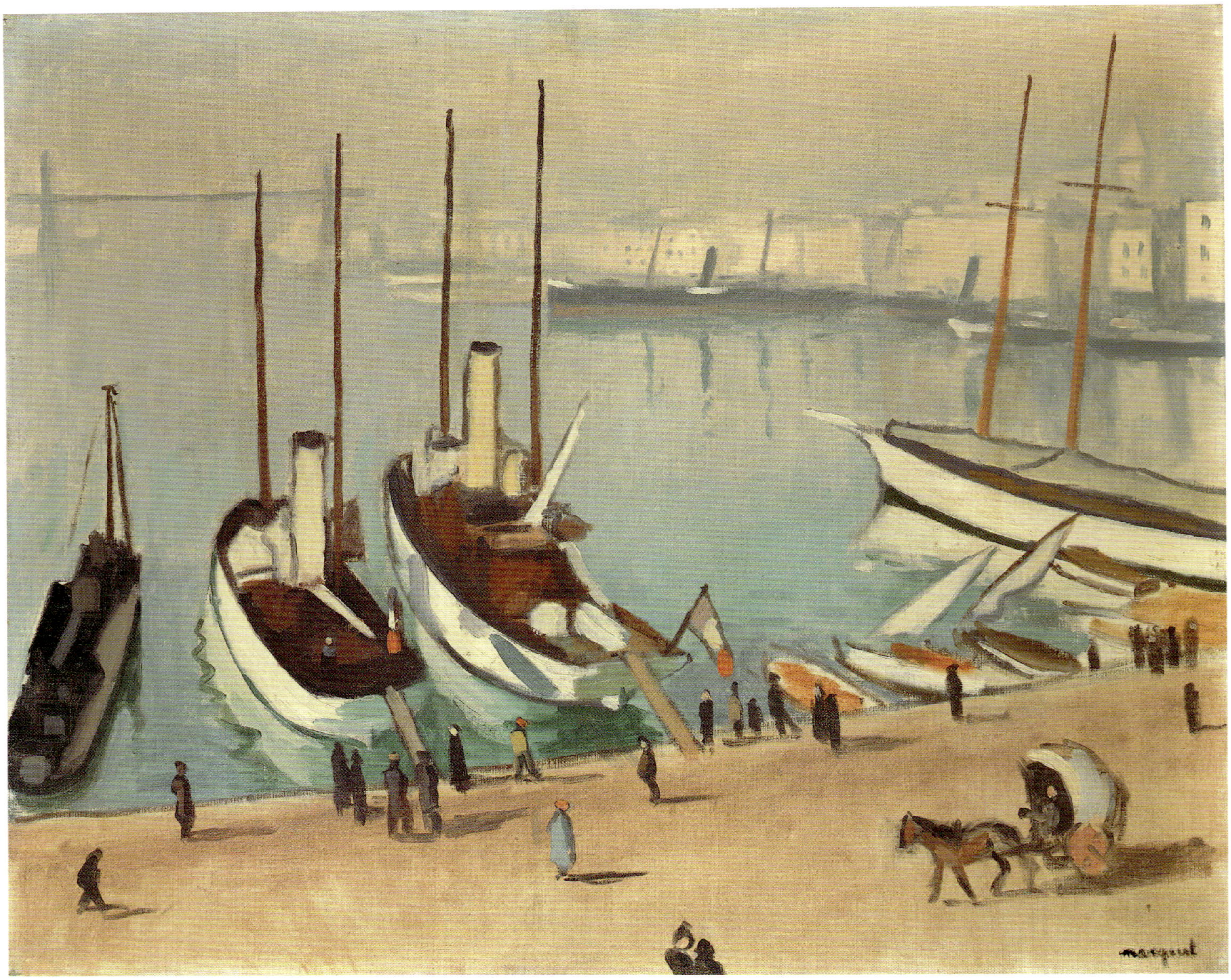

21 *Le Vieux-Port à Marseille,* 1917

Oil on canvas

60 x 73 cms

Donation of Adèle and Georges Besson, 1963

On deposit at the Musée des Beaux-Arts et

d'Archéologie de Besançon

AM 4224 P

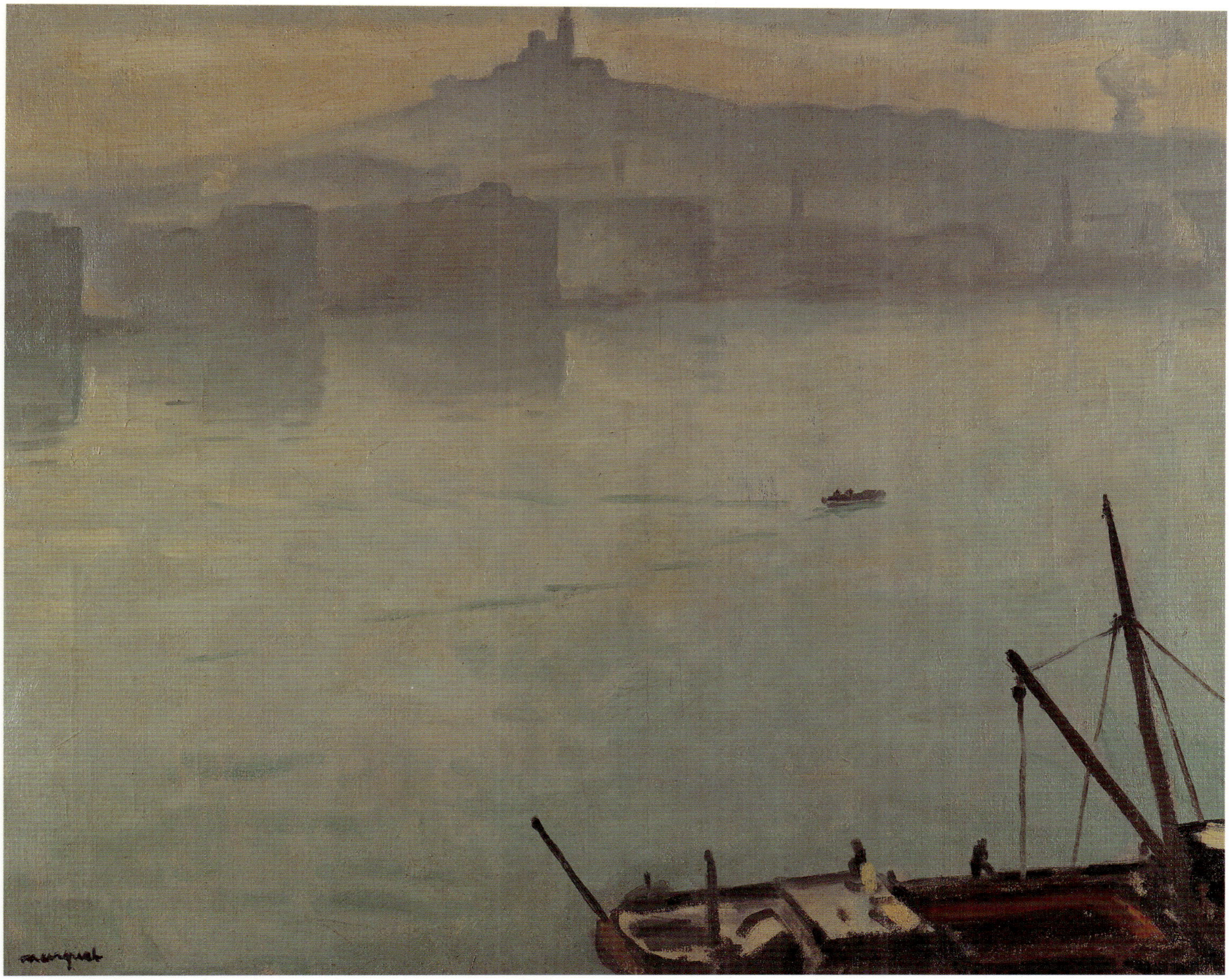

22 *Port de Marseille*, 1918

Oil on canvas

64 x 80 cms

Georges Grammont bequest to the national museums,

exclusively for the Musée de l'Annonciade de Saint-Tropez, 1959

On deposit at the Musée de l'Annonciade de Saint-Tropez

AM 3825 P

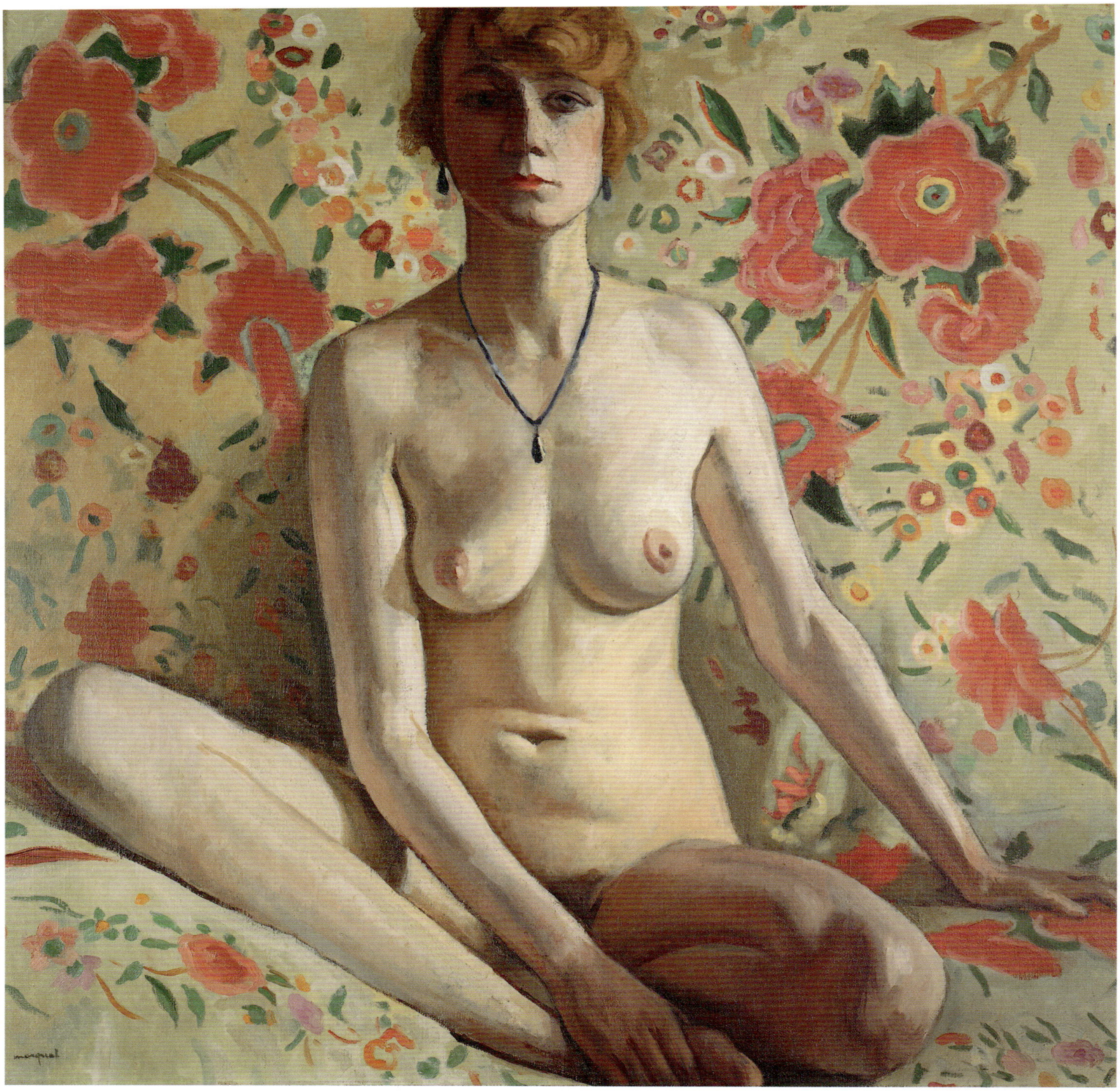

23 *La femme blonde*, 1919

Oil on canvas

98.5 x 98.5 cm

Gift of Olivier Senn, 1939

AM 2229 P

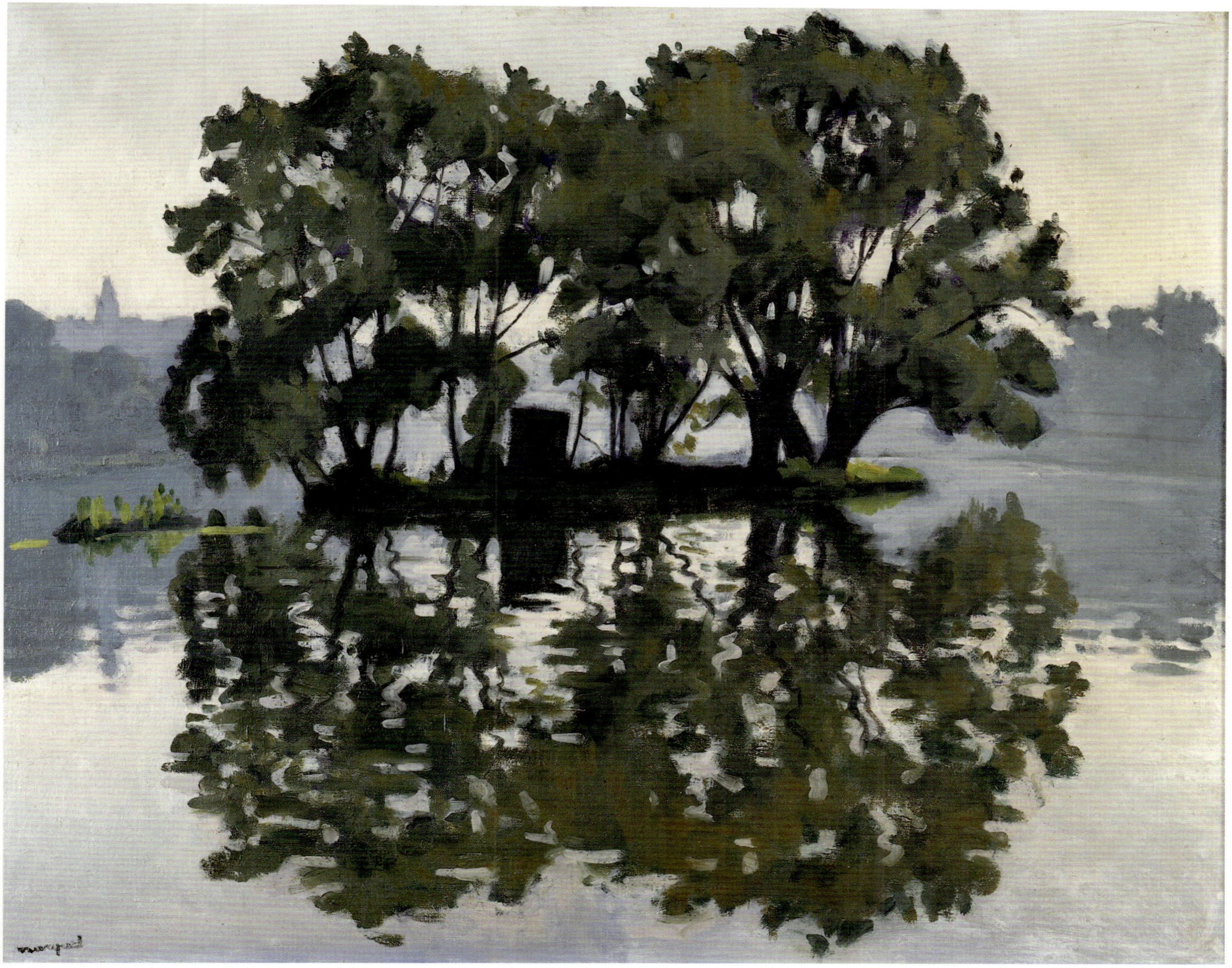

24 *L'Ile aux cygnes*, 1919

Oil on canvas

75 x 81 cms

Bequest of Carle Dreyfus, 1953

AM 3196 P

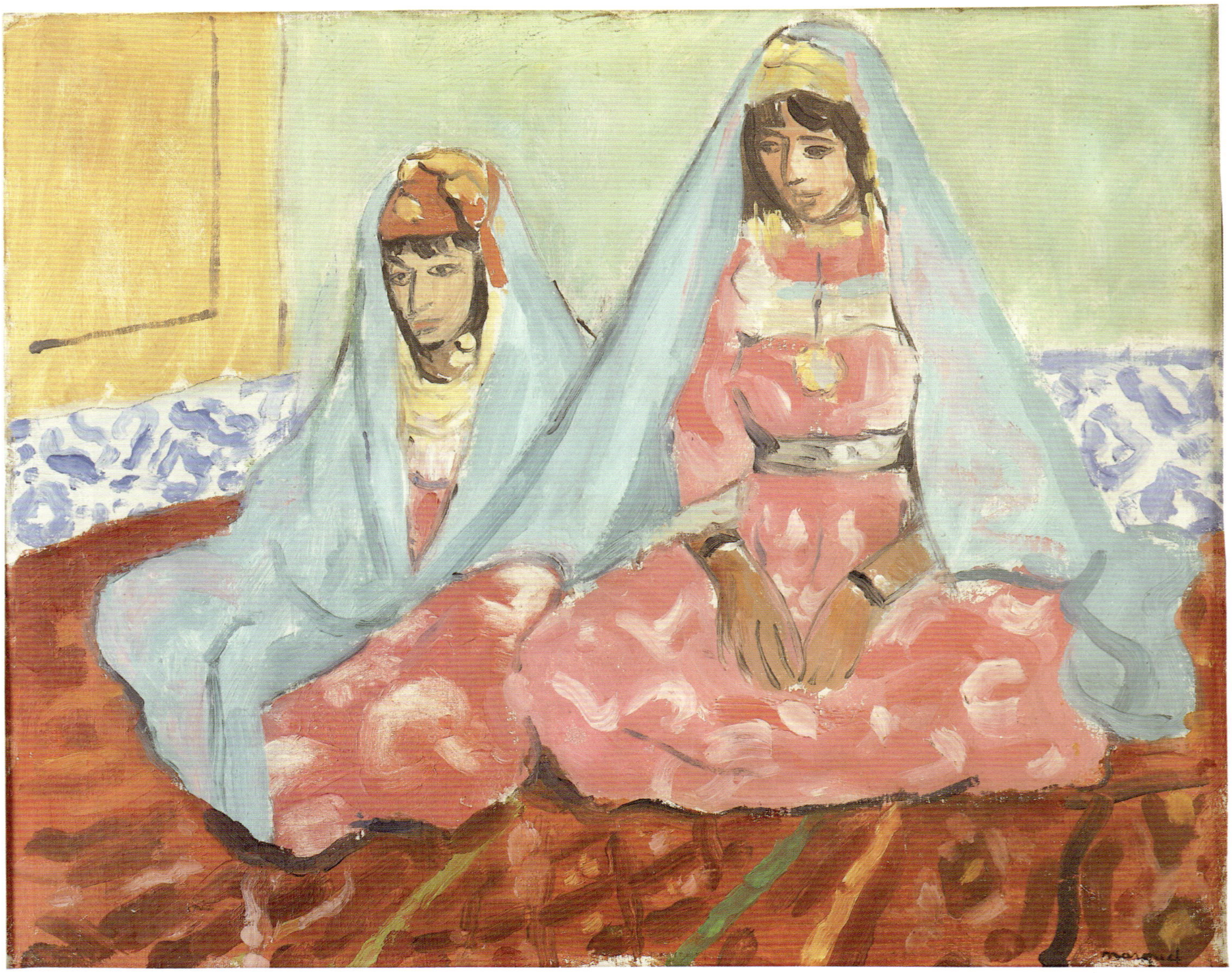

25 *Femmes de Laghouat, ca. 1921*

Oil on canvas

34.5 x 41.5 cm

Purchased from the artist in 1924 and assigned to the Musée national d'art moderne

AM LUX.0.128 P

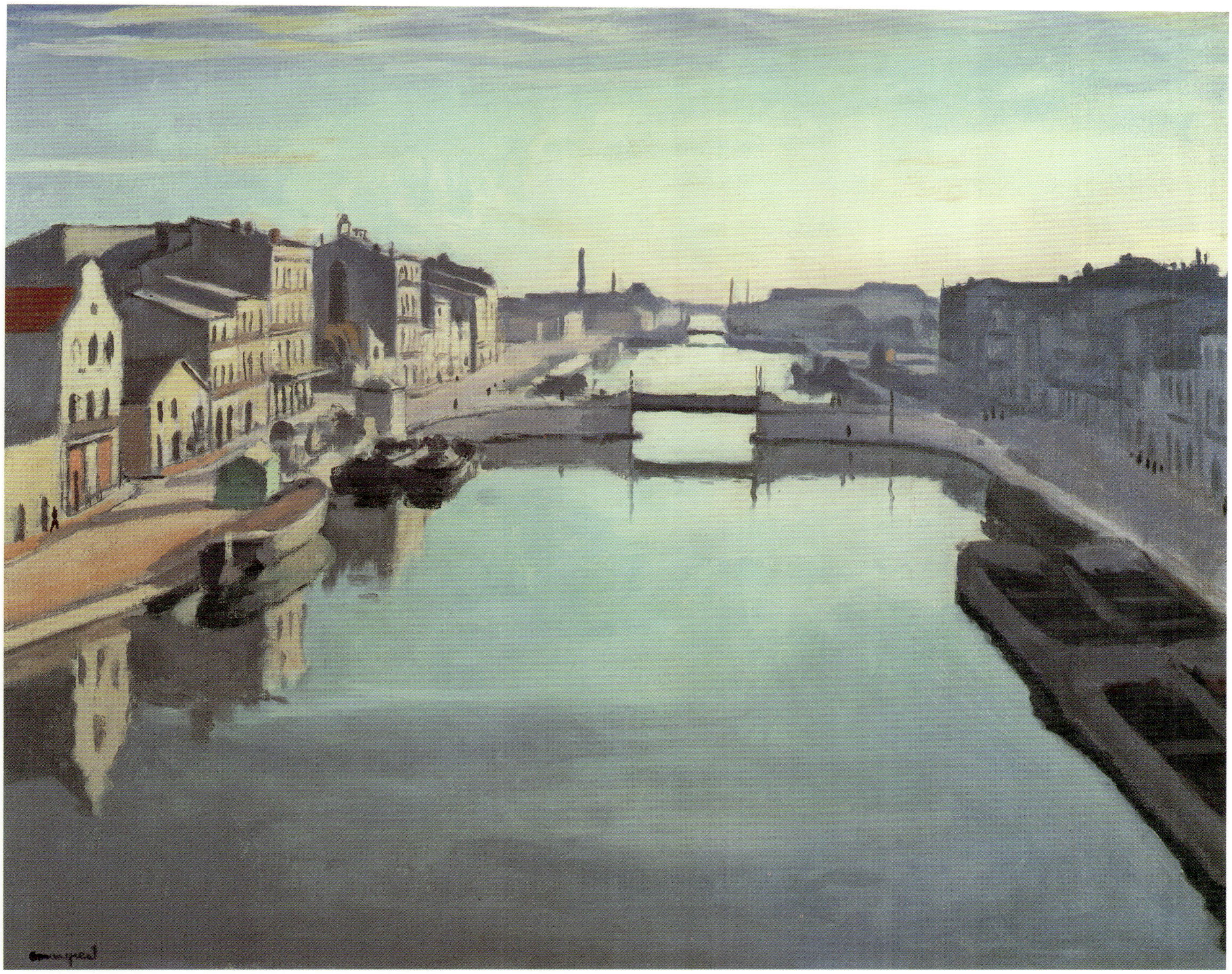

26 *Sète, le Canal de Beaucaire,* 1924

Oil on canvas

64 x 80 cms

Georges Grammont bequest to the national museums,

exclusively for the Musée de l'Annonciade de Saint-Tropez, 1959

On deposit at the Musée de l'Annonciade de Saint-Tropez

AM 3824 P

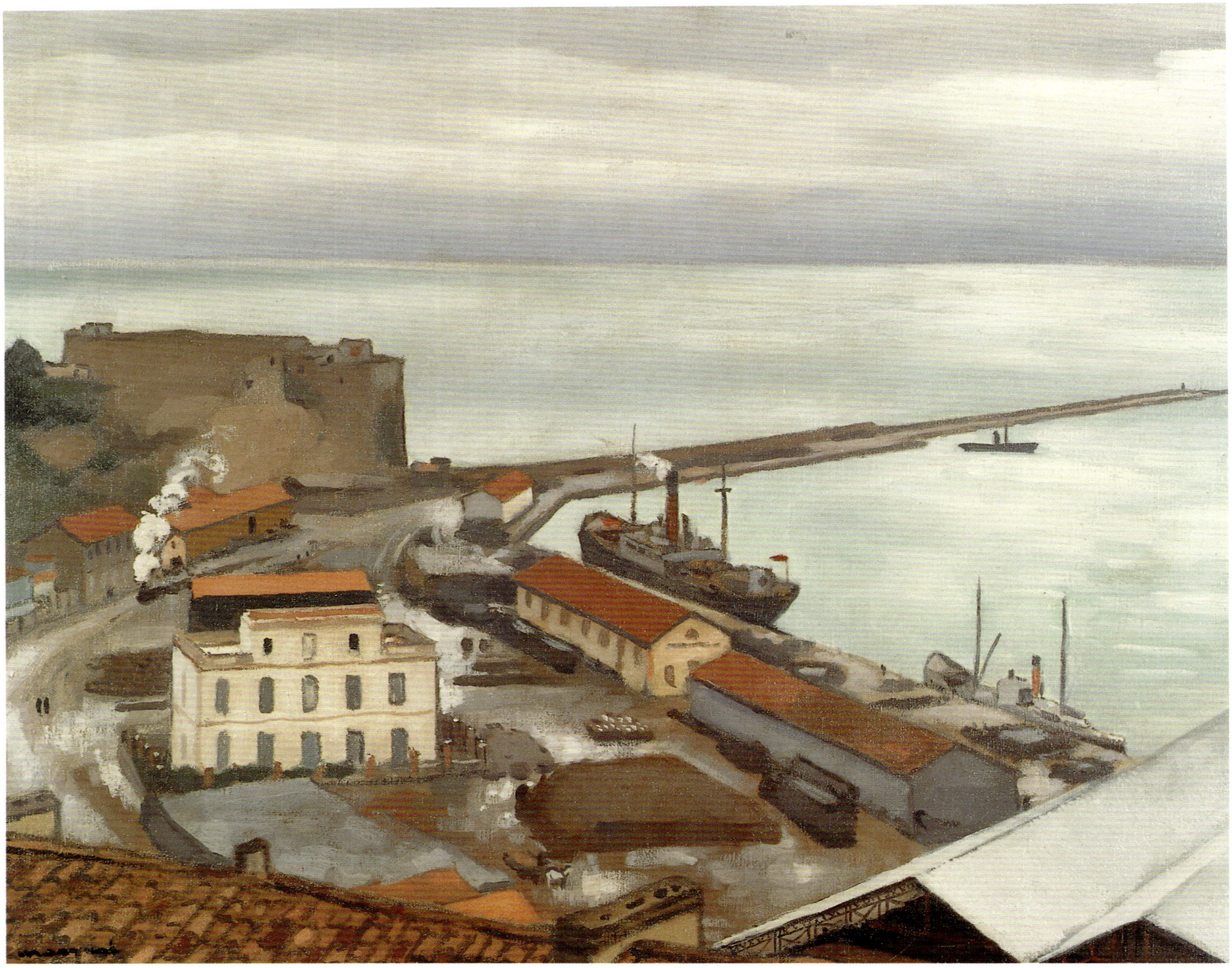

27 *Le port de Bougie par temps gris*, 1925

Oil on canvas

65 x 81 cms

Bequest of Mme Frédéric Lung, 1957

On deposit at the Musée d'art et d'industrie de Roubaix

AM 3903 P

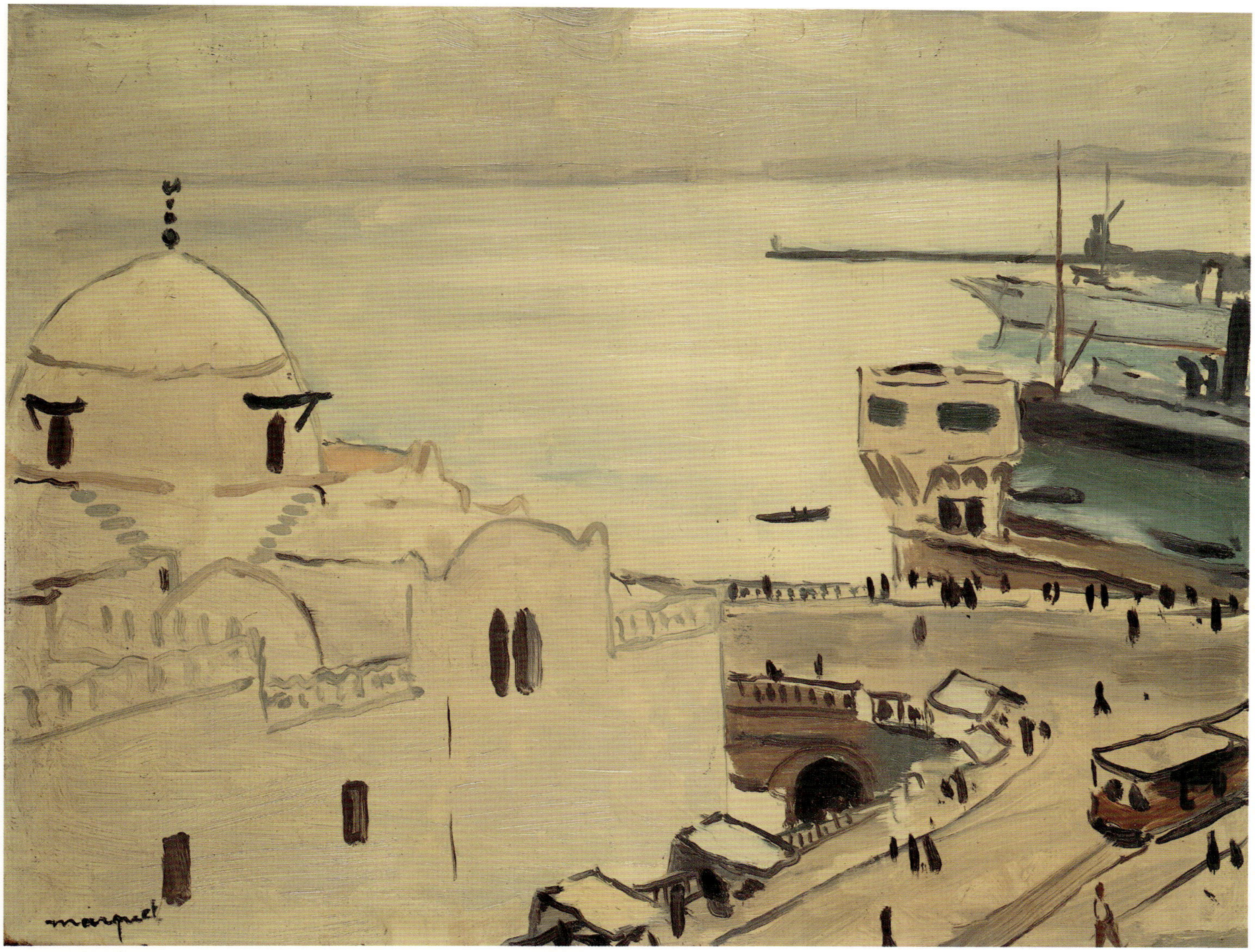

28 *La place du gouvernement à Alger*, 1927

Oil on wood

32.5 x 41 cms

Bequest of Mme Frédéric Lung, 1957

AM 3905 P

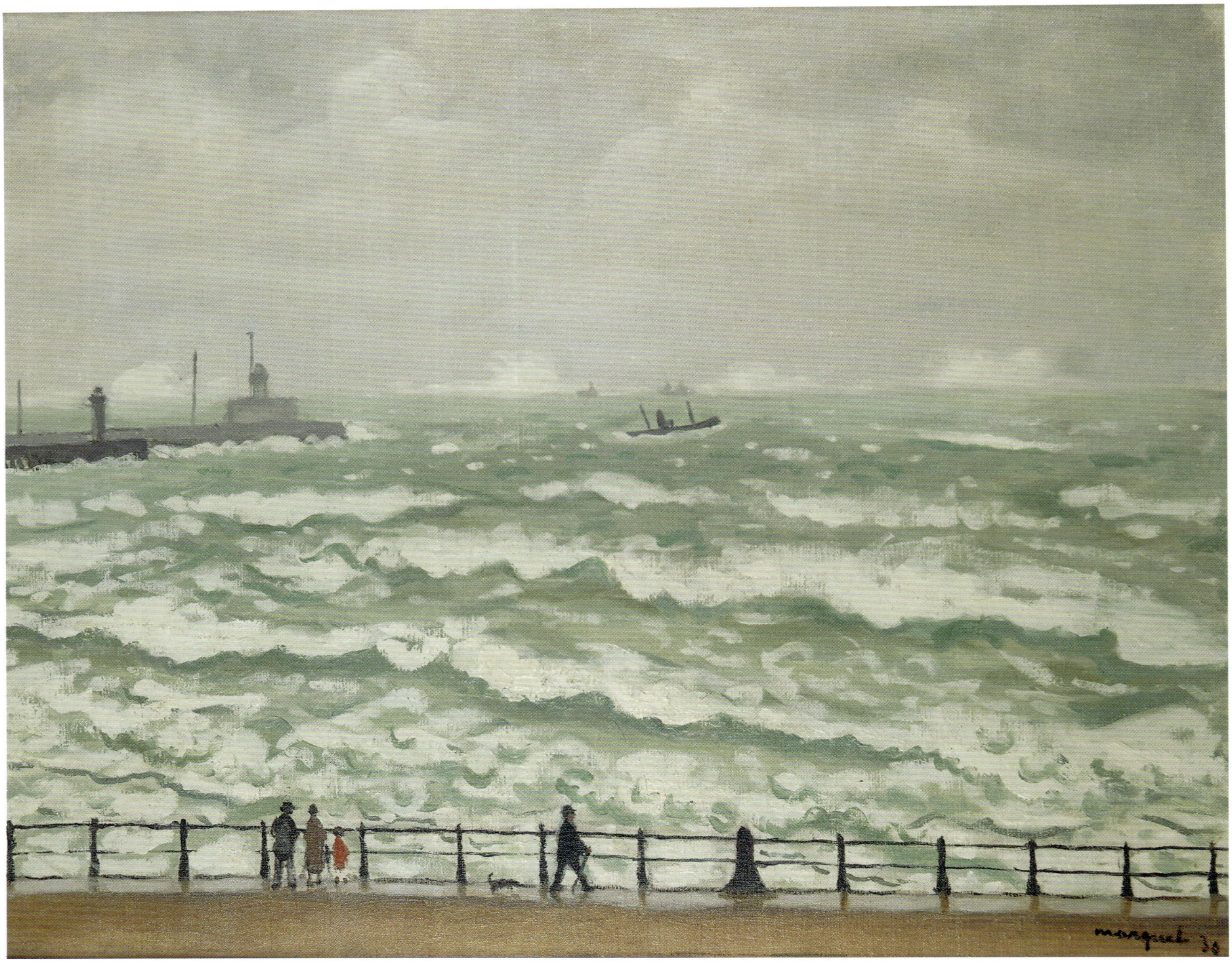

29 Port de Boulogne, 1930

Oil on canvas

65 x 81 cms

Georges Grammont bequest to the national museums, exclusively for the Musée de l'Annonciade de Saint-Tropez, 1959

On deposit at the Musée de l'Annonciade de Saint-Tropez

AM 3851 P

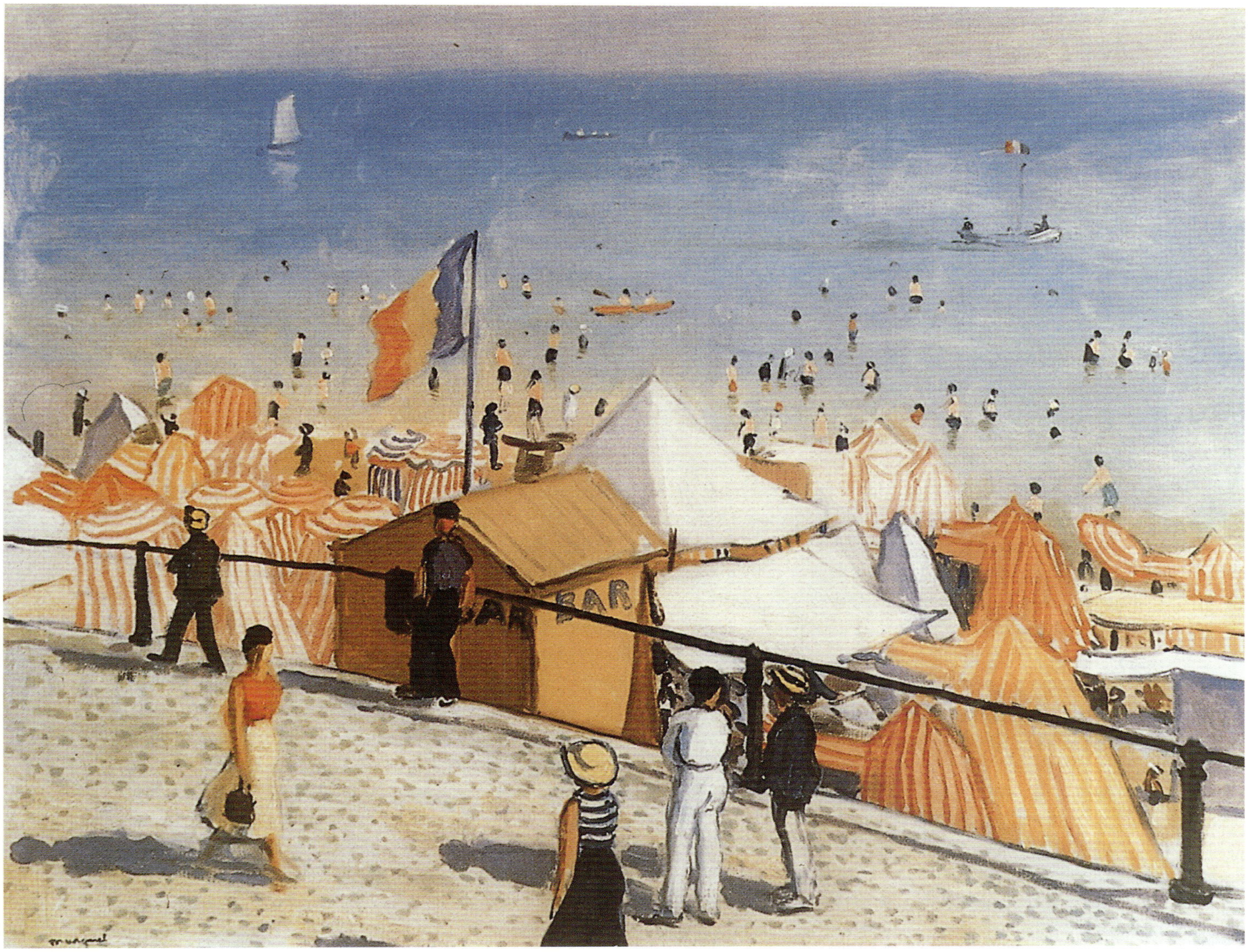

30 *Eté, la plage des Sables-d'Olonne*, 1933

Oil on canvas

65 x 82 cms

Purchased from the artist, 1934

On deposit at the Musée de l'Abbaye Saint-Croix, Les Sables-d'Olonne

AM 1976 P

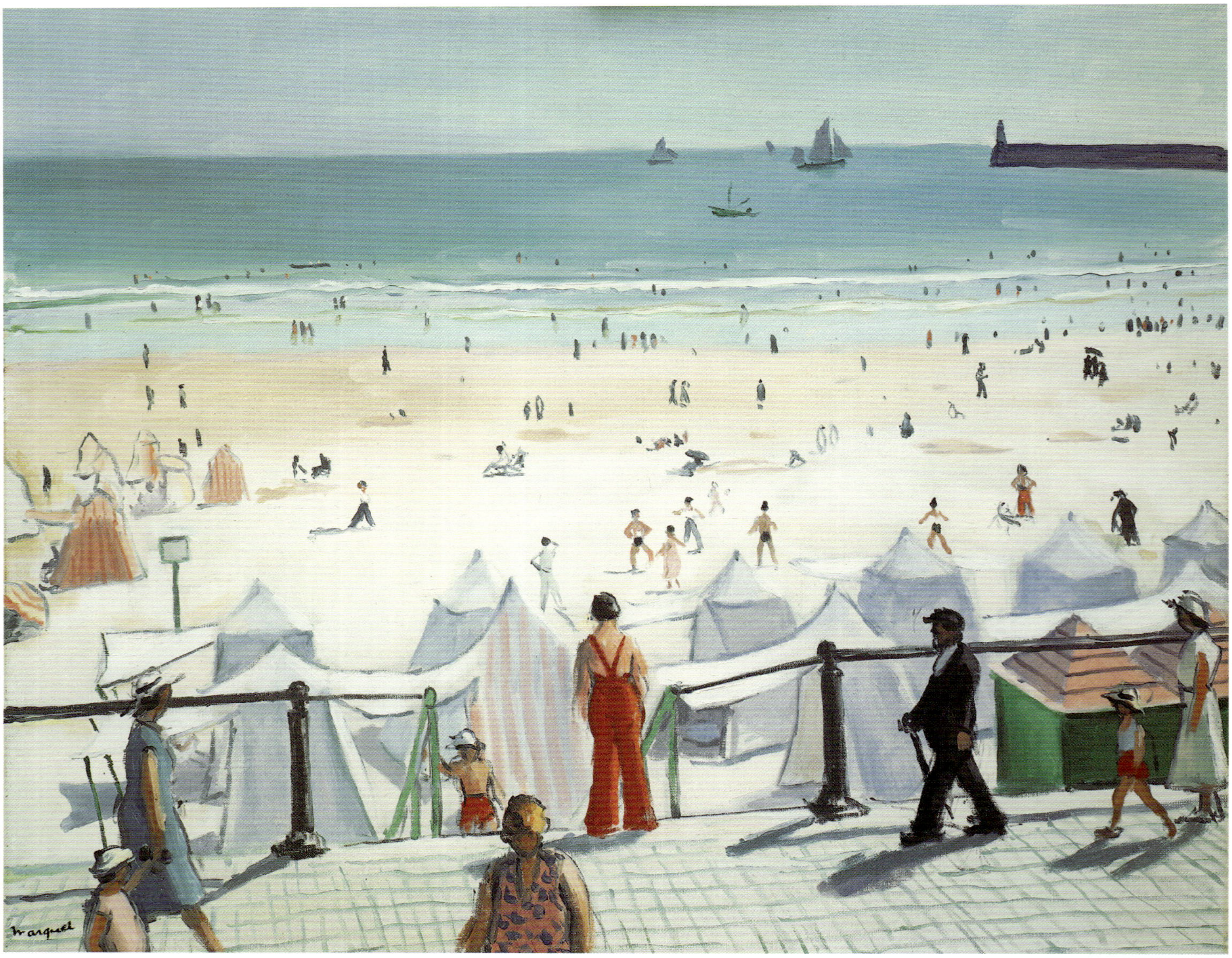

31 *Plage des Sables-d'Olonne*, 1933

Oil on canvas

65.3 x 81.1 cms

Purchased with the participation of the Société des Amis du Musée de Poitiers, 1957

On deposit at the Musée Sainte-Croix de Poitiers

AM 3443 P

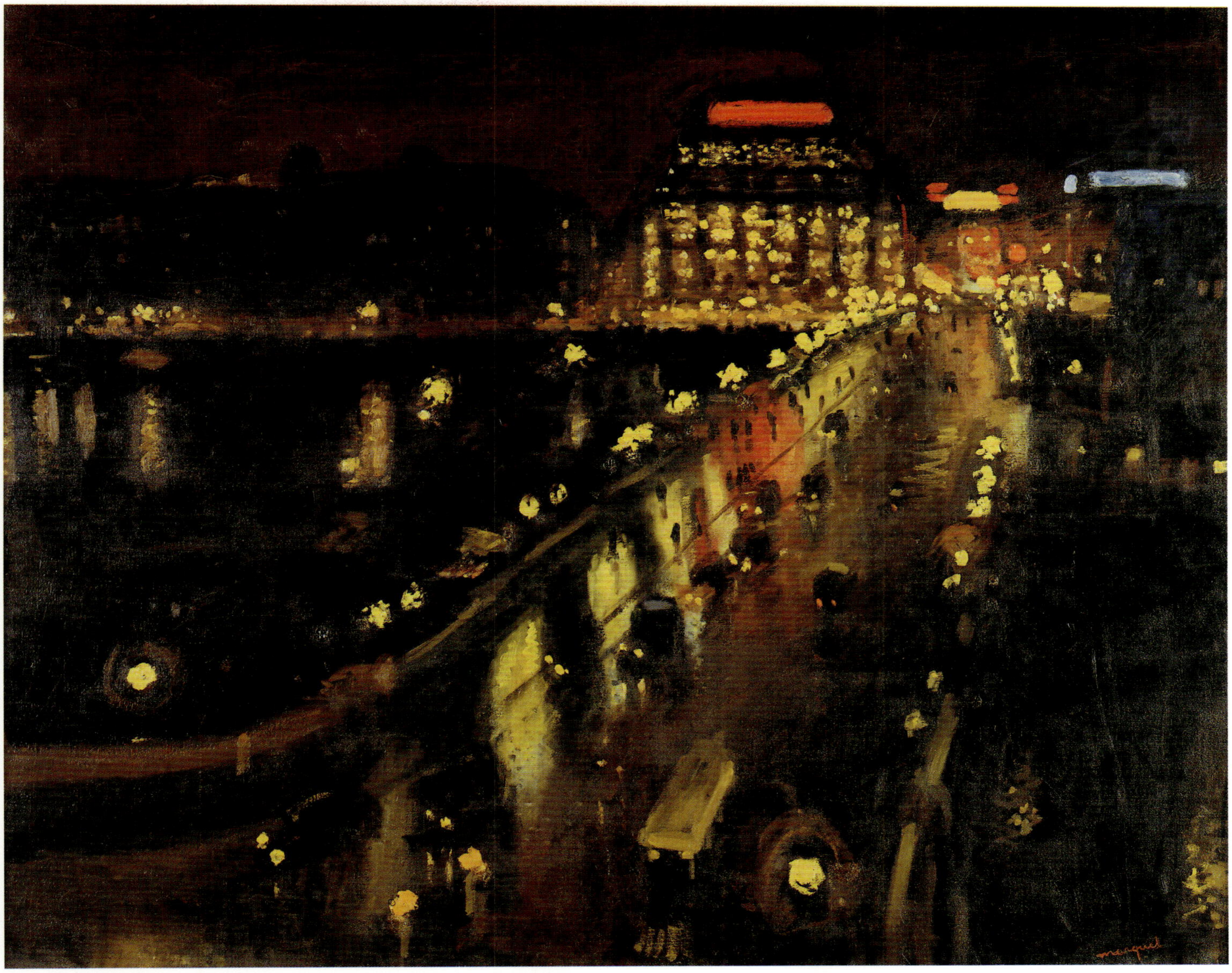

32 *Le Pont Neuf, la nuit*, ca. 1935–1939

Oil on canvas

82.5 x 100.5 cms

Gift of the artist, 1940 and assigned to the

Musée national d'art moderne in 1942

AM 2354 P

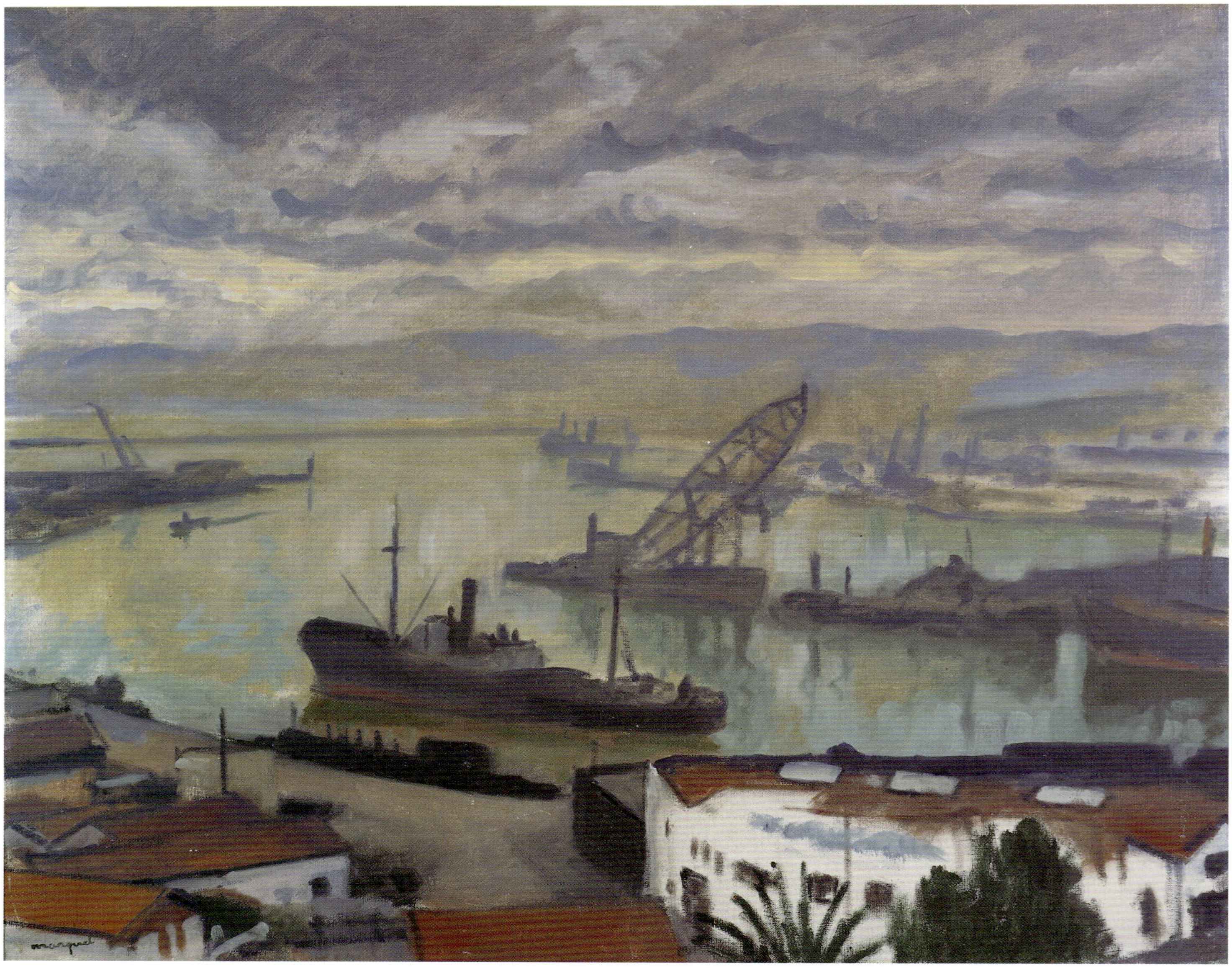

33 *Port d'Alger*, 1935

Oil on canvas

63 x 80 cms

Georges Grammont bequest to the national museums,

exclusively for the Musée de l'Annonciade de Saint-Tropez, 1959

On deposit at the Musée de l'Annonciade de Saint-Tropez

AM 3839 P

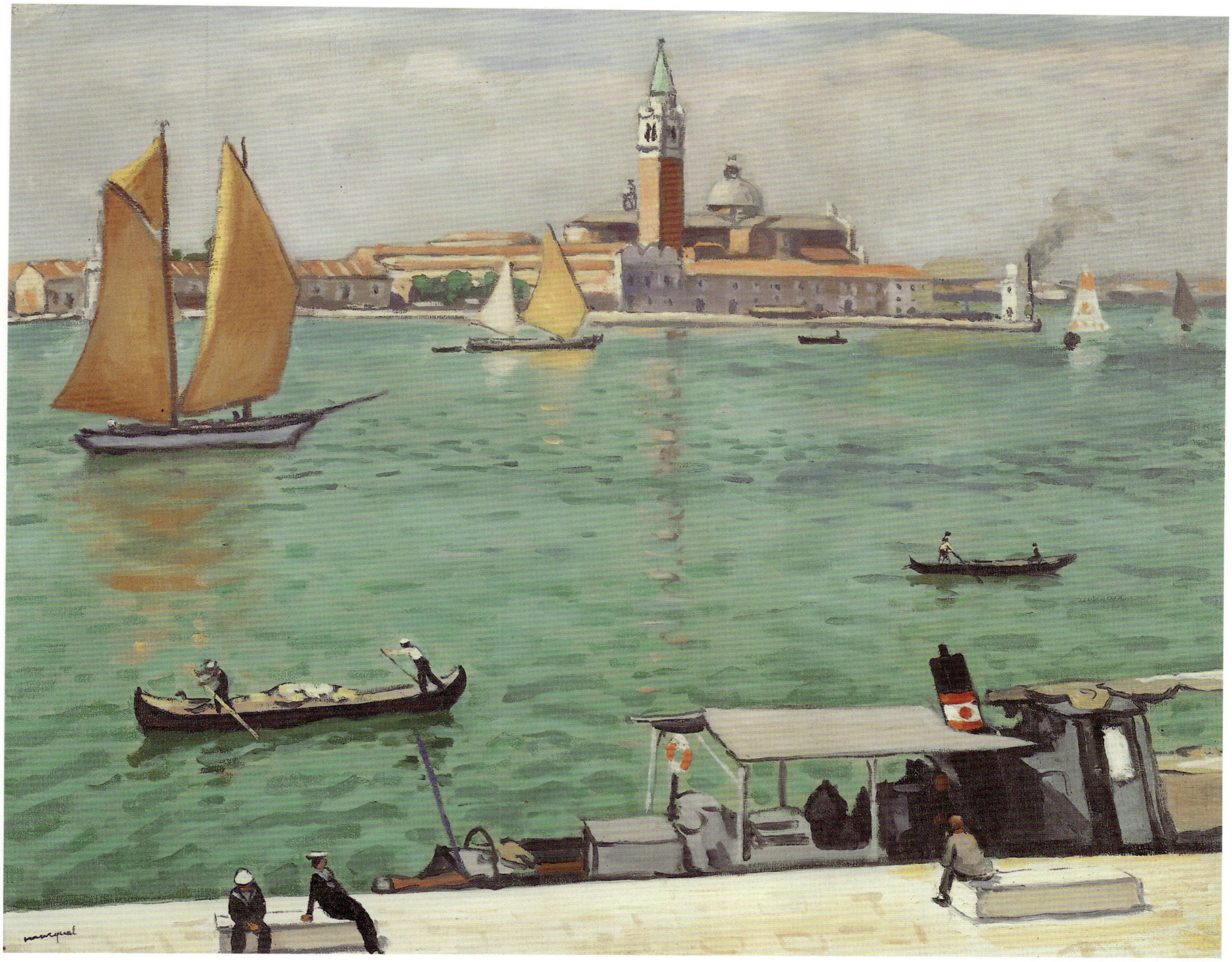

34 *Venise. La voile jaune,* 1936

Oil on canvas

65 x 80.5 cms

Purchased from the artist and assigned to the Musée national d'art moderne, 1937

AM 2115 P

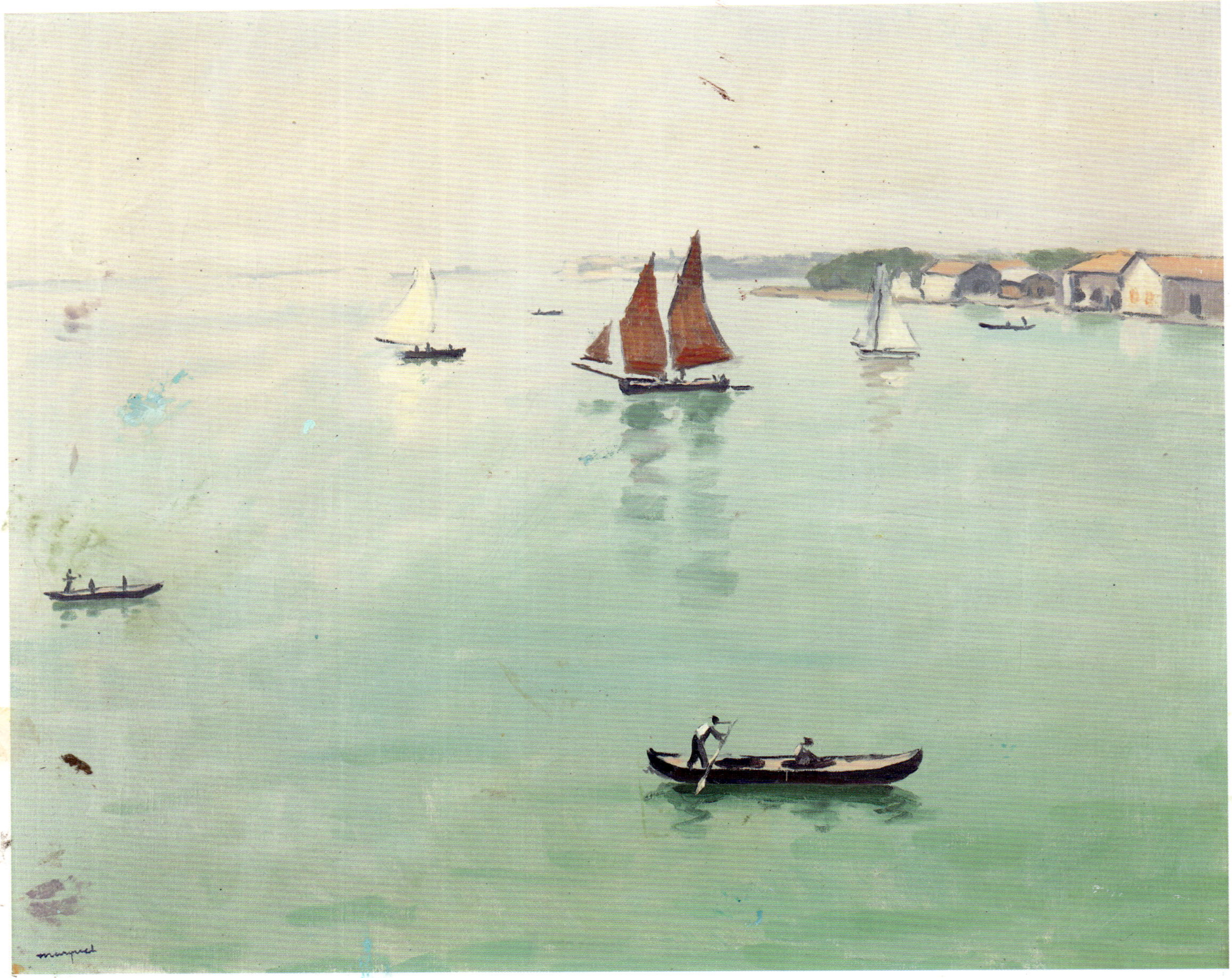

35 *La lagune à Venise*, 1936

Oil on canvas

65.2 x 80 cms

Purchased from the artist, 1937

AM 2116 P

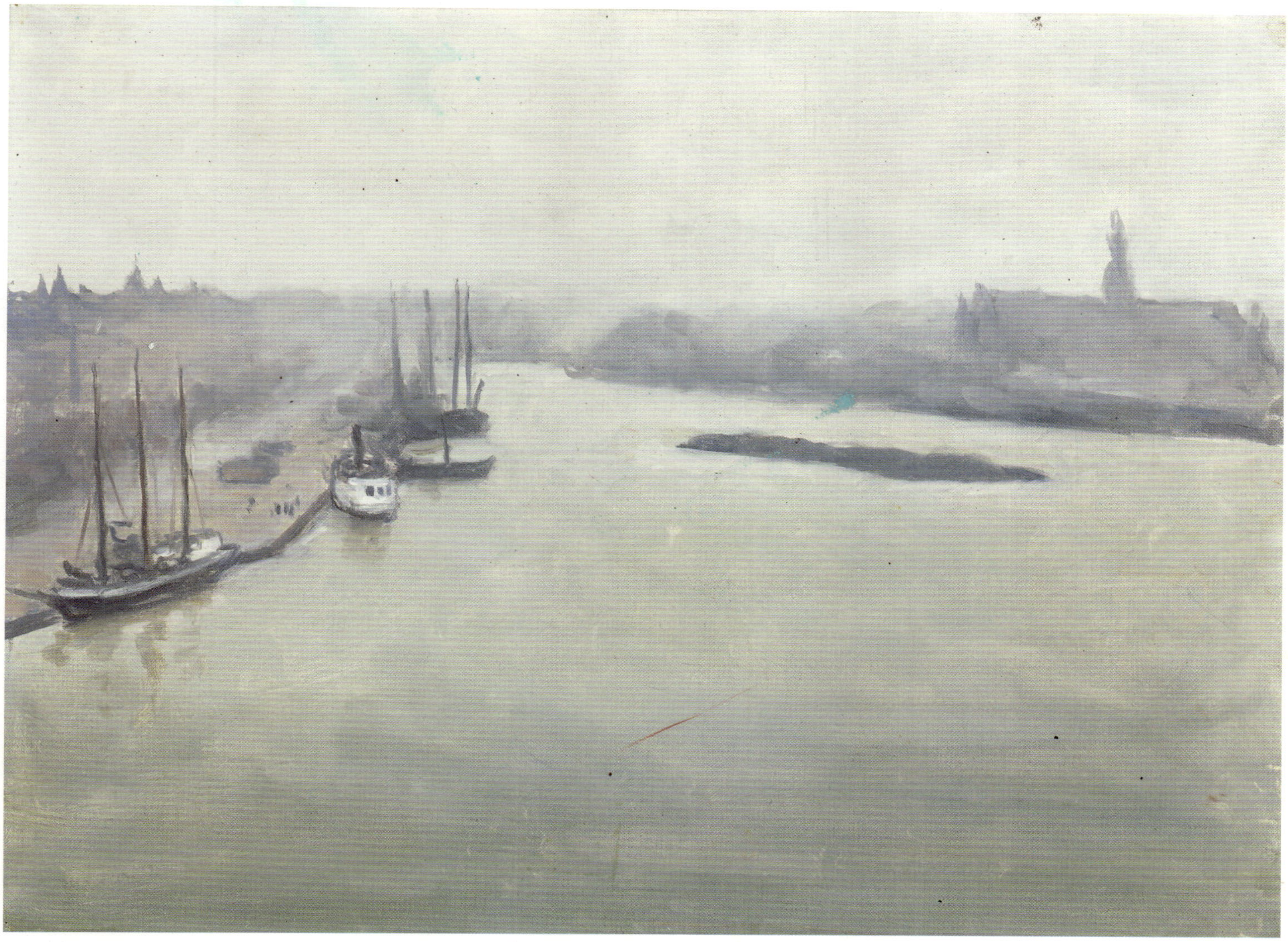

36 Brume à Stockholm, 1938

Oil on canvas

46 x 61 cms

Purchased from the artist in 1939 and assigned
to the Musée national d'art moderne

AM 2627 P

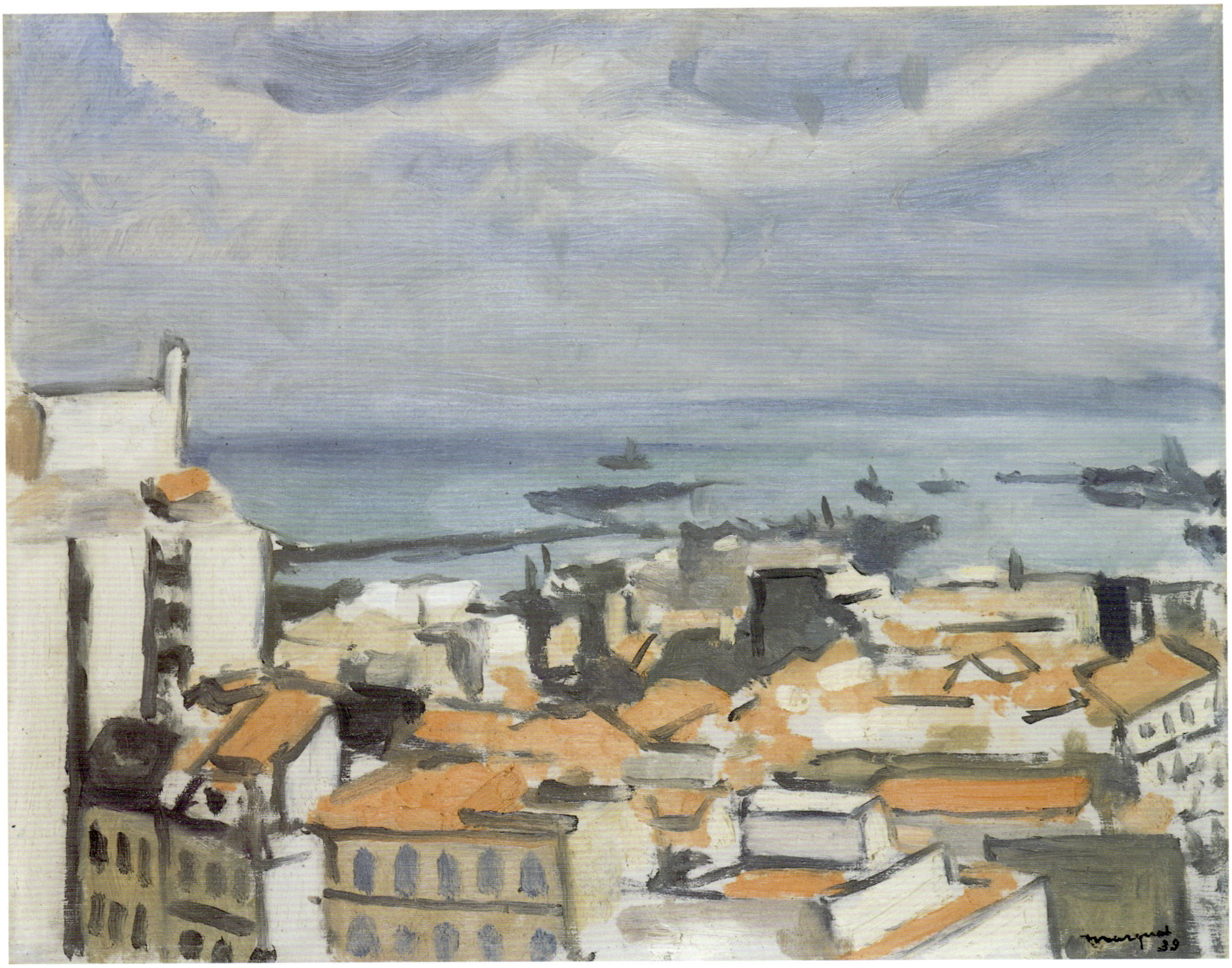

37 *Le port d'Alger*, 1939

Oil on wood

33 x 41 cms

Bequest of Mme Frédéric Lung, 1957

On deposit at the Musée des Beaux-Arts de Bordeaux

AM 3904 P

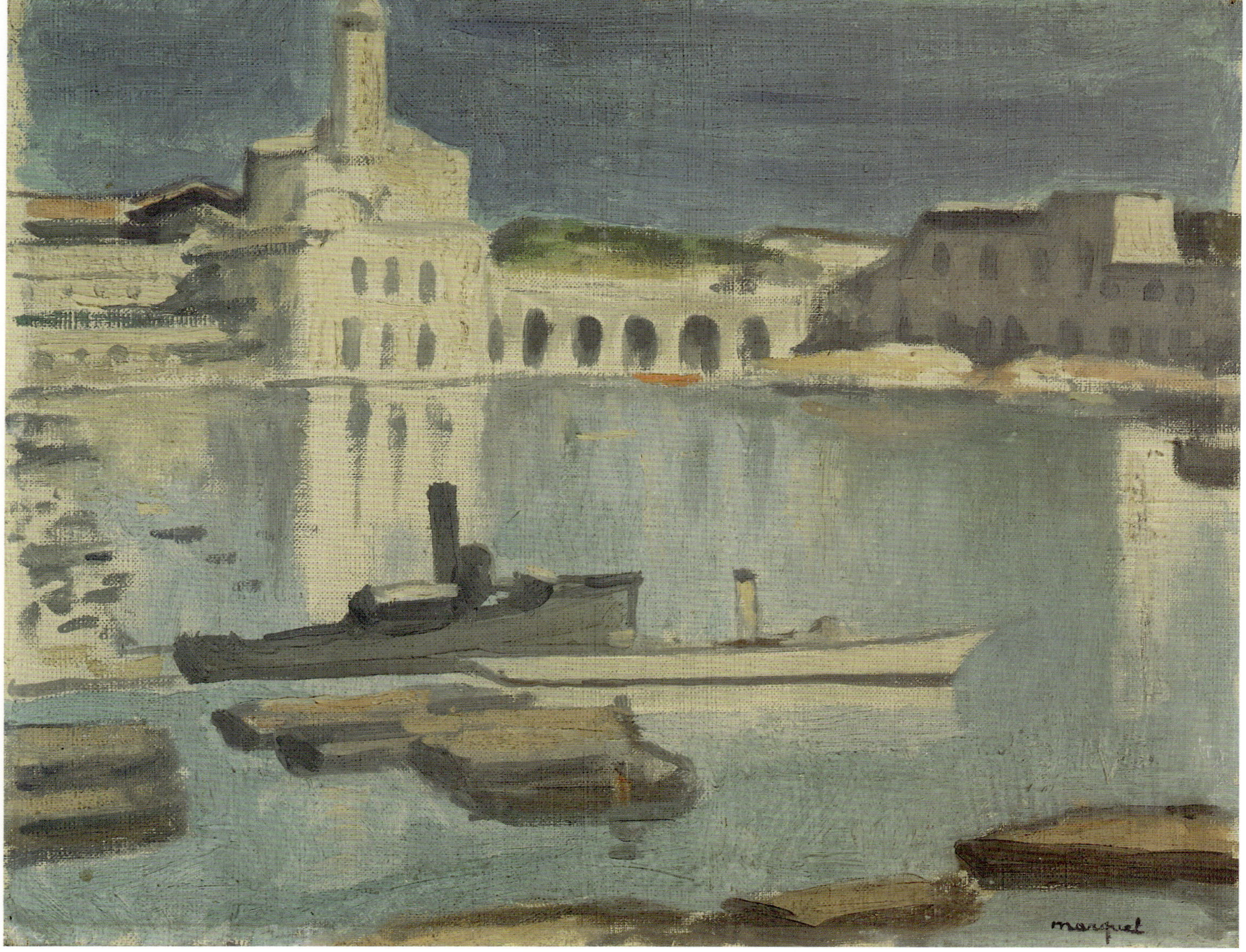

38 *Paysage au remorqueur*, 1939

Oil on cardboard

34 x 42 cms

Donation of M. Jean-Pierre Hugot and Mademoiselle

Louise Hugot, 1968

AM 4475 P

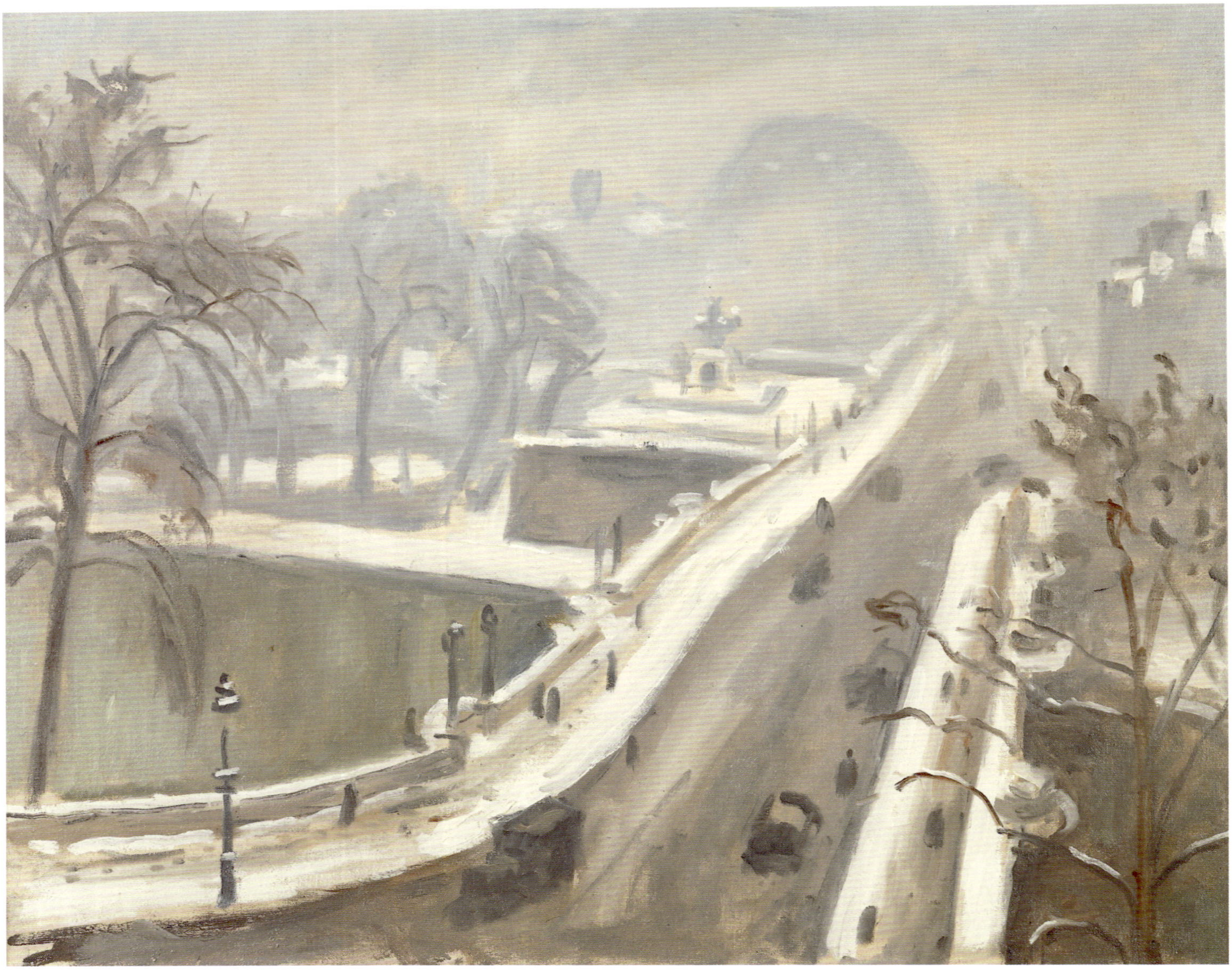

39 *Le Pont Neuf sous la neige*, 1947

Oil on canvas

65.2 x 81.5 cms

Gift of Mme Albert Marquet, 1955

AM 3372 P

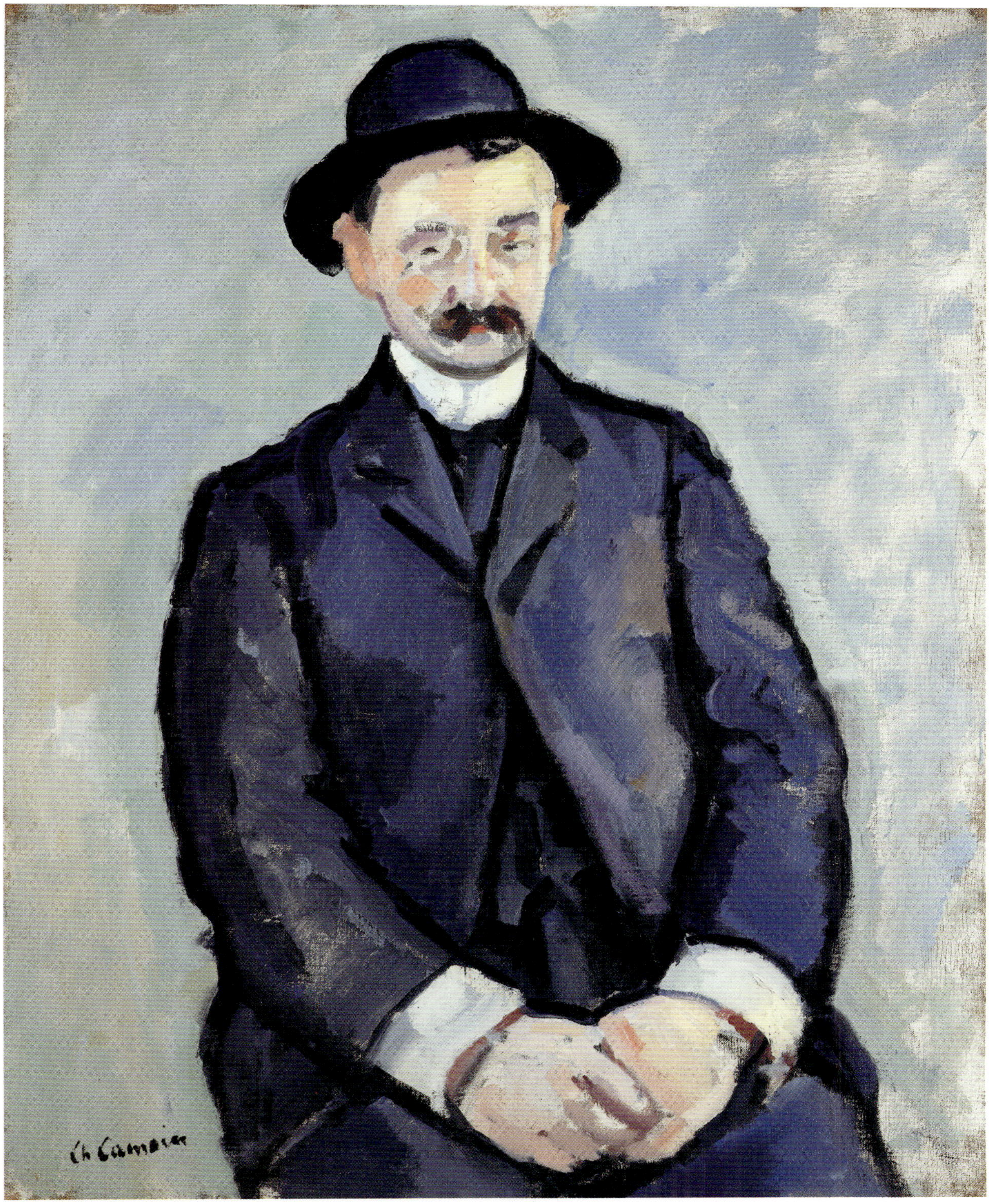

40 *Portrait d'Albert Marquet*, 1904

by Charles Camoin

Oil on canvas

92 x 72.5 cms

Gift of Mme Albert Marquet, 1948

AM 2857 P

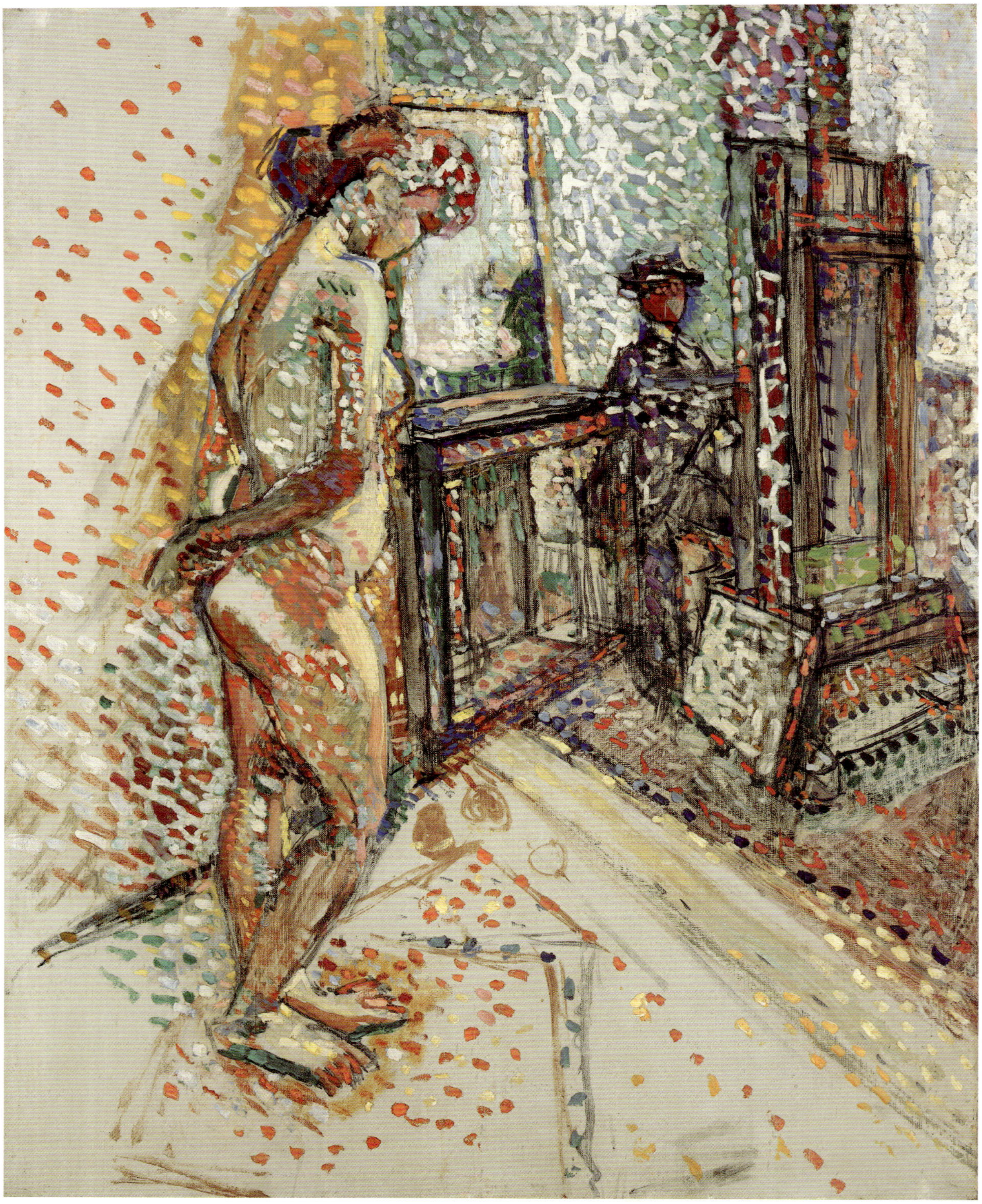

41 *Nu dans l'atelier,* 1904–1905
by Henri Manguin

Oil on canvas
91 x 72 cms
Purchased from M. Martinet with the participation
of M. Pierre David-Weill, 1957
AM 3489 P

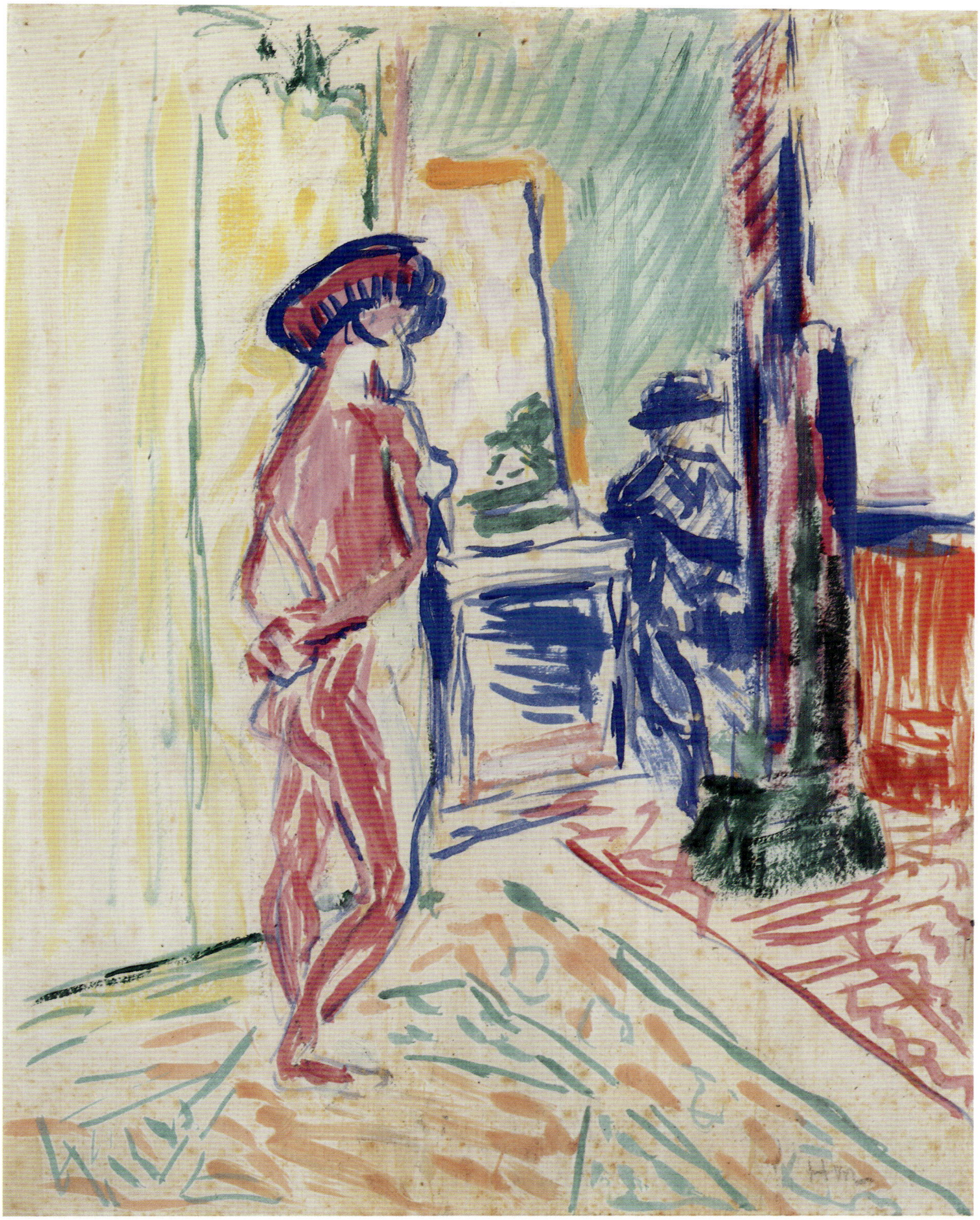

42 *Marquet peignant un nu dans l'atelier de Manguin*, 1904–1905

by Henri Matisse

Oil on paper

31 x 24 cms

Purchased from M. Martinet with the participation of M. Pierre David-Weill, 1957

AM 3490 P

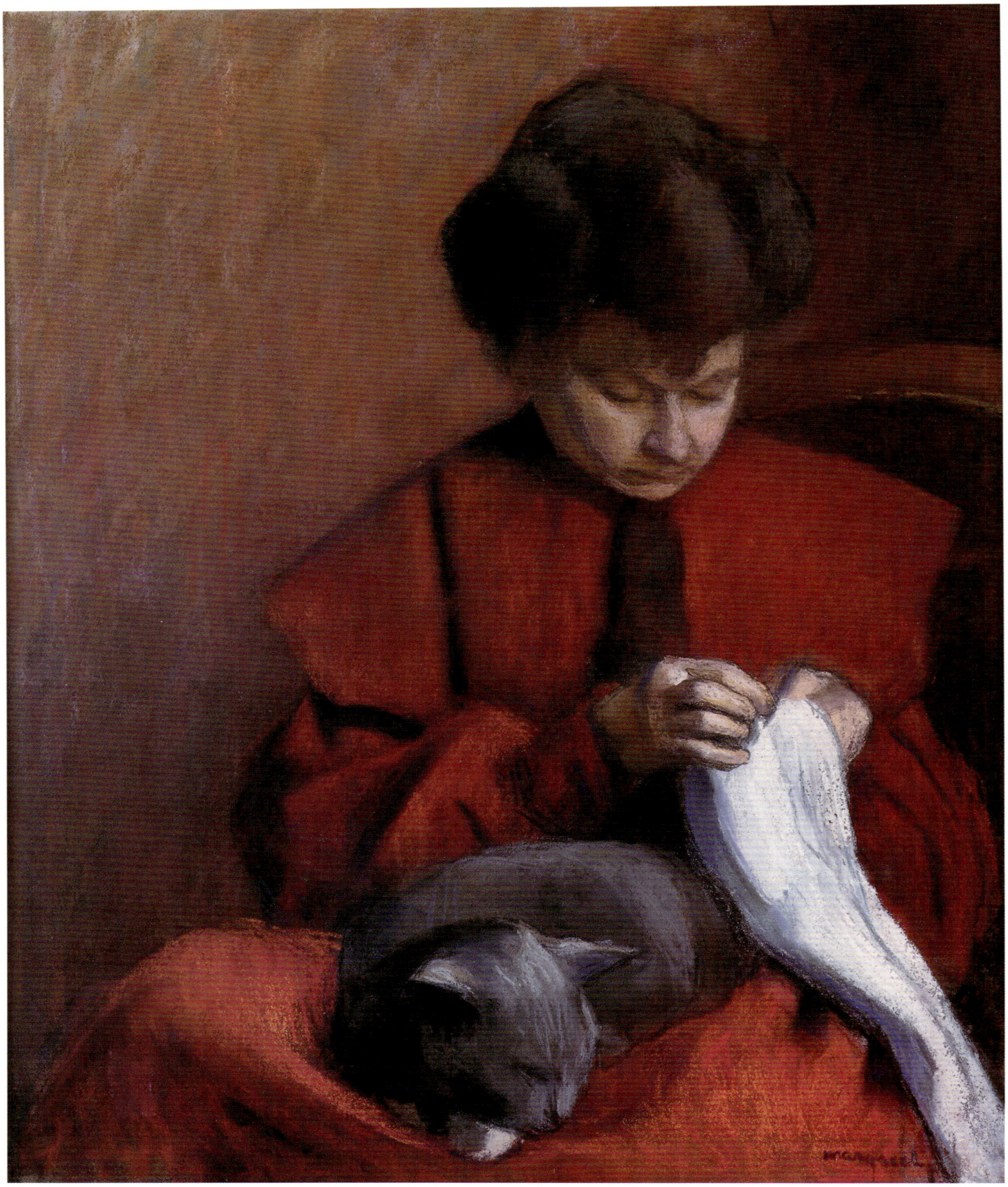

43 *La mère de l'artiste*, ca. 1905–1906

Pastel on paper

61 x 50 cms

Bequest of the artist, 1948

On deposit at the Musée des Beaux-Arts de Bordeaux

AM 2461 D

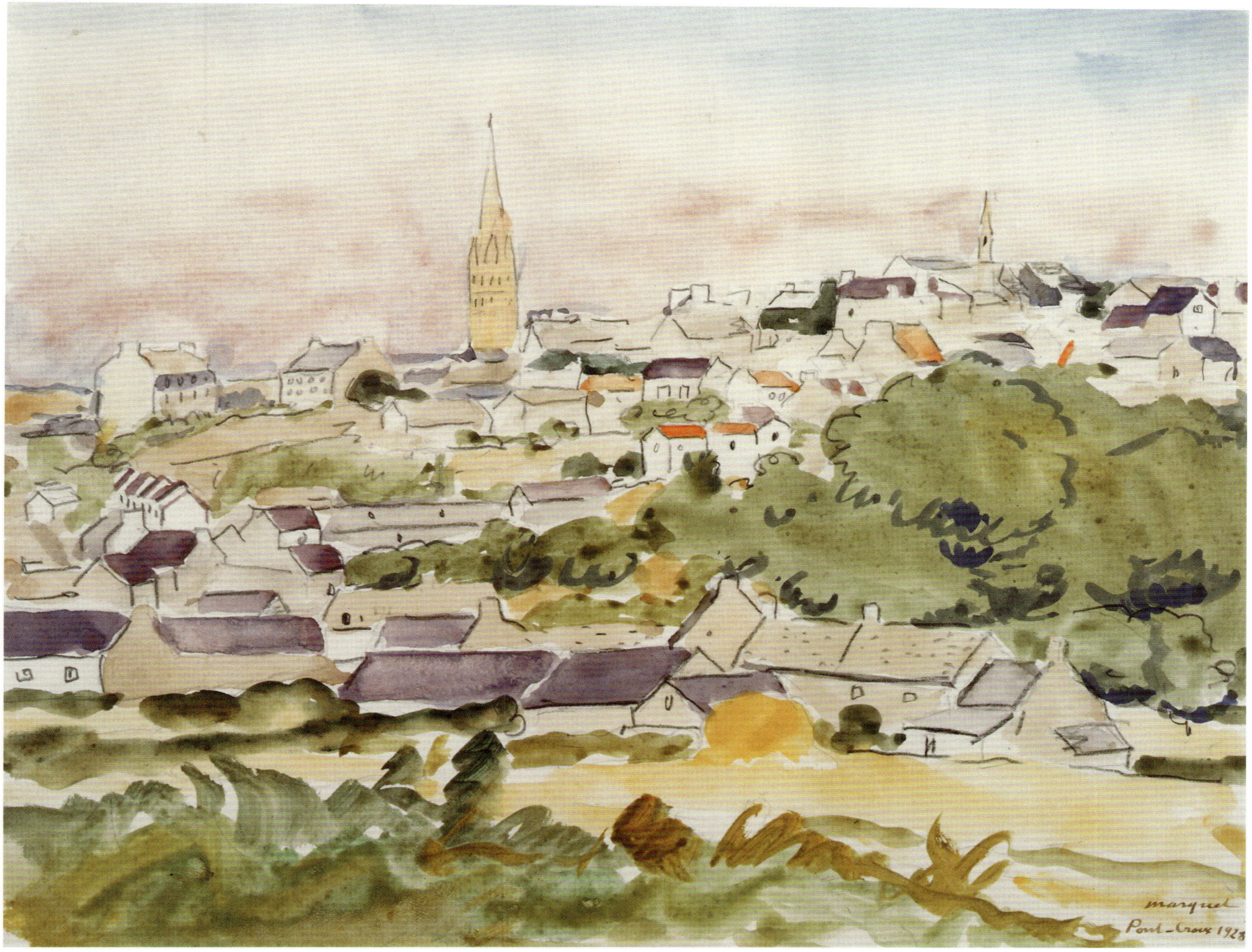

44 Pont-Croix, 1921

Watercolor on paper

22 x 28.5 cms

Bequest of Carle Dreyfus, 1953

AM 1815 D

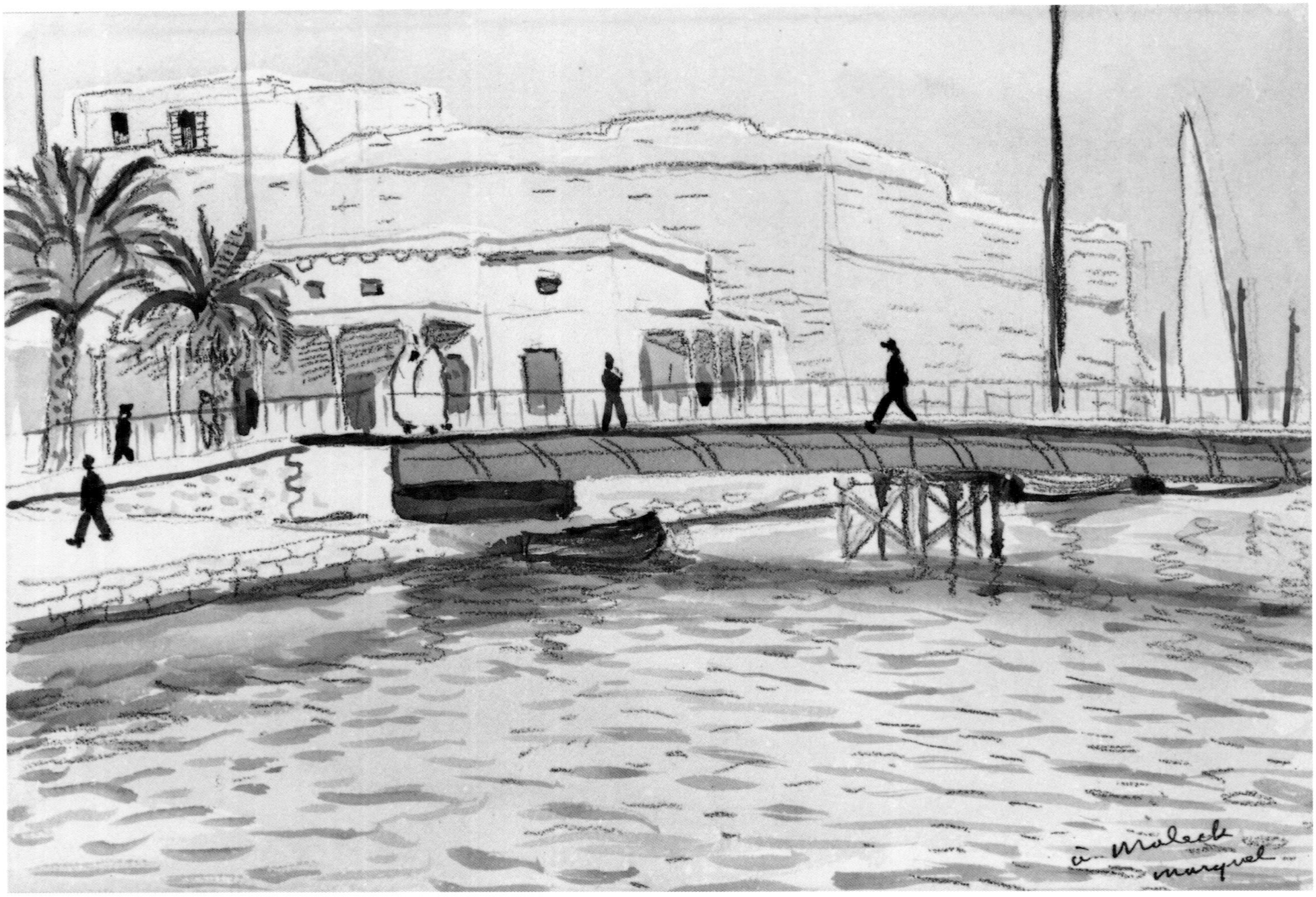

45 *La Goulette, Tunis,* 1926

Watercolor on paper
17.5 x 25 cms
Gift of Jacqueline Brétégnier-André and assigned
to the Musée national d'art moderne in 1968
On deposit at the Musée du Château de Montbéliard
AM 3675 D

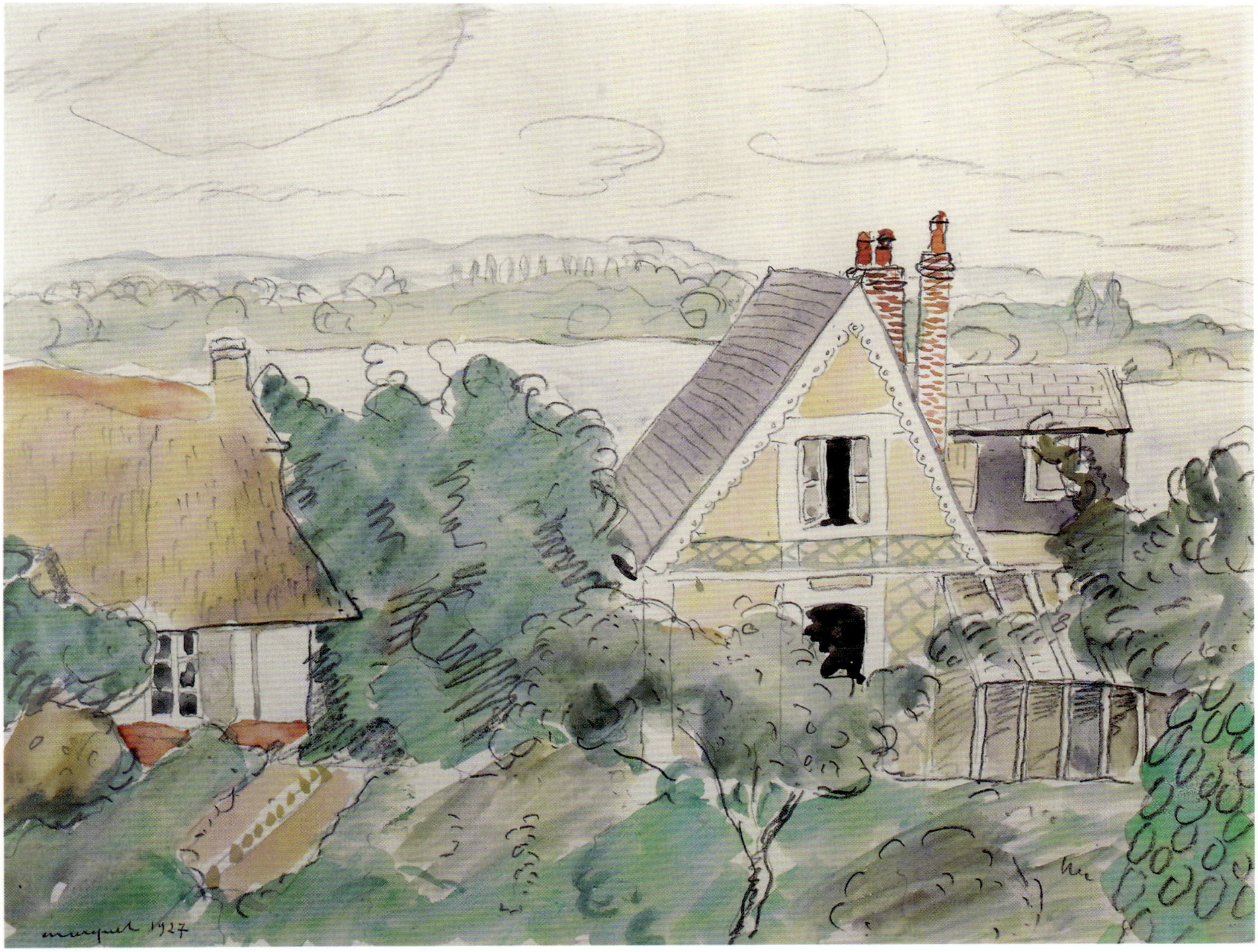

46 *Saint-Jean-de-Luz*, 1927

Watercolor on paper

38 x 44 cms

Purchased in 1939

AM 1419 D

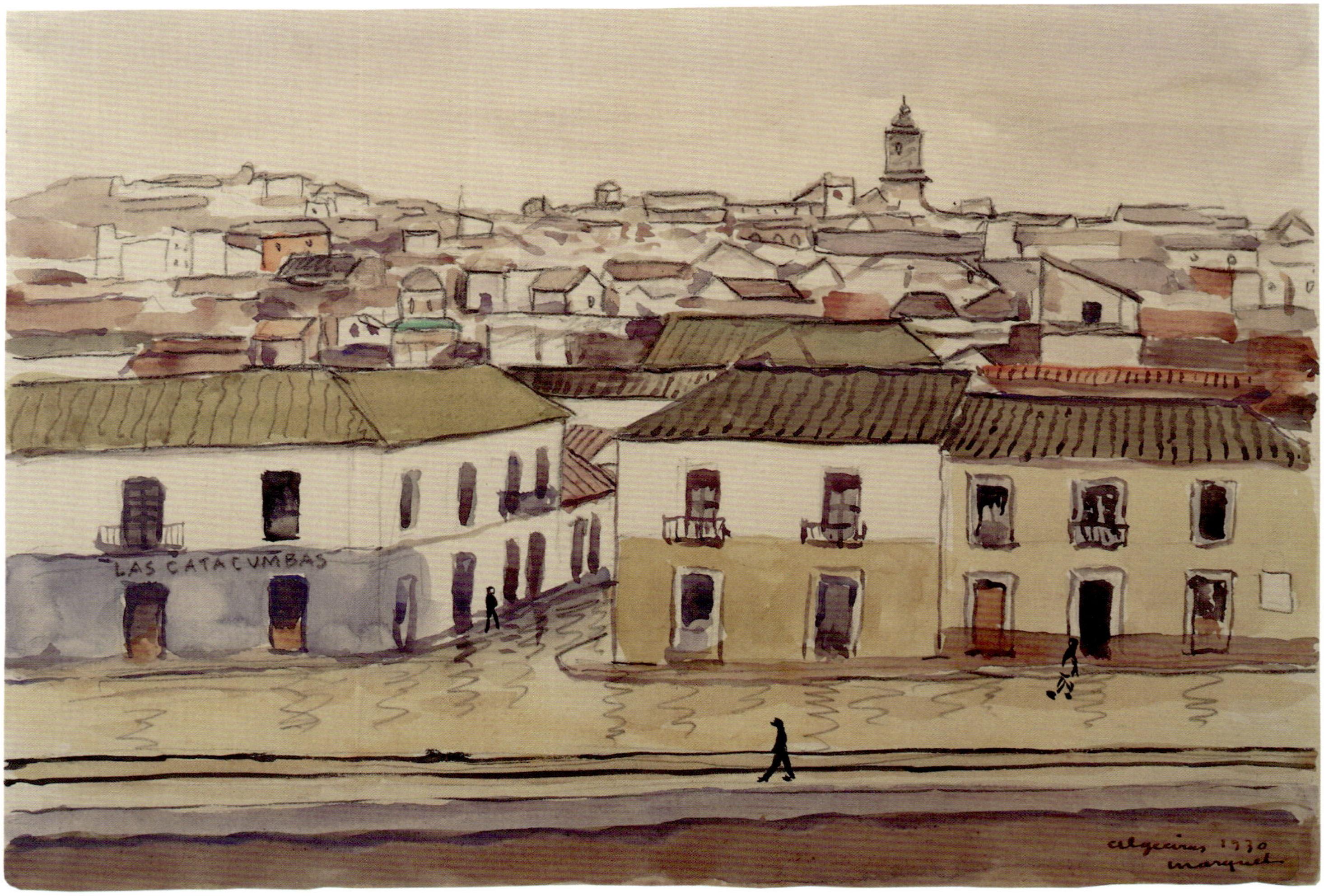

47 *Algesiras,* 1930

Watercolor on paper

32 x 38 cms

Purchased in 1939

AM 1418 D

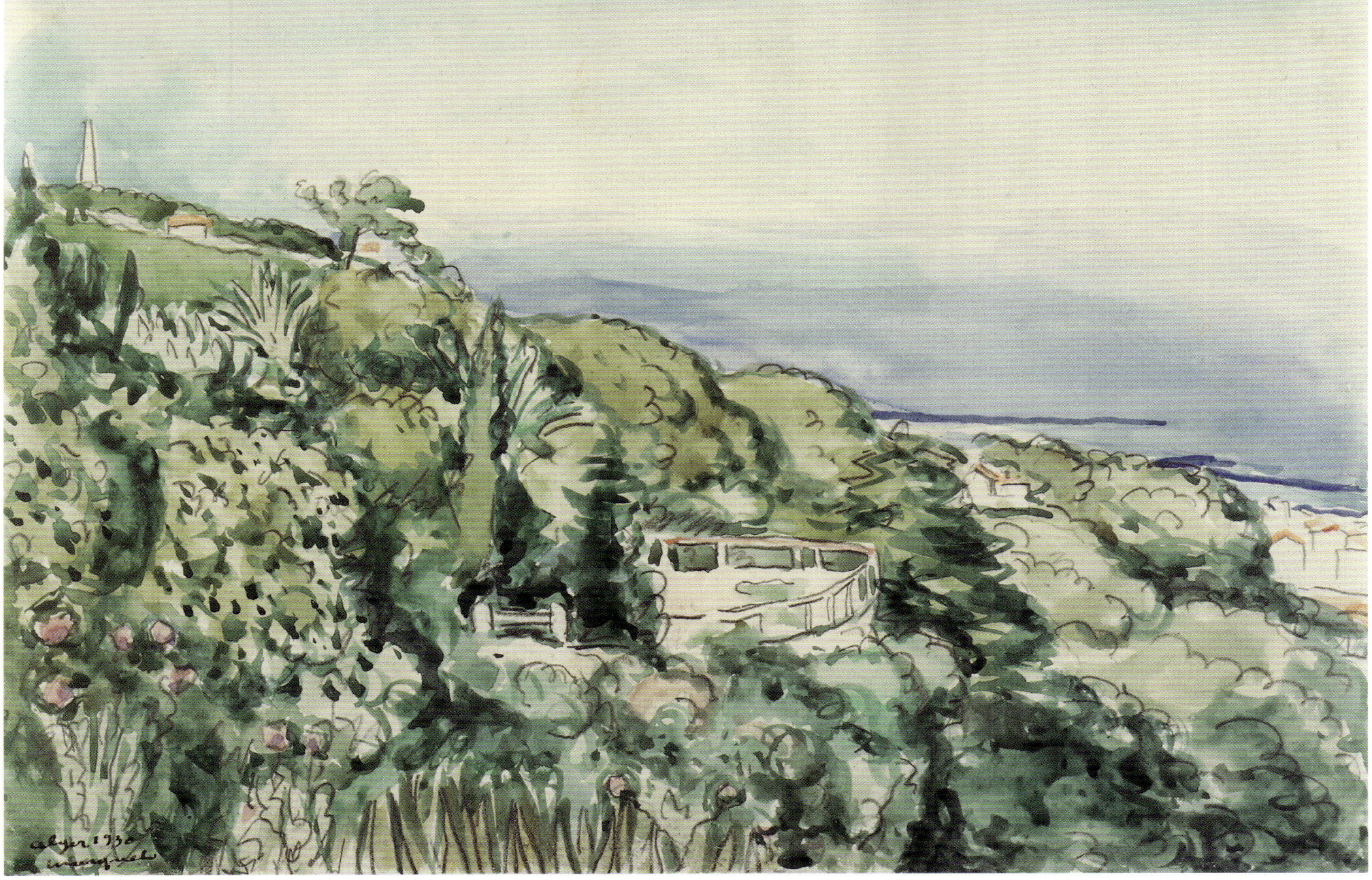

48 *Alger*, 1930

Lead pencil and watercolor on paper

17.5 x 25 cms

Purchased in 1932

AM 1068 D

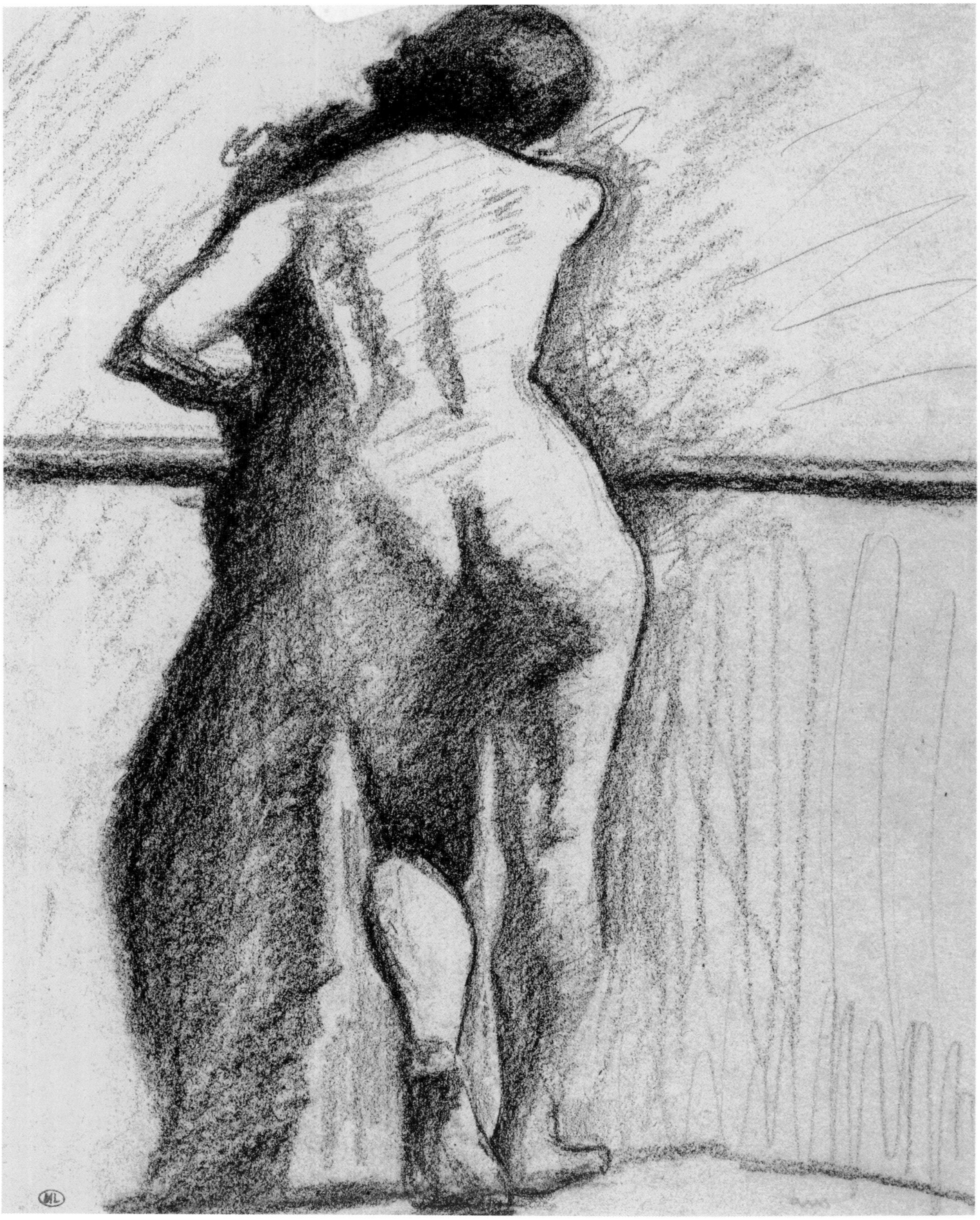

49 Nu de dos contre un mur, 1898

Charcoal on paper laid on cardboard

27.5 x 21.9 cms

Donated by Paul Jamot, 1943

AM 1716 D

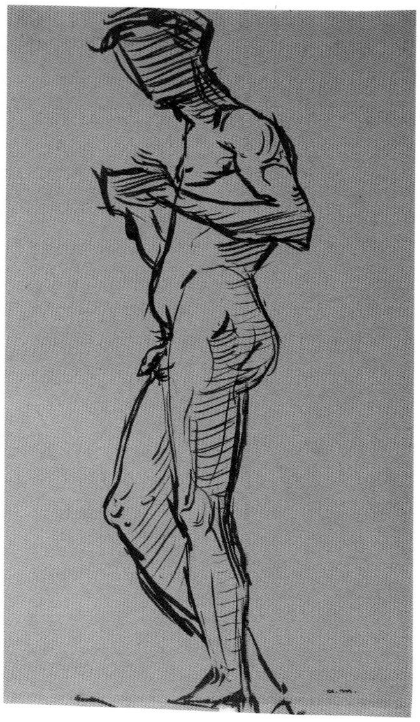

50 *Nu de profil*, ca. 1898

China ink on paper

32.5 x 20 cms

Gift of Mme Albert Marquet, 1959

AM 2030 D

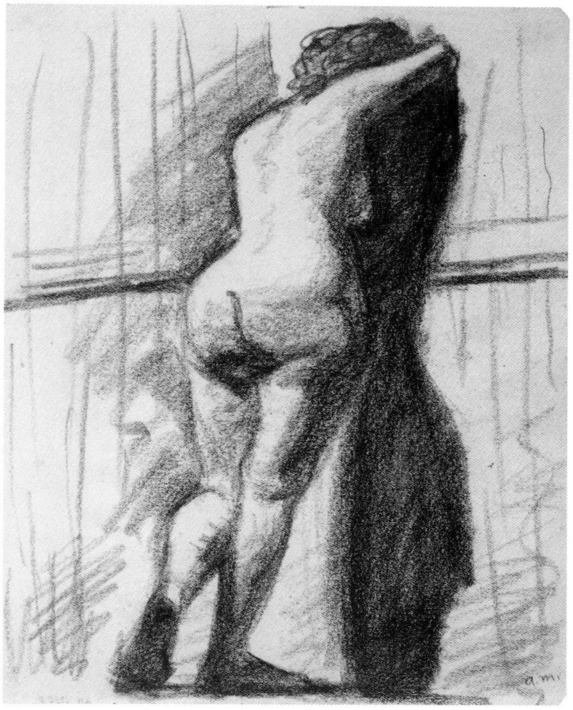

51 *Nu de dos appuyé contre un mur*, ca. 1899

Charcoal on sketchbook paper

21.8 x 17 cms

Gift of Mme Albert Marquet, 1959

AM 2035 D

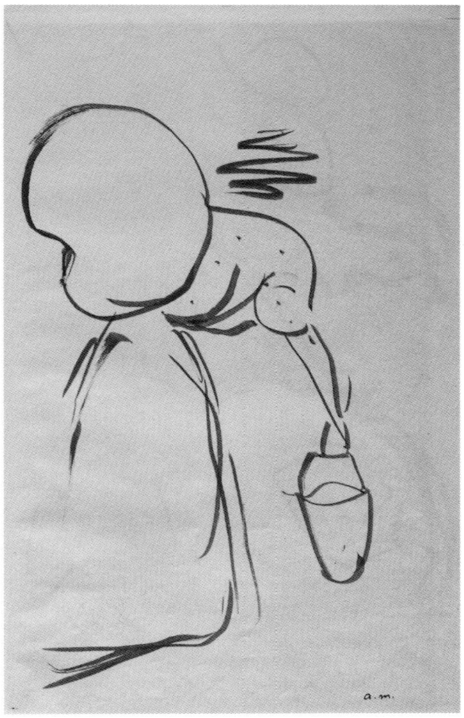

52a *Blanchisseuse*, 1903

China ink on paper

32.7 x 21.4 cms

Gift of Mme Albert Marquet, 1959

AM 2029 D RECTO

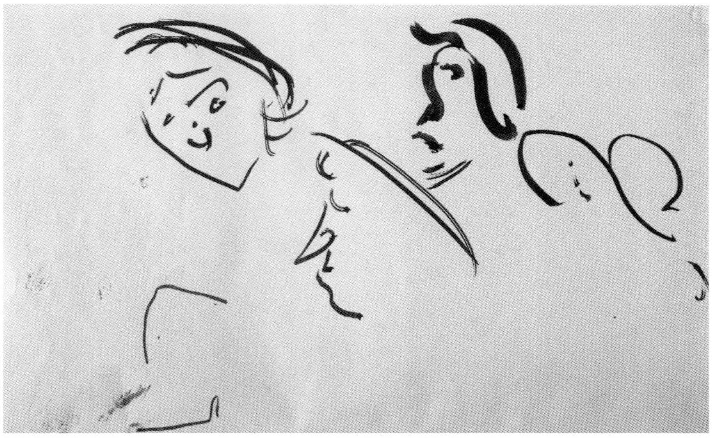

52b *Croquis de visages*, 1903

China ink on paper

21.4 x 32.7 cms

Gift of Mme Albert Marquet, 1959

AM 2029 D VERSO

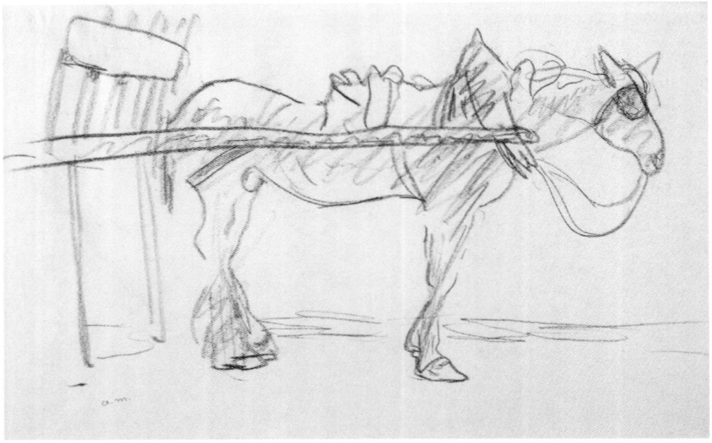

53 *Cheval attelé,* ca. 1904

Charcoal on paper

20 x 32 cms

Gift of Mme Albert Marquet, 1959

AM 2032 D

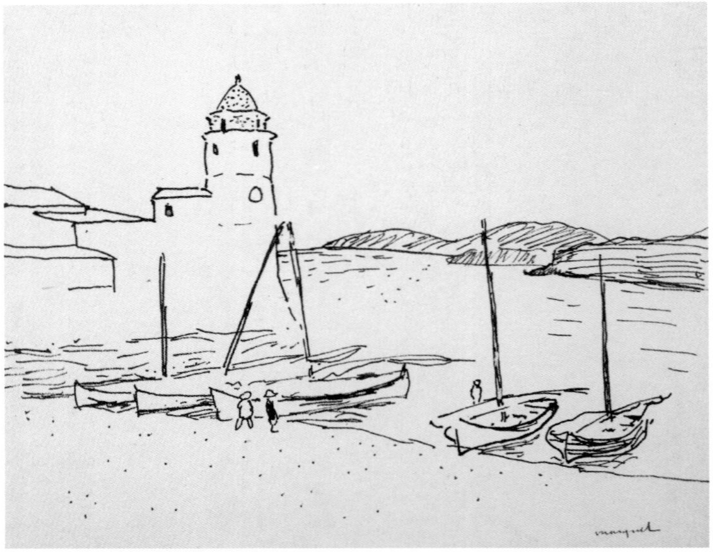

55 *Le port de Collioure,* ca. 1912–1914

China ink on paper

16.5 x 21 cms

Bequest of Carle Dreyfus, 1953

AM 1871 D

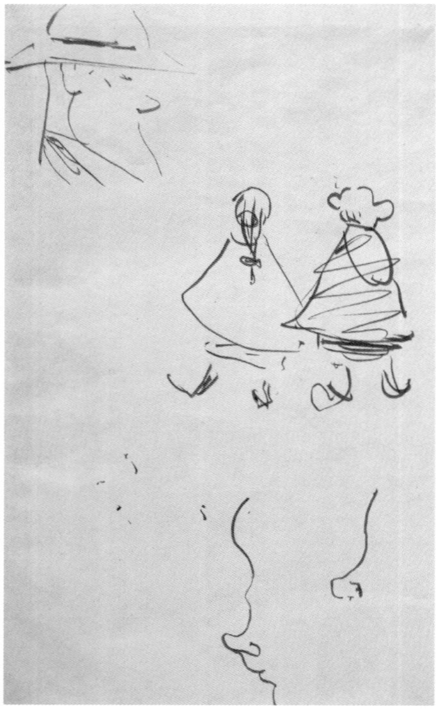

54a *Croquis de vieillard, d'enfants et deux profils,* ca. 1904

China ink on paper

33 x 20.5 cms

Gift of Mme Albert Marquet, 1959

AM 2028 D VERSO

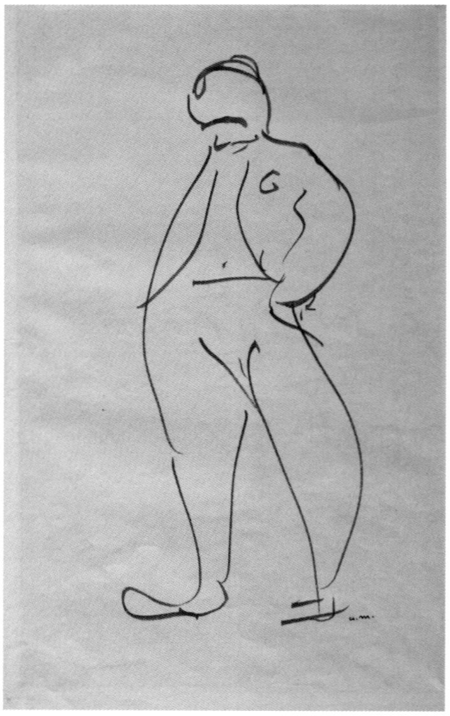

54b *Croquis d'homme,* ca. 1904

China ink on paper

33 x 20.5 cms

Gift of Mme Albert Marquet, 1959

AM 2028 D RECTO

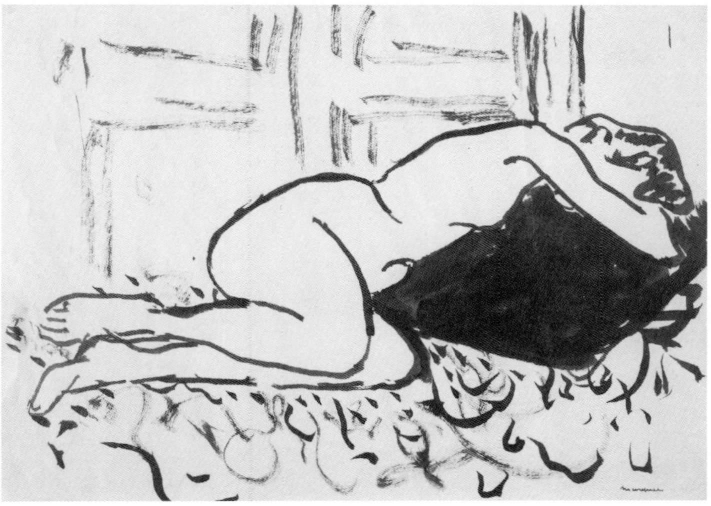

56 *Study for Nu sur un divan rouge*, 1912

China ink on paper

24.5 x 34 cms

Gift of Mme Albert Marquet, 1959

AM 2027 D

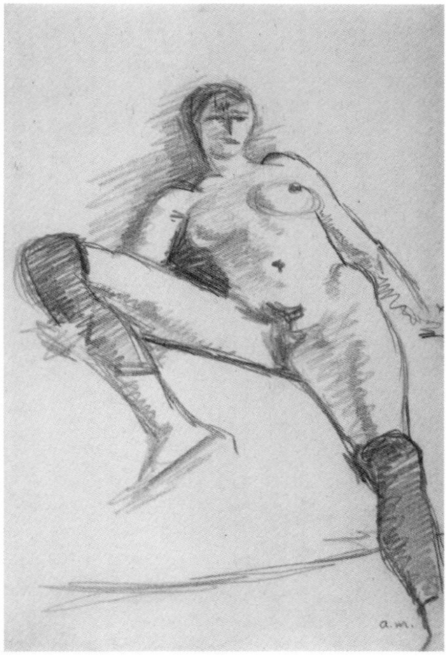

57 *Study for Les deux amies – femme à demi-étendue*, 1912

Pencil on paper

25 x 13.3 cms

Gift of Mme Albert Marquet, 1959

AM 2033 D

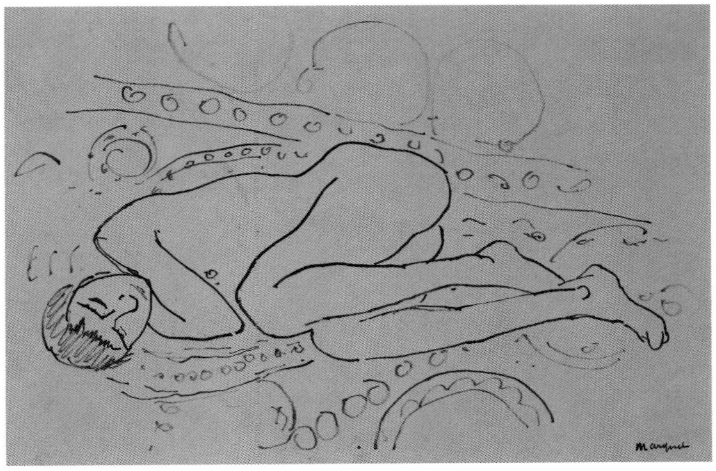

58 *Nu au tapis oriental*, ca. 1912

China ink on paper

19.8 x 29.3 cms

Donation of Adèle and Georges Besson, 1963

On deposit at the Musée des Beaux-Arts et d'Archéologie de Besançon

AM 2921 D(13)

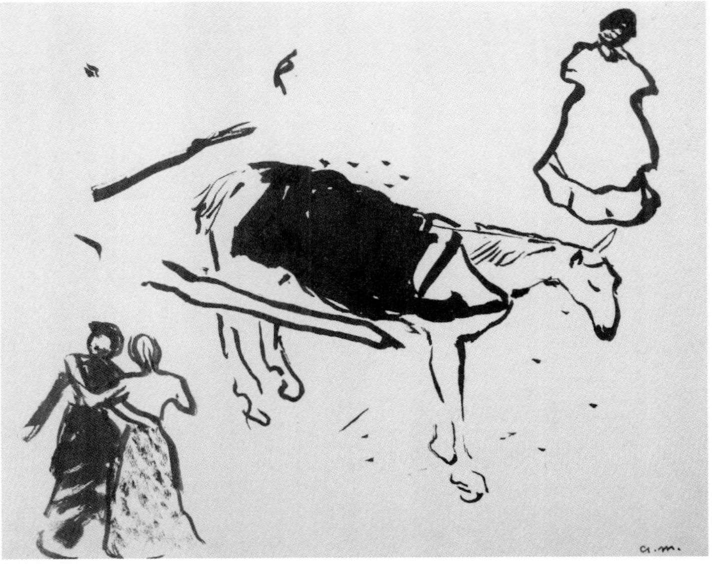

59 *Passantes et cheval*, 1916

China ink on paper

17 x 21.2 cms

Gift of Mme Albert Marquet, 1959

AM 2036 D

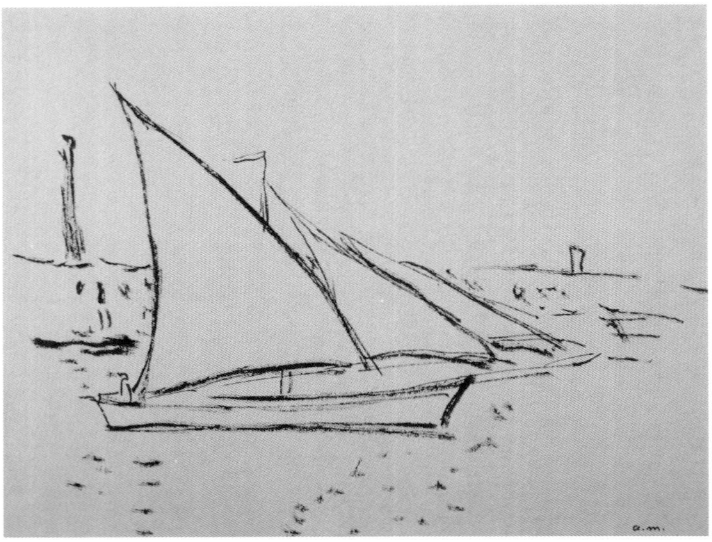

60 *Voiliers à Marseille*, 1916

China ink on paper

20 x 26 cms

Gift of Mme Albert Marquet, 1959

AM 2037 D

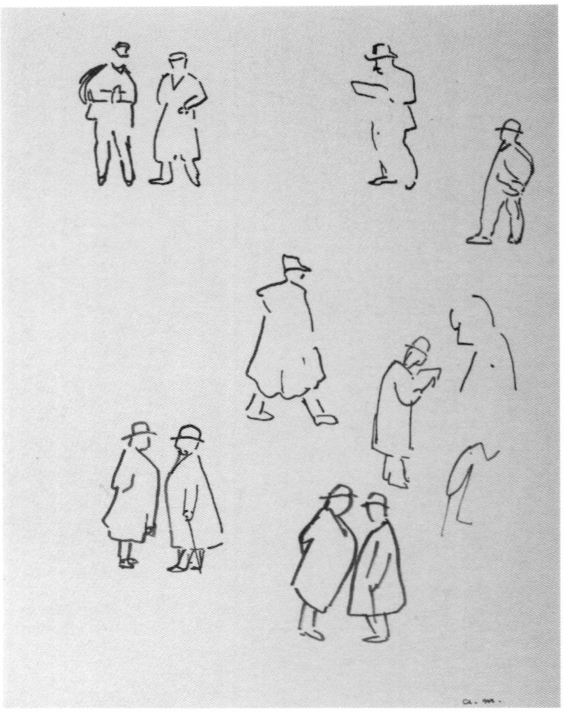

61 *Passants*, 1916

China ink on paper

25.4 x 19.5 cm

Gift of Mme Albert Marquet, 1959

AM 2038 D

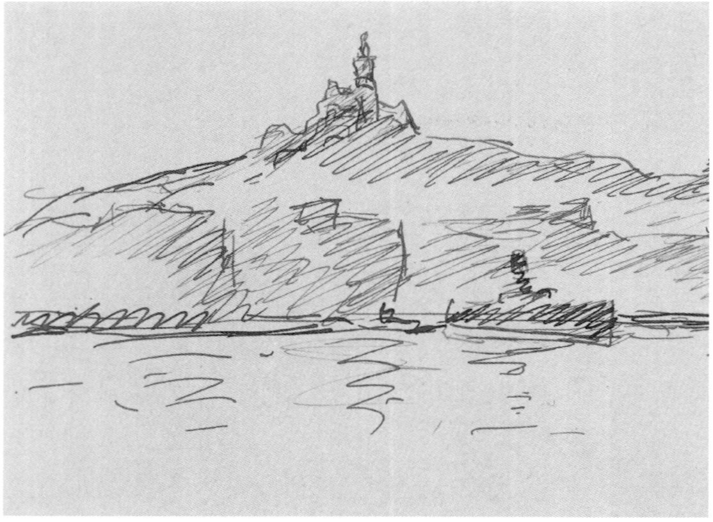

62 *Marseille*, 1916

China ink on paper

18 x 24 cms

Gift of Mme Albert Marquet, 1959

AM 2039 D

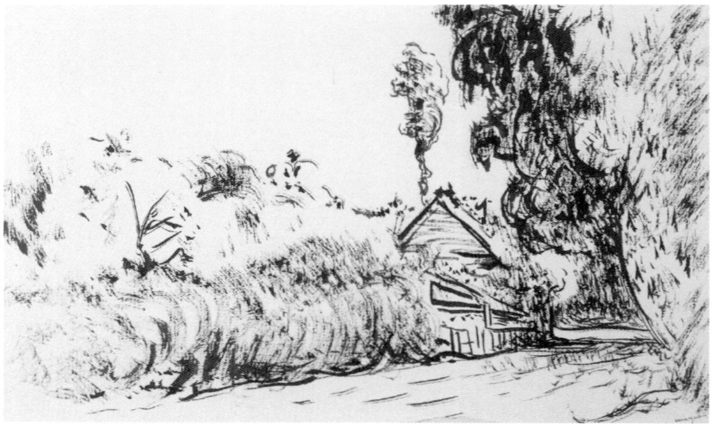

64 *Paysage*, 1921

China ink on paper

21.4 x 34.8 cms

Bequest of Carle Dreyfus, 1953

AM 1870 D

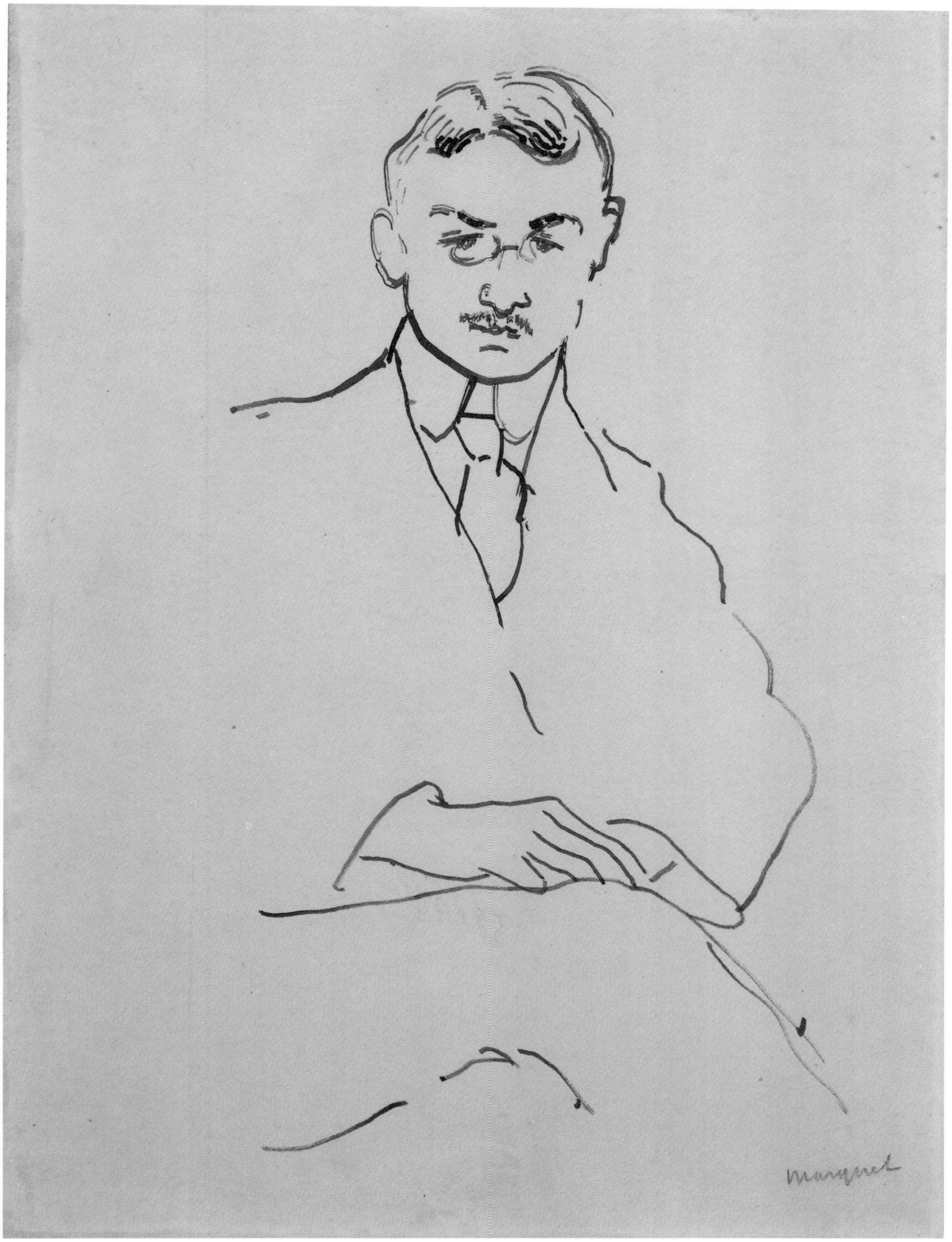

63 *Portrait de George Besson*, 1917

China ink on paper
27 x 20.2 cms
Donation of Adèle and Georges Besson, 1963
On deposit at the Musée des Beaux-Arts et
d'Archéologie de Besançon
AM 3841 D

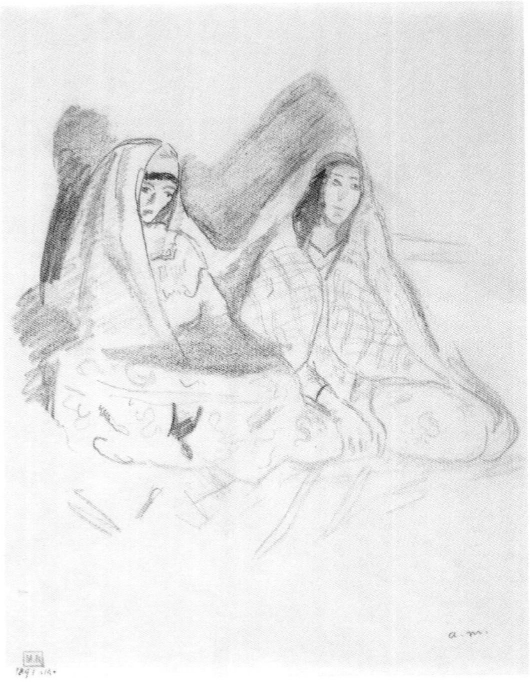

65 Study for Les femmes de Laghouat, ca. 1921

Lead pencil on paper

27 x 20.2 cms

Gift of Mme Albert Marquet, 1954

AM 1893 D

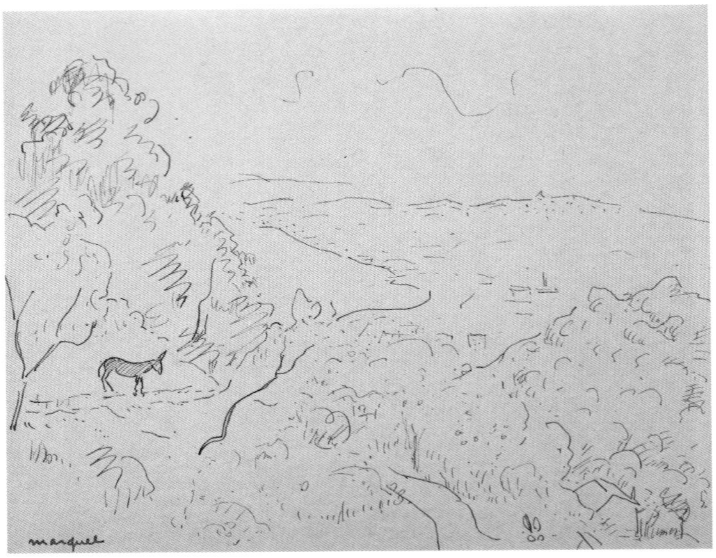

66 *Alger*, 1921

Ink on paper

16.7 x 21 cms

Gift of Mme Albert Marquet, 1959

AM 2034 D

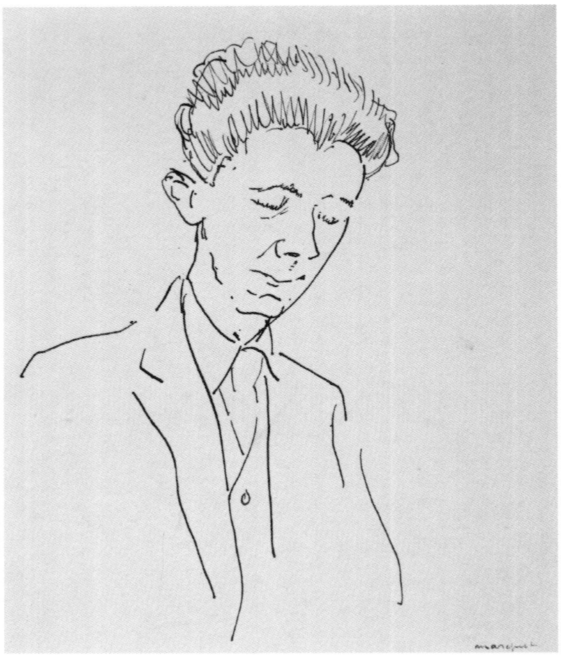

67 Portrait d'un journaliste americain, 1934

China ink on paper

23.5 x 19.5 cms

Gift of Mme Albert Marquet, 1959

AM 2031 D

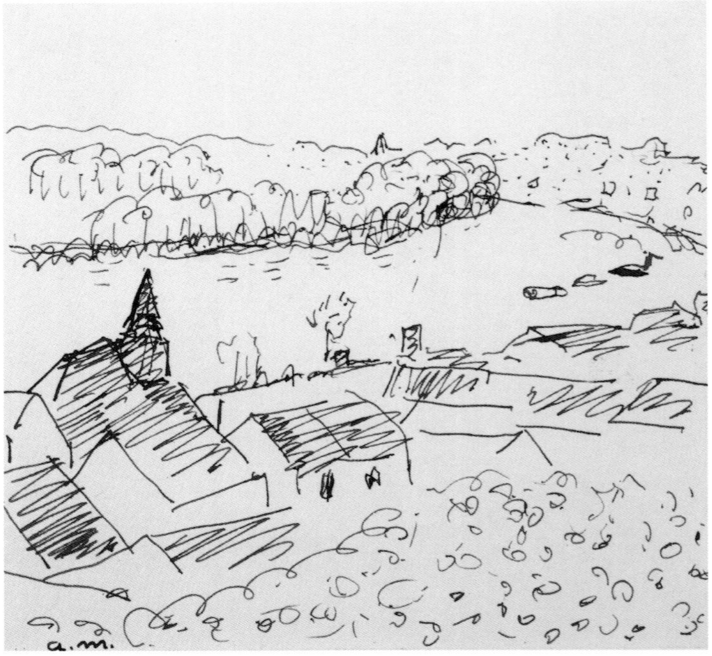

68 La Frette vue d'en haut, 1945

China ink on paper

10 x 10 cms

Gift of Mme Albert Marquet, 1959

AM 2025 D

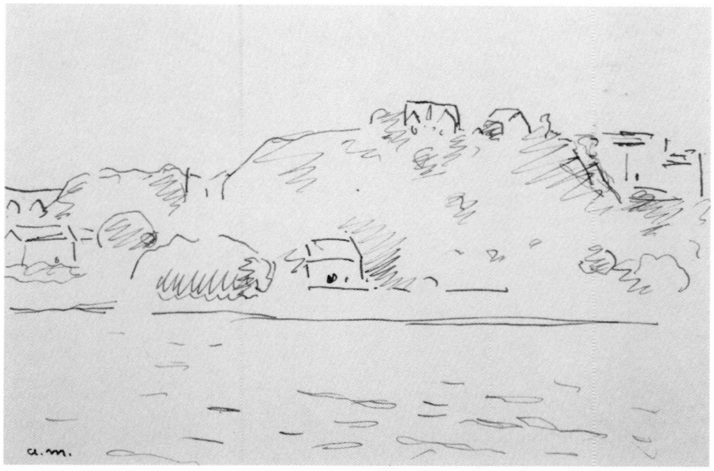

69 *La Frette au bord de l'eau*, 1945

China ink on paper

10 x 15 cms

Gift of Mme Albert Marquet, 1959

AM 2026 D

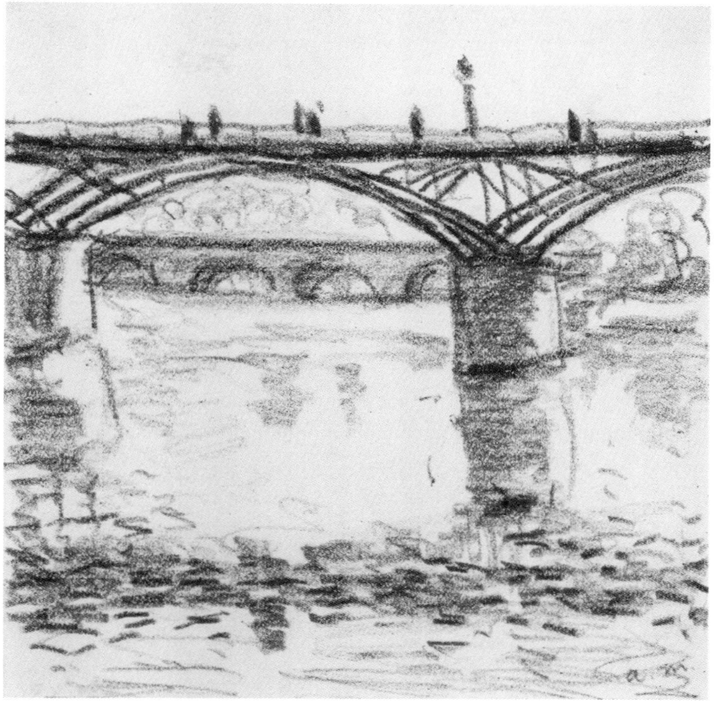

70 *Le Pont des Arts*, 1946

Pencil on paper

10.7 x 10.5 cms

Gift of Mme Albert Marquet, 1959

AM 2024 D

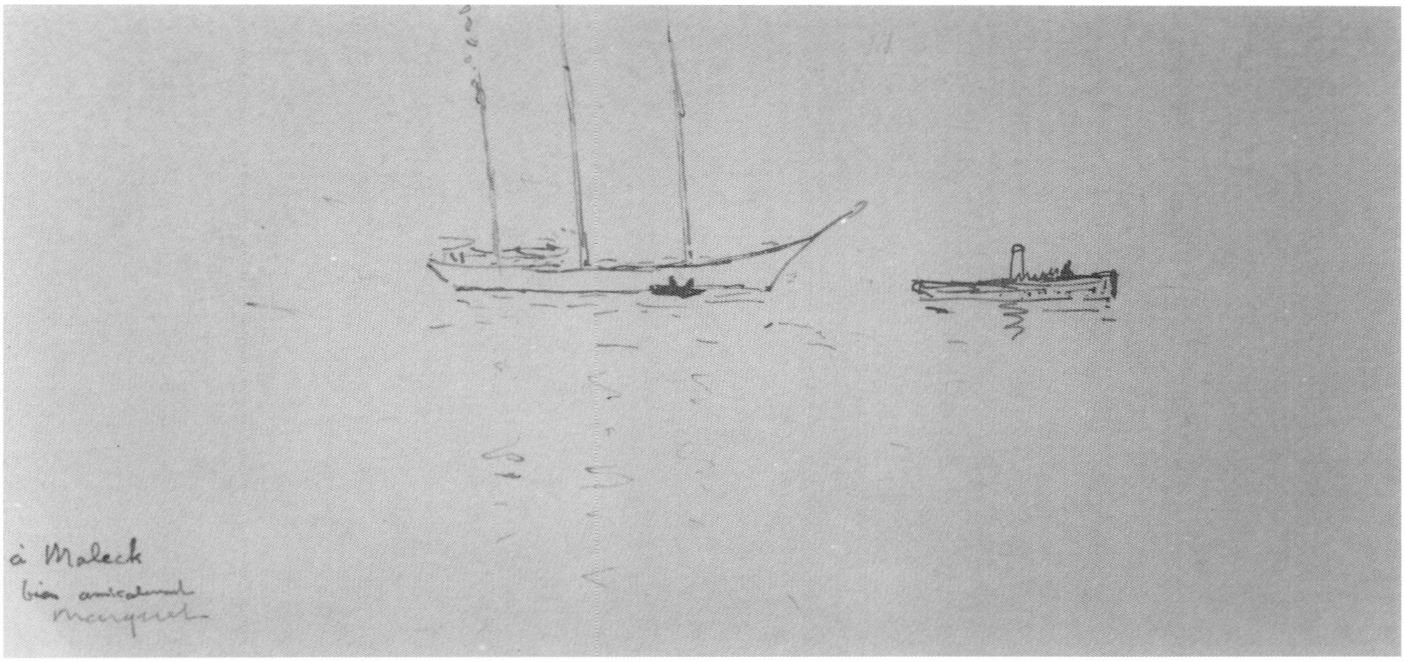

71 *Deux bateaux*, 1947

China ink on paper

10 x 20 cms

Gift of Jacqueline Brétégnier-André and assigned
to the Musée national d'art moderne in 1968

On deposit at the Musée du Château de Montbéliard

AM 3676 D

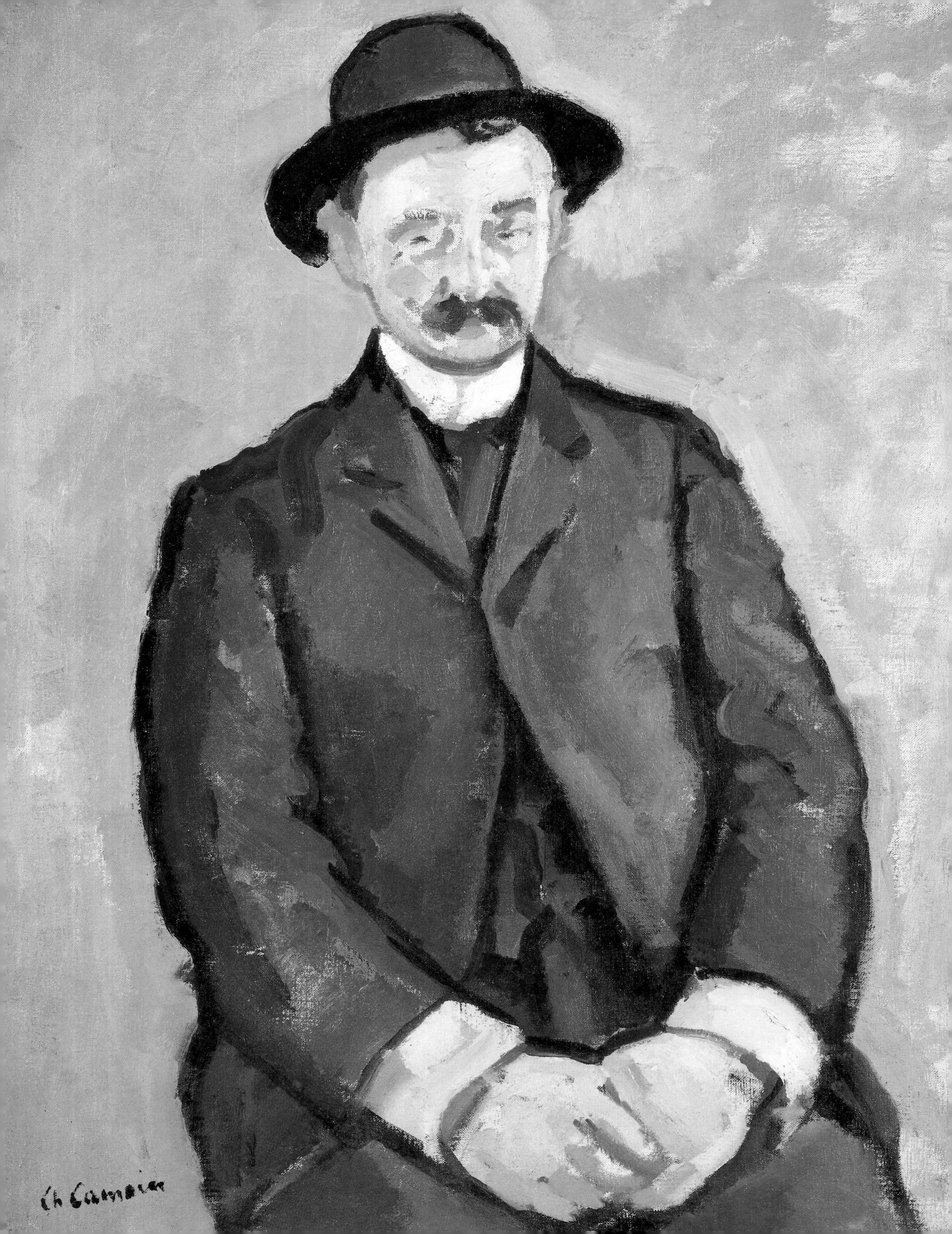
Ch Camoin

Biography

by Michèle Paret

1875

Pierre Léopold Albert Marquet is born on March 26, in Bordeaux, at eight in the morning. His father, Joseph, in a state of distraction, forgets to register him at the town hall. The following day, going to the registry, he does not dare to admit his mistake for fear of paying a fine. The official date of birth of the artist is therefore March 27: "Son of Joseph Marquet, forty years of age, employee, and of Marguerite Deyres, twenty-six years of age, his wife."[1]

1880–1890

From his infancy, Marquet draws. At school, he is not a good student. Timid, he suffers from his infirmity: a clubfoot sets him apart from the other children with whom he would like to run and play. He has bad vision, but does not wear glasses until he is fifteen. His teacher, "that chain-gang guard," thinks he is an idiot.

He takes refuge in the port of Bordeaux, and is enthralled by the movement of the water and the boats, as well as the colors.

In the summer, his vacations are spent in the Arcachon basin, with his mother's family, where he draws, watches cows, and lives like a peasant. His mother is his only support, and plays a great role in his life. "Petite, slender and lively," she knew her son very well and figured very quickly that with his gifts he should pursue his study of drawing in Paris, so as to find a career from which to live. She sells "a small plot of ground" belonging to her "in the Arcachon basin, a slip of a house at Teich," so as to buy a little shop, and they leave Bordeaux.[2]

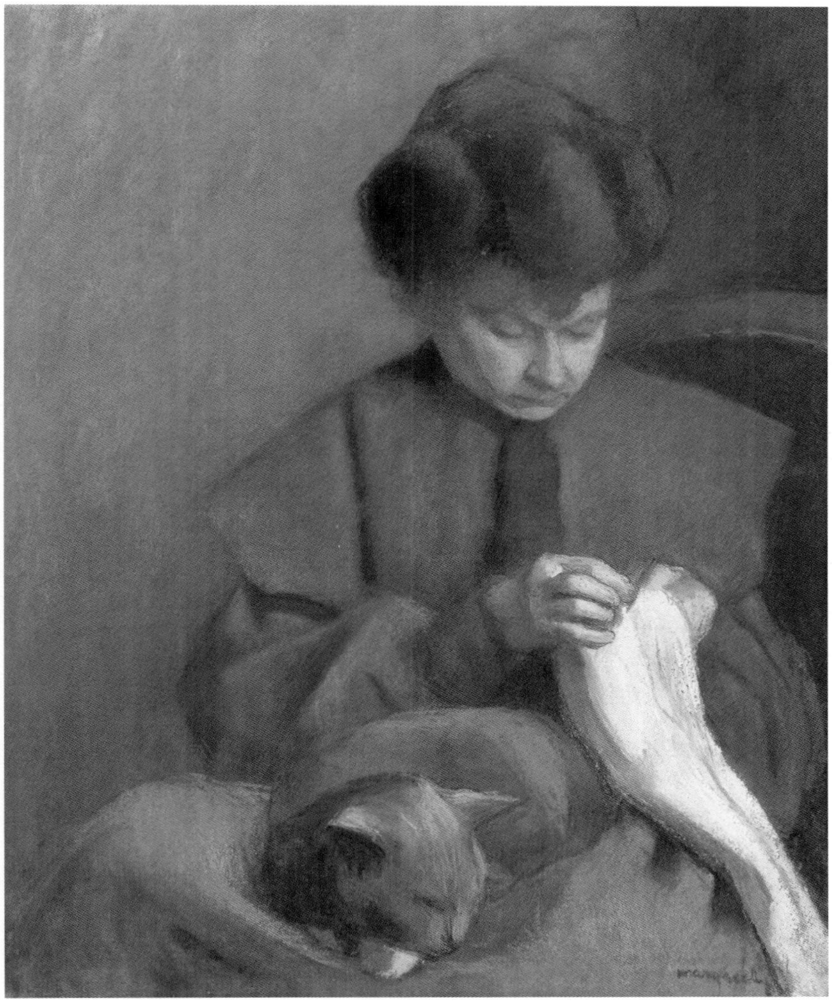

La mère de l'artiste, ca. 1905–1908 (#43)

1890–1893

Madame Marquet opens a corner-shop, *Jours et Broderies*, which she will run with one of her nieces, at 38, rue de Monge, in Paris. Marquet's father disagrees with his wife, he does not approve of her project, and has no confidence in art as a way of earning a living. He stays in Bordeaux, his retirement is near, and as a junior employee of the railways, he cannot leave his job. Admitted in 1892 to the *Ecole Nationale des Art Decoratifs* (National School for the Decorative Arts), Marquet meets young artists who are "rather a bad lot."[3] Hoffbauer, Géo Dupuis, Marcel Lenoir, Flandrin and Matisse, with whom he bonds. Matisse, a few years his elder – he was born on December 3, 1869 – who is free and easy and full of self-confidence, wins the friendship of the young man, who is timid but full of soul. A letter from Paul Baudoin, a teacher at the *Ecole Nationale des Art Decoratifs*, dated July 23, 1893, asks Gustave Moreau, professor at the *Ecole des Beaux-Arts* (School of Fine Arts), to take on his pupil Marquet.[4]

1894–1897

At the *Ecole des Beaux-Arts*, Matisse and Marquet follow the courses of Gustave Moreau, "great educator, respecter of individuality,"[5] who advises them first and foremost to be themselves and to study the ancient painters. Created professor and *chef d'atelier* (studio chief) on July 23, 1892, he occupies the position until his death on April 18, 1898.[6]

In 1894, Marquet takes the test for admission to the *Ecole*. He is received in the life-study class on May 1, 1895, and at the *Ecole* on July 13, 1897, a nomination confirmed by the delivery on May 21 of a students' card valid until October 15.[7] With his *atelier* friends and companions Matisse, Bussy, Evenepoel, Flandrin and Camoin (from 1898), the artist goes to the Louvre to copy the masters; he learns his trade in oil and pastel with Poussin, Claude, and Titian.

Life is "hard and gay:" during the day, work from models at the *atelier*, and in the

Opposite: detail, *Portrait d'Albert Marquet*, 1904 (#40) by Charles Camoin

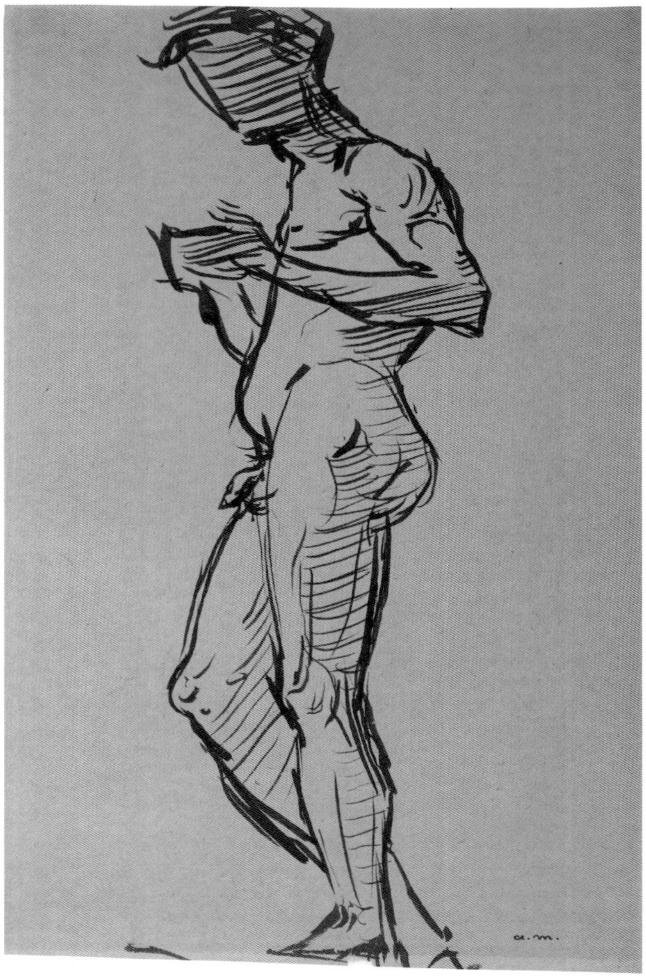

Nu de profil, ca. 1898 (#50)

evening, comradely reunions in the *cafés*. At the Café Procope, they joke, draw, and reform the world.

This type of camaraderie does not last long for most of the students, but a solid friendship grows between Marquet and Matisse, Manguin, Camoin and, a few years later, the future art critic George Besson.

Madame Marquet, an affectionate mother, attentively follows and encourages the studies of Albert. In July 1896, she writes to Gustave Moreau asking for a meeting, to find out what he thinks of her son.[8]

During those years, vacations are spent with family, In Teich, a commune in the Arcachon basin in which his mother was born, Marquet rediscovers his youthful customs. In 1895 and 1896, at Châtenois, in the Vosges, where his father hails from, he paints a few pictures. These works are still awkward – a *Rue de Châtenois* (Road at Châtenois) survives to this day, kept by a young cousin of the artist.

A few paintings of the Arcachon basin are also extant and date from this period (1895–1897).

In Paris, his first works are views of the *quais* (quays) and a few portraits.

1898

Charles Camoin joins the *Ecole des Beaux-Arts* in January, at a time when Gustave Moreau is already very ill. He meets Marquet and Manguin. Matisse has already left the *Ecole* and Paris. In a letter of February 28 to his friend Marquet he announces that he is in Corsica: "They have just managed to deliver to me here, in Corsica, the card and the congratulations from you and Fluchaire. I suppose therefore that you have heard of my marriage."[9]

Marquet goes to Arcueil to paint with Jules Flandrin. He is to return in future years with Matisse, and they will also paint in the *Jardin du Luxembourg* (Luxembourg Gardens). After the death of Moreau, the youngsters join different studios: either the Académie Julian or the Académie Camillo, where Eugène Carrière comes to critique.

They make the acquaintance of André Derain and Jean Puy and work from life; they paint a series of "school" nudes. However Marquet and Camoin are stifled in class, and escape to the streets and *quais* of Paris. They make little sketches of passers-by and carriages, hidden in tradesmen's entrances or on the terraces of *cafés*. The lack of money makes itself cruelly felt, despite Mme. Marquet's (modest) shop, they have to content themselves with vacations with family or friends.

1899

Marquet exhibits for the first time in May, at the *Salon de la Société Nationale des Beaux-Arts* (National Society for the Fine Arts), on the Champs-de-Mars. The work is *Saint-Etienne-du-Mont*.

In July-August, he sends *Panier de Pommes* (Basket of Apples) to the *Salon de Grenoble*, as well as a *Route au Soleil* (Road in the Sun).

With Matisse at Arcueil and at the Jardin du Luxembourg, he paints in a manner that will later be called "Fauve". Matisse, in a letter to his friend in June 1947, evoked the souvenir of those days when their means obliged them to "do landscapes in Paris in the morning, and at Arcueil in the afternoon…(they) sat on the sidewalk, making (their) landscapes at the bottom of (their) boxes."[10]

Manguin moves in to the rue Boursault and invites his friends to come and work with him in his studio.

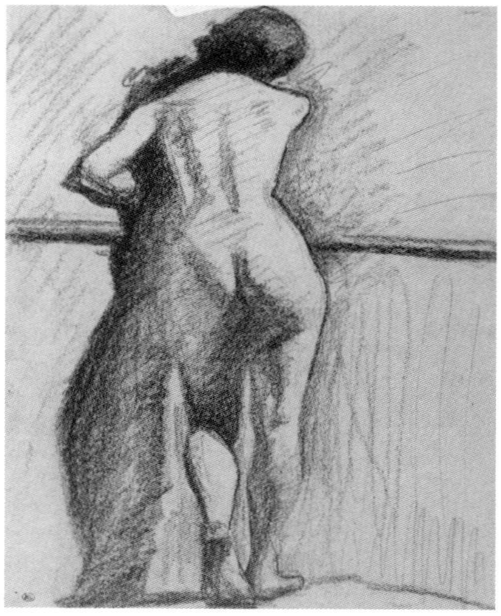

Nu de dos contre un mur, 1898 (#49)

1900

Camoin does his military service with the 55th infantry regiment. On the 18th of January he writes to Marquet "I am waiting impatiently for April to come around when we can see each other again and do the old Louvre together."[11]

To make ends meet, Marquet and Matisse accept work for "the frieze painter Jambon who is to decorate the Grand Palais for the *Exposition Universelle* (Universal Exhibition)…They were paid 1,25 francs per hour."[12] This exhausting work does not stop them from painting for themselves, and to continue work at the *atelier*.

In the spring, a young cousin from Teich arrives in Paris: Clementine. The young lady, who had come to visit the *Exposition Universelle* with her father, does not leave until 1903.

First she helps her aunt with her business and then when her aunt has no more need of her, she takes courses. Marquet will paint several pictures of his cousin: *Une jeune fille à la robe rouge* (A Young Woman in a Red Dress), as well as a few portraits. A bit of a grumbler, he does not appreciate the laughter and singing of youngsters.

The journalist Gustave Coquiot contacts Marquet with the idea of studying his work for publication in a revue. This project never seems to get off the ground.

To the little group of friends is added Jacqueline Marval, a friend of Jules Flandrin: "Since 1900 Marie Vallet, now known as J. Marval, made a sensational entrance into the group of friends."[13]

1901

Marquet participates for the first time in the *Salon des Indépendants* (Salon of the Independents), which is under the Presidency of Paul Signac. The artist exhibits alongside Matisse, Jean Puy, Laprade and Marval. He shows 10 paintings of Arcueil and the Luxembourg. After this exhibition, his name will appear in newspaper criticism, amongst others in *Gil Blas*, under the banner of Gustave Coquiot: "Mr. Marquet also sings of the glory of the town and its gardens. But he is brutish and uneven, though not without charm."[14] A small exhibition held at 13, rue Laffitte, the premises of the publisher Hessèle, has work by George Besson, Braquaval, and Charles Guerin. On March 2nd, in *La Chronique des Arts*, one reads: "In the same ensemble as Charles Guérin, in *Au jardin du Luxembourg* (In the Luxembourg Garden), Mr. A. Marquet researches by preference violent synthesis, the sonorous juxtapositions of which are softened by his pastel"[15]

Refused at the *Salon du Champ-de-Mars*, Marquet is never again to appear in this show, which is too bourgeois for his taste.

Opening on December 1 of Berthe Weill's gallery at 25 rue Victor Massé, where young painters are welcomed. Berthe Weill "became one of the great sources for modern art…(and) from 1902, she began to show the work of the group. She starts with Matisse and Marquet.[16]

1902

The year sees the first joint exhibition, at Berthe Weill's, for Matisse and Marquet. "Frantz Jourdain buys for 50 francs a little *Effet de neige* (Impression of Snow) by Marquet."[17] In her book, Madame Weill gives the wrong date for the purchase. Frantz Jourdain settles up for this work with Marquet in May 1905.

Camoin returns to Paris on leave and continues visits to the Louvre with his friends. Marquet rents a room at 25, quai de la Tournelle, from where he paints his series of *Absides de Notre-Dame vue du quai de la Tournelle* (Apse of Notre-Dame seen from Quai de la Tournelle).

He contributes to the *Salon des Indépendants* ten works of which five are recent, with subjects such as Notre-Dame and the Jardin du Luxembourg. In August he receives a letter from Matisse who is in Switzerland: "I've certainly met more Parisians and foreigners than Swiss. Among other Parisians I've met Roger-Marx who has given me much to tell you. I think that he is really interested in you."[18]

He receives some postcards from Jean Puy who is at Belle-Île-en-Mer. "Old Marquet, look at these landscapes waiting modestly for you twiddling their thumbs...nice country, but lacking in nude women."[19]

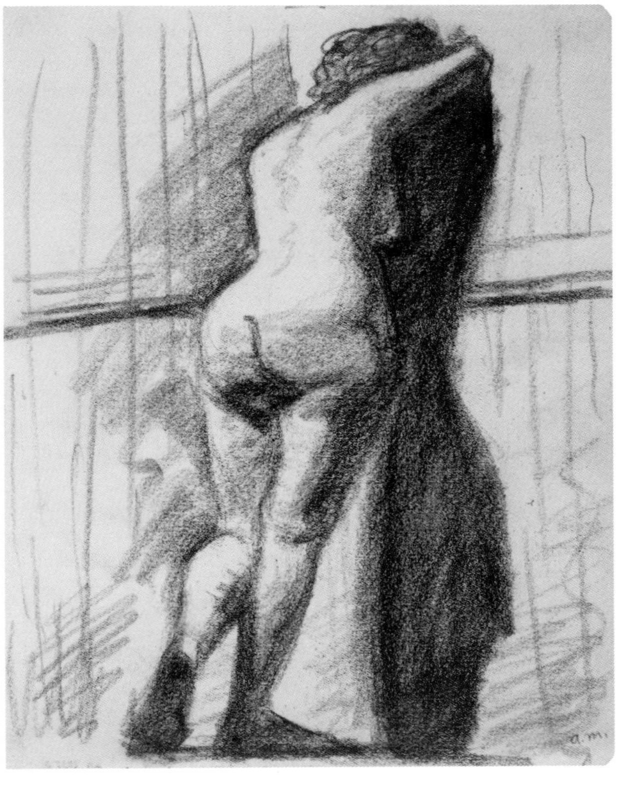

Nu de dos appuyé contre un mur, ca. 1899 (#51)

1903

Marquet and his parents move to 211 bis avenue de Versailles where they are to live a little more than a year.

From the windows of their apartment (a habit he is to retain for the rest of his life), the artist will paint the avenue and the Point du Jour district, as well as views of roofs.

His timidity and his complexes (he considers himself ordinary and misshapen), make him hesitate to go out. Later he is to refuse to have children in case they resemble him. Notwithstanding, intelligent and delicate, his spirit and his personality make him many friends among painters and in the intellectual circles of his day, friendships he is to retain all his life.

On March 5, Matisse, sick and discouraged, announces that he is off to rest in the Midi. From Bois-Guillaume, he asks Marquet to tell Luce that he is "suffering from a general anemia" and that it will be impossible for him to fulfill his obligations at the *Salon des Indépendants*.[20]

At Berthe Weill's gallery until May 31, there is a group exhibition that includes Luce, Marquet, Matisse and Prunier.

Marquet passes the summer in Normandy. The artist leaves with Manguin and his family for La Percaillerie. The two artists streak up the coast, go to Falaise and spend their time working "and joking." Matisse sends them several letters from the Aisne *département*, where he spends the summer regretting he is not with them.[21] In September, he writes to Marquet: "Your letter of this morning which announces that you are not happy with your season, reconciles me to my own. So in the sad life of friends do we console our own...I aim to return to Paris around the first days of October. You will of course be warned of my arrival and you can come and see my ugly daubs in which you will see "wonderful things" and once again I will be happy with myself."[22]

At the first *Salon d'Automne* (Autumn Salon), the young painters exhibit under the Presidency of Eugène Carrière and Frantz Jourdain. Marquet shows a few Normandy paintings: *Une falaise* (A Cliff), *En Normandie* (In Normandy) and *La Barrière* (The Barrier).

1904

The writer Charles-Louis Philippe asks Marquet to illustrate his novel *Bubu de Montparnasse*.

Marquet shows five paintings at the *Salon des Indépendants*, which takes place from February 21 to March 24.

At Berthe Weill's gallery, Marquet takes part in a new group show along with Matisse, Jean Puy, Camoin and Manguin. In March-April he copies at the Louvre with his friends Matisse and Manguin. Eugène Druet starts to be interested in picture dealing. Formerly the owner of a *bar-tabac* at the place de l'Alma, he got to know the painters who show their work at the Salon des Indépendants. Also an amateur photographer, he becomes Rodin's hired photographer, and starts to get closer to the young painters, without giving up his own art. In 1904 he exhibits the work of a group of young artists at the gallery that he opened the year before at 114, rue du Faubourg Saint-Honoré: "At the back of the shop, you could generally find Maurice Denis, Marquet, Laprade, Manguin, Flandrin, Vallotton, and Marval arguing with Romain Coolus, Tristan Bernard, Denys Cochin, at the same time as riffling through the

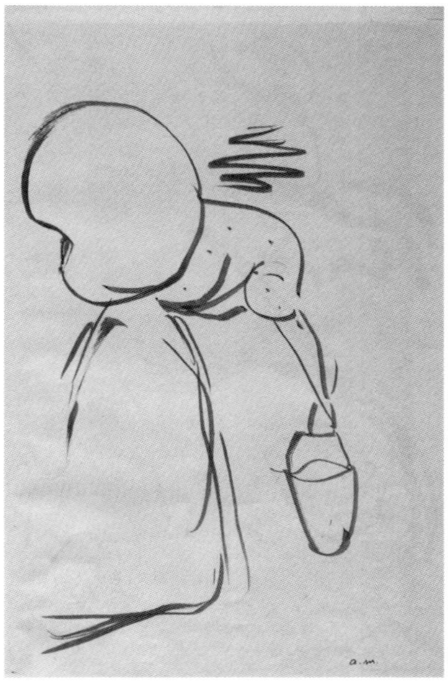

Blanchisseuse, 1903 (#52a)

first installments of the *Nouvelle Revue Française* and the works of Gide, Claudel, and Charles-Louis Philippe, for whom Druet stocked books.[23]

Marquet rents a room in a little hotel at the corner of the rue Dauphine, at the same place where, in 1931, he will keep house with his wife in a new apartment that will be built on the site of the hotel.

On June 8 Marquet receives an affectionate letter from his mother, on holiday at Teich with her family: his father is in the Vosges.

He goes with Dufy for "a day of regattas and painting at Fécamp."[24]

Staying in Paris to complete the designs for *Bubu de Montparnasse* for Charles-Louis Philippe, Marquet writes to his friends throughout the summer, notably to Matisse who is staying at St. Tropez: "Preoccupied as I am with Bubu, I've had to give up all thoughts of landscape." He does not feel as gifted as in the past and though Philippe seems enthusiastic, the publisher hardly looks at the drawings.[25] Mr. De Noussane rejects them without having looked, and gives the commission to the draftsman of *l'Assiette au buerre*, Grandjouan. Charles-Louis Philippe, desolate, sends Marquet an indignant letter on September 7.[26] On the 11th, Marquet writes to Matisse, "This time, *Bubu*, is totally dead."[27] During the summer, Camoin is in Italy. Marquet and his father stay in Paris and receive letters full of recommendations from Madame Marquet who is still in Teich, with her family.

The little group of artists begins to attract the attention of connoisseurs. Eugène Descaves, who visits Marquet's studio, comes away with a large number of paintings for next to nothing, even though Marquet and his family are fighting financial worries

1905

Marquet and his parents move once more. They install themselves in an apartment at 25, quai des Grands-Augustins.

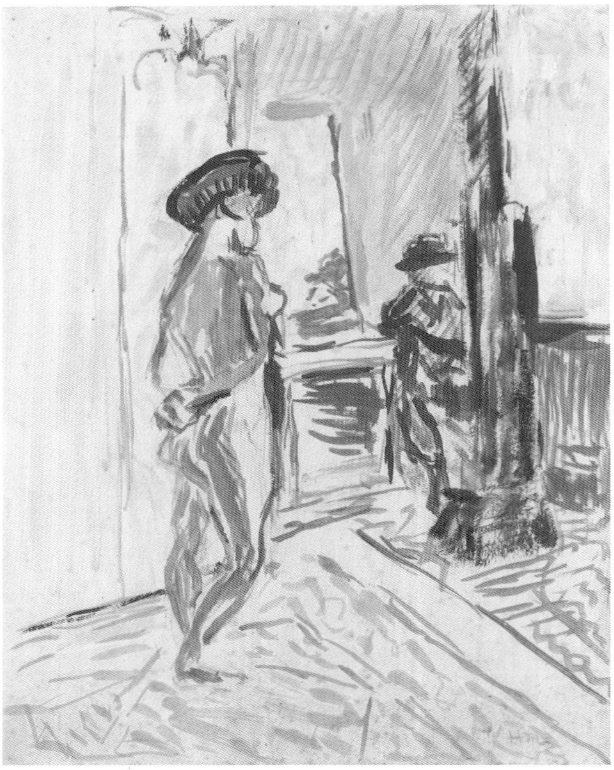

Marquet peignant un nu dans l'atelier de Manguin, 1904–1905, by Henri Matisse (#42)

He begins at this time the series of paintings of quays in all weathers and at all times of day. On March 7, Ambroise Vollard offers to buy six works for one thousand francs.[28]

Frantz Jourdain settles the balance of his debt, he buys from him a small *Effet de neige*, and thanks the artist for the egoistical pleasure he finds in his work.[29]

From March 24 to April 30, Marquet exhibits as always at the *Salon des Indépendants*, and from April 2 to April 23 at Berthe Weill's gallery. At the *Salon*, the state buys one work, *Notre-Dame au soleil* (Notre-Dame in the Sun).[30]

On April 6, Camoin, Matisse and Marquet attend a dinner given in Rodin's honor at the *Closerie des Lilas*.

Thanks to his sales, and liberated from financial worry, Marquet can envisage leaving Paris for a long stay in the Midi, where Manguin and his family are waiting for him. They rent a villa on the outskirts of St. Tropez, the "villa Demière".

On May 6, Manguin writes to him, "Marseilles admirable, try to stay there a day or two…St. Tropez seems very pretty, have not seen much yet, been having a bit of a sea which reminds me of La Percaillerie."[31] The bad weather was also there to welcome Marquet, when he arrives at his friend's. They have a visit from Francis Jourdain, the son of Frantz. The artist despairs of seeing the sun, and, finding himself too far from St. Tropez, he decides to install himself at the Hôtel Sube, on the port.

On June 6, Matisse sends a long letter to Marquet and Manguin, with news of friends and his work at Collioure. "I have been content to know that you are reunited so as to support each other through the bad weather and the mistral…what are you up to? Have you been to Ramatuelle, to Gassin, to Grimaud? To see Cross, and Valtat, that is to say, have you been to Agay?"[32] And Marquet writes back: "The bad weather continues and our studies are getting nowhere."[33] In turn, on June 9, Manguin writes to Matisse: "The only troublesome thing is that we are a bit far from the sea and St. Tropez which is really very pretty. Also, old Marquet has dropped us and moved to the port, he has a superb view."[34] With Paul Signac, who they visit at his villa La Hune, and John Antoine Nau, they spend a lot of time at the *café*. The friends are not bored, but neither do they get to work.

The little port of St. Tropez, filled with boats and hogsheads, offers them a calm and simple life that they appreciate, and on June 12 Marquet tells Camoin: "(I have) started to work rather recently, there's not much done."[35]

He encourages Camoin, who is staying at Cassis, to come and join them. The latter writes to Matisse from St. Tropez on June 28: "Luckily, we have the Bon Bock *café* to fall back on!" With Marquet we have had fits of laughter that couldn't be paid for, and which are undescribable."[36] They paint together the girls in the Bar des Roses. Having profited rather too much of the pleasures offered by the "young ladies," the pair leave St. Tropez. On July 5, they are in St. Raphaël, then they go to Agay where Cross and Valtat invite them to spend a few days "collecting burning memories…and an extensive pharmacy."[37] They stay at the Grand-Hôtel at Agay.

Marquet continues on his own towards Le Trayas and Nice, Camoin returns to Cassis to recuperate.

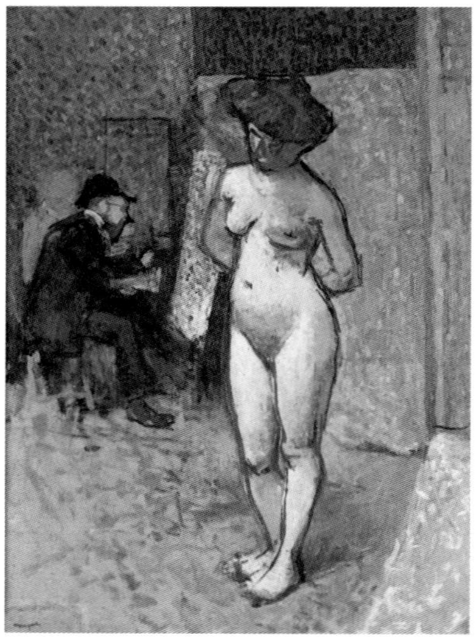

Matisse dans l'atelier de Manguin, 1905 (#8)

At Menton Marquet stays at the Hôtel des Négociants, where on August 18, he gets news of his friend, with whom he has corresponded, having given him addresses beforehand for his entire pilgrimage.[38]

Back in St. Tropez, he rejoins the Camoins at Cassis and paints his friend in front of his easel in the garden of the Hôtel Cendrillon. At Marseille, the group, having been somewhat dispersed by work during the summer, re-group before they return to Paris. Derain and Matisse are returning from Collioure.

In September, Marquet goes to Teich to fetch his mother, and takes advantage of the opportunity to rediscover Bordeaux and tour the region. He hopes to get back to Paris and the *Salon d'Automne*, where, from October 18 – November 25, he will show, in room VII, his paintings *Anthéor, Menton, Agay*, and *les Roches rouges au Trayas* (Red Rocks at Trayas), next to works by his friends Manguin, Matisse, Camoin, Flandrin, Rouault, Girieud, Puy, Derain, Vlaminck, Valtat, Friesz and Van Dongen. This collection creates a scandal and Louis Vauxcelles, in the supplement to *Gil Blas* of October 17, christens the group "Fauves": "In the middle of the room, a torso of a child and a little marble bust by the sculptor Albert Marque, which are modeled with delicate skill. The color of these busts is surprising in the middle of all those pure tones: Donatello among the *fauves* (wild beasts)." In October and November, a group exhibition is held at Berthe Weill's gallery.

1906

At the beginning of the year, Marquet prepares his entries for the exhibitions at Brussels and Paris.

Elie Faure whom he still only barely knows, but with whom he will bond, asks him to join in the exhibition *Libre Esthétique* (free aesthetic) in Brussels. On January 3, Marquet accepts, also recommending his friend, Matisse.[39] From Rueil, Vlaminck asks him for tips about the show where Manguin is also represented.[40] The exhibition takes place from February 25 to March 25, and Matisse shows there for the first time.

From Corsica, Camoin checks up on the send-in dates for the *Salon des Indépendants*, which will be held from March 20 to April 30 in the conservatories of the City of Paris.[41] Marquet exhibits there a series of landscapes that can be identified as the *quais* of Paris, in particular the quai des Grands-Augustins.

From 1906 Georges-Jean Aubry regularly organizes a series of exhibitions in Le Havre that aim to introduce modern art to the art buffs of Normandy. Marquet is a regular contributor. On May 26, the show opens. Marquet refuses Aubry's offer to buy his paintings[42] and announces his forthcoming arrival. He exhibits with Braque, Camoin, Derain, Dufy, Friesz and Manguin.

Eugène Druet is unable to keep the exclusivity of his contract with Marquet, and has to share the artist with the galerie Bernheim-Jeune. In a letter addressed to Manguin, dated May 13 (collection Jean-Pierre Manguin), Marquet tells of the death of his father. His mother is "once again ill, as in the winter."[43]

For a couple of months, Marquet rents a room on the quai du Louvre. During the spring and summer, he creates a series of canvases of the *quais* looking towards the Ile de la Cité and the Eiffel Tower.

On June 14 Camoin, in Marseille, advises his friend to leave for Le Havre "as soon as possible."[44] With Dufy, Marquet goes there and they stay at the Hôtel du Ruban Bleu, the address to which Camoin and Matisse write to him on June 29. The stay lasts at least until July 14, as several paintings feature the French national holiday. At the end of the year, Marquet sends Matisse their new address at Fécamp,[45] the Hôtel Duhamel. They then go on to paint at Dieppe and Trouville.

Returning to Paris in mid-September he prepares submissions for the *Salon d'Automne*, and he informs Matisse, in Collioure, of the relevant dates.[46] Matisse puts him in charge of his paintings, and writes: "What do you think of my daubs?"[47] Having been part of the jury the year before Marquet is not part of it in 1906 but he helps his friends to organize their submissions and keeps up a correspondence with them in relation to this. On September 21 he explains to Manguin that "(his) paintings have all been received...Matisse has had a great deal of success...two of Camoin's works were plucked...Dufy, Friesz and Van Dongen are mostly plucked."[48]

The *Salon d'Automne* opens its doors on October 6 at the Grand Palais. *Le Port de Fécamp* figures among the state's purchases. Excellent notices in the papers at this time, in particular in December from Paul Jamot in the *Gazette des Beaux-Arts*.

A group exhibition is held at the galerie Berthe Weill from November 7 to 30.

Marquet wants to move. He finds a little lodging house at 29, place Dauphine, and installs himself and his mother.

At the end of the year, Druet sends a series of canvases by his painters to Germany for an exhibition that will last until January of 1907 and will take place in Munich, Frankfurt, Dresden, Karlsruhe and Stuttgart.

1907

From February 11 to 23, the galerie Druet holds Marquet's first one-man show. His fame continues to grow, and more and more connoisseurs buy his work. In the *Chronique des Arts* of February 16, Pierre Jamot hypothesizes that "in the ideal exhibition reuniting the best and most original painters of Paris ...(Marquet)...would deserve a place at the top of the list."

Marquet's account book, kept at the musée de Bordeaux, gives us the number of paintings purchased in the year, and their prices, unfortunately in no greater detail.

Druet wants to gets his artists known abroad. After the traveling show in Germany, he sends works by Marquet to Vienna and then to Prague.

In January, the artists receives several postcards from Gublin, a comrade from Moreau's studio, whom he still sees when Gublin passes through Paris.[49]

From March 20 to April 30, he exhibits at the *Salon des Indépendants*. On April 26 he replies to Jean Aubry, who had told him of the vicissitudes of his painting purchased by the state at the *Salon d'Automne*, which had been sent to the musée du Havre, where the curator refused to exhibit it or keep it in his museum.[50]

At the end of April Camoin, Friesz and Marquet visit London.

His mother, exceedingly tired, writes to him on May 4: "I received your card this morning, it gave me great pleasure, as with all the bad weather we've had, I've been mortally anxious."[51]

The painters elicit a mocking interest from the English: "Camoin was wearing a red velvet costume which was a little loud, Albert a bowler which he was not used to and had just purchased...making them a fairly exuberant and remarkable trio."[52] After this voyage of pleasure and discovery, the artist picks up the threads of his Parisian activities.

In May he exhibits at the *Cercle de l'Art moderne* (the modern art circle) at Le Havre, where thanks to Jean Aubry he sells two paintings. At the beginning of June, Marquet gets ready for another trip to London this time in order to work and bring back a few paintings. Camoin is in Spain. Arriving between July 8 and 10 in London, Marquet stays at 44 Dean Street, Soho Square, and finds a little difficulty making himself understood, as he speaks no English.

Recalled to France a few days later by his mother's family, he stays with her in Teich until her death on August 25. He is very touched by the death of the person who had always supported him and who dedicated to him a large portion of her life.

Manguin writes to him from Saint-Tropez. Camoin is still in Spain.

Not having been able to work sufficiently in London (he brought back two paintings), in August he goes off to Ciboure and Saint-Jean-de-Luz.

From October 1 to 22, Marquet shows two paintings at the *Salon d'Automne*, of which one is a London scene, *Le Pont de Blackfriars* (Blackfriars' Bridge). With Matisse, he is one of the jury. From October 24 to November 10, an exhibition is held at the galerie Eugène Blot, with Camille Claudel, Puy and Manguin.

At the end of the year, on December 30, he sends his greetings to Manguin and announces that he is "thinking of moving in eight to ten days."[53]

1908

During the first days of the year, Marquet moves to the 5th floor of 19, quai Saint-Michel, to the studio that Matisse has just left, wanting a larger apartment for his family. In this building, artists live on all floors, and Matisse returns to live on the 4th floor several years later.

On February 4 Marquet tells Camoin: "I have at last got down to it (work) as well, it has been a bloody long time since this has happened."[54]

Several exhibitions this year show his works: Bernheim-Jeune (*Portraits d'hommes*, or portraits of men), the *Salon des Indépendants*, the *Sécession de Berlin* (Berlin Secession), an exhibition in Moscow in April, and one in Liège in May-June, for which Marquet receives a card from Tyge Möller: "Returning from Liège, I wanted to give you news of your two paintings which are admirably placed and are arousing lively interest."[55]

In June, Marquet and Manguin travel to Italy. From Fiesole, then from Naples, Marquet sends his impressions to his friend Matisse. In Naples, they find Raoul de Mathan, and the writer Eugène Montfort who invite him to Capri, the "Villa Croce."[56] On July 7, he asks Camoin to send him news, "*poste restante*, beautiful country, very amusing town, what an adventure!"[57]

In July, in Paris, a group exhibition is held at the galerie Druet.

Returning to France in mid-August, after a detour to Cassis to see Camoin, Marquet goes to work in Poissy, and stays at the Hôtel de Rouen. Eugène de Montfort continues to send him cards from Naples: "For three days I have been the happy husband of your fiancée!"[58]

The weather is very bad at Poissy and he works less than he had planned. He waits impatiently for the visit of his friends.

From the beginning of September, Matisse is with Marquet at Poissy so as to fish and boat on the Seine. The two artists decide to go on a trip, they pass through Bordeaux where Marquet's aunt expects his visit and continue their odyssey in the direction of Dakar where they stay a week from September 24 to October 3: "We're going to show negresses at the private view of the *Salon d'Automne*," Marquet writes to Manguin on September 23.[59]

At the *Salon d'Automne*, in October, Marquet, the vice-president, is represented by a series of drawings. In December, there are several group exhibitions in Paris, at Eugène Blot's, Berthe Weill's, and at the galerie Druet.

1909

At the beginning of the year, Marquet participates in an exhibition at the galerie Berthe Weill, from January 22 to February 22. In Moscow, at the *Salon de la Toison d'Or* (salon of the golden fleece), from January 24 to February 28, he is represented by three of his works. In March, he shows two works in Paris, at the *Salon des Indépendants*.

Matisse, returning from Germany where he spent the month of December 1908, encourages his friend to go there also. He gives him many letters of introduction, addresses of relatives and painters who he can visit. When he arrives in Hamburg, at the beginning of March, Marquet stays at the Hôtel Wiezals à Sankt Pauli, and on March 9 writes to Matisse: "Thanks to your good recommendations I have found in Hamburg some very amiable people who have just about done the trick for me."[60] He leaves the hotel quickly to live at 4, Reimerusstrasse, near the port. At the beginning of April Matisse, in touch with his work and his preoccupations, replies to him: "Today I saw Mr. Nolken and he came into my studio this morning as a pupil. I was pleased to learn from him that you are working. I say from him as from Manguin I only heard that you were thinking of getting down to it; I had made up my mind that you were pulling our dear friend's leg."[61] Around April 15, Matisse sends to Marquet a new letter including several addresses for his friend's stay in Berlin, and on May 1 he sends some addresses in Munich, where the painter does not stay.[62]

In Hamburg, in the snow the rain and the cold, Marquet paints, and draws a lot. From Berlin, Dresden and Munich he brings back only souvenirs. On his return to Paris, on May 10, he writes to Camoin: "The German campaign is over. It was joyful enough but not very glorious."[63]

After this northerly voyage, Marquet shows his works in Le Havre in June. At the beginning of June, with Eugène Montfort who has just started the review *Les Marges* (the margins), they return to Naples where the artist had worked only a little the preceding year. Eugène Montfort, a great fan of Italy, rents an apartment or a villa at 20 Vico Santa Teresella degli Spagnoli. Marquet calls on Jean Aubry for help and asks him to send him some money.[64]

On July 24, he sends a card to Matisse from Paestum, and another on August 21 from Naples, where he still is. He announces that he has just climbed Vesuvius and is off to Sicily, and that he will be in Marseilles around September 1, that he will then go to Tangiers, and at the end of his trip will visit a few Spanish towns.[65] On September 19 he is in fact in Seville.

In October, at the *Salon d'Automne*, six canvases by Marquet, belonging to Druet and Jean Aubry, are shown.

1910

The winter is spent in Paris. Marquet paints in his studio several pictures of the pont Saint-Michel. He continues to go to the Académie Ranson to work with his friends.

From February to March, there is an exhibition of the Société Manès in Prague: in March, *La Libre Esthétique* in Brussels shows five of his paintings of Paris and Naples. From March 18 to May 1 he shows two paintings at the *Indépendants*.

In April Marquet goes to London with the intention of working there, but struck down by flu he is able to achieve nothing.[66]

From May 2 to 14, the galerie Druet organizes a Marquet exhibition in its rooms. Fifty-three works are recorded, but the photographs of the galleries lead one to suppose that the number of canvases and drawings was in fact greater. Excellent notices in *La Presse* of May 4, and in the *Paris-Journal* of May 9.

On May 10, he receives a card from Camoin, who is in Corsica for a few weeks.[67]

In Russia, several of his works are shown in different exhibitions during the year.

In August, Manguin is in Villennes-sur-Seine for a month, Marquet for two months. They have rented the Villa des Cytises on the Ile de Villennes. The two painters will work together painting *en plein air*. Orthon Friesz announces his forthcoming visit on September 13: "One of these days I will come to shake your hand and get the shit out of my eyes on your island..."[68] Manguin has left.

In October, Marquet tells Camoin "as of my return to Paris, the holidays are over."[69]

After a few days spent with his family in Bordeaux, in November he undergoes a hernia operation and passes his convalescence at the Maison Velpeau, 7, rue de la Chaise.

His friends Jean Puy, Manguin, Matisse and Camoin regularly send him postcards from their travels.

In December, he once again finds himself at 19, quai Saint-Michel, and on December 27 Matisse, still in Spain, writes, "I am glad to hear you're back to full strength."[70]

1911

On January 7, Marquet writes to Matisse: "I'm always between colds and rheumatic attacks... I don't really have the taste for work at the moment."[71]

From 1911, he embarks on a series of nudes done in the studio. Surrounded by numerous young models, single artists like Marquet and Camoin, having fun as much as they painted, often formed attachments with one or other of their models. For many years, up until his meeting with Marcelle Martinet in 1920, Marquet goes out and travels with different lady-friends, but one among them, Yvonne – whose real name was Ernestine Bazin – serves as his model for most of his nudes and often accompanies him on his travels around France.

On January 20, a card from Matisse tells of his return from Spain,[72] while Marquet is busy executing views of the *Eglise de la Trinité* (Church of the Trinity) from the apartment window of the publisher Paul Gallimard. A lover of art, Gallimard will buy paintings from the young Fauves. Marquet has already abandoned that manner of painting, which he only used for a little while in the Arcueil and Agay period of 1905.

In April he exhibits with the group at the dealer Druet.

At Munich, at the galerie Tannhauser, there is an exhibition of several young French artists including Marquet, Camoin, Girieud and Matisse.

In May, he spends fifteen days at Conflans-Sainte-Honorine which he had already visited in 1908 while staying at Poissy. He stays at the Hôtel de la Gare and paints the bridges and barges that are moored on the banks of the Oise.

On June 4 he writes to Camoin: "Disgusting weather. Returning to Paris tomorrow."[73]

On May 7 and 8, the Henry Bernstein sale takes place in Paris, one of the first collectors' sales to include a work by Marquet, a *Port de Naples* (Port of Naples). Marquet is surrounded by the likes of Besnard, Bonnard, Cézanne, Fantin-Latour, Matisse, Monet and Renoir.

From Paris the artist heads for Honfleur to paint the port and the boats. On June 22 he sends an enthusiastic postcard to Camoin. In July Eugène Montfort sends him news, from Morgat, at the Saint-Siméon farm where he has been staying a few weeks: "I met Ernestine before I left who showed me all your postcards."[74]

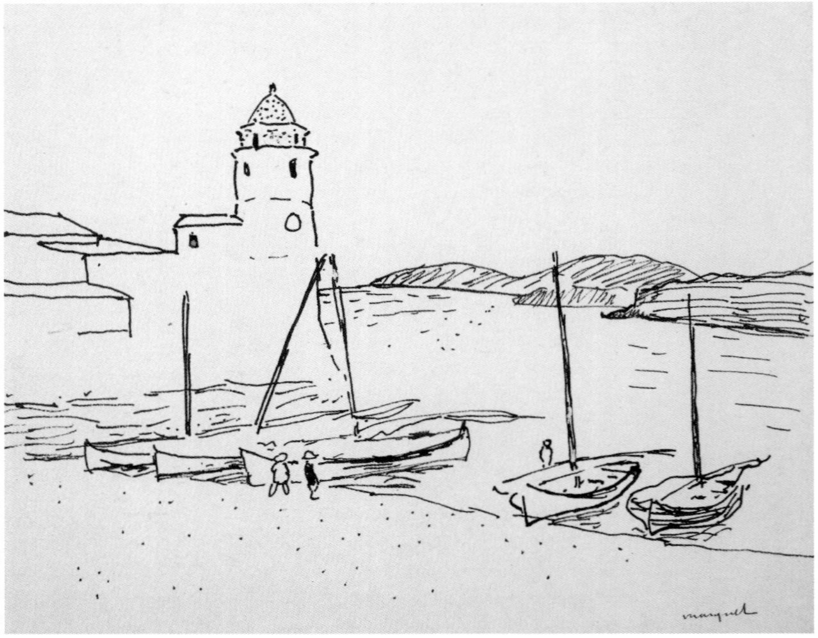

Le port de Collioure, ca. 1912–1914 (#55)

On July 7 he writes to Manguin, who is at Sanary: "Here there have been a few days of abominable weather, now a starry sunlight. Vallotton is broken-hearted. I am working a bit, but I'm only doing the sea."[75]

He receives greetings from Orthon Friesz, who is on holiday in Portugal.

At the end of July, he tells Manguin of his return to Paris, and his forthcoming departure to the Midi.[76] On July 30, Matisse tells his friend that he will be staying in Collioure another month, to work there and tells him that they would see each other on Marquet's return from warmer climes. He later sends him a letter recommending Fez. "I hope that you are less hot in Tangiers than we are here," adds Olga Meerson on the postcard.[77]

Marcelle Marquet in her book *Voyages de Marquet* of 1968 mentions a trip to Morocco with Matisse in 1911, which seems impossible on reading these rediscovered documents. They are never there together, Matisse preferring the winter, and his friend the summer.

In August, Marquet leaves for Morocco with Eugène Montfort. They are to make a voyage of discovery: Tangiers, Rabat, Fez, Tetouan, and Casablanca. The artist vows to do nothing and to profit from his vacation. They meet acquaintances, have a lot of fun, and ride horses. Camoin, who is finishing his time in the military, getting bored in Cassis, is envious. On August 31, Marquet writes to Matisse, "I am at the moment in Tetouan where we arrived after eleven hours, on horseback...Haven't done any painting yet."[78] In fact, from this whole summer in Morocco, he only brings back a few gouaches.

He announces his return at the end of August from Casablanca: "where he is awaiting a boat for France."[79] His return at the beginning of October is later than he had hoped. Marquet stops a few days in Bordeaux before getting back to Paris. On September 25, he is still being sent his press cuttings at Teich.

In October, he exhibits at the *Salon d'Automne*: *La Place de La Trinité* (Trinity Place), *Les barques roses* (The Red Boats), *Conflans*, and *Le Port de Honfleur* (The Port of Honfleur).

Druet sends his paintings abroad throughout the whole year, so as to get him better known.

During the winter, Marquet continues to paint nudes and the Pont St-Michel.

1912

On January 23, Olga Meerson asks Marquet to gift one of his paintings to the Pinacoteca in Munich.[80]

At the beginning of January, an exhibition of drawings and paintings at the Druet Gallery: "Landscapes from the pen of Mr. A. Marquet, of an amplitude, a delicacy, a mastery of the first order, do they not directly evoke Nicolas Poussin in their spirit and their beautiful sepia?" comments René Jean.[81]

The whole group, reunited at Druet's, send their wishes to Henri Matisse in Tangiers.[82] Matisse sends his friends despairing cards because of the rain and the incessant storms he has suffered since his arrival at the end of January. In these postcards he frequently asks Marquet to come and join him.

In March, still in Paris, Marquet sends a few canvases to Switzerland, to the Vallotton Gallery in Lausanne.[83] On March 8, he writes to Matisse who is still in Tangiers: "Here...we are to have the *Indépendants*, and we will be able to double up with laughter among the cubes and other novelties."[84]

On April 13, Marquet's aunt, the sister of his father, dies at Châtenois. The artist goes to spend a few days there.

On his return, he goes to Rouen where in May he writes to Camoin: "I am at the Hôtel de Paris, quai de Paris, at Rouen. It really is fascinating and I count on doing a lot of work."[85] Unfortunately torrential rain hampers him a little, so he decides to study the effects of rain and to profit from the bad weather.

Very quickly tiring of the bad weather, he exhorts his friends to join him.

On May 13, he announces to Manguin that he will be back in Paris at the end of the week.[86]

In June, Camoin leaves for Collioure, where he finds the painter Etienne Terrus.

On June 27, his friend and model Ernestine announces to Marquet that she will be twenty on the following Friday. This postcard is addressed to 1, rue Duquesne, Rouen, where the painter is again staying. Sun and heat have replaced the rain, and, in mid-July, he plans "a little trip down Marseilles way," where Eugène Montfort is asking for him. With Matisse, who has come to spend a few days in Rouen, they decide to go and join Camoin at Collioure passing via Marseilles, where they will pick up Montfort. On September 23, in Marseilles, Eugène Montfort writes to Marquet a letter whose style one can appreciate: "I had to leave, with the aunt of the little proprietress, my umbrella. This umbrella is like an old servant become deaf and gouty...it has become useless, but you hang on to it. My umbrella is rusted, the whalebone worn out, it is bent out of shape but it is my old and faithful umbrella...I would always take it with me on my travels...now I do not have it. I look forward to its comfort when I return home."[87]

Marquet returns to Paris at the end of September. During the first half of September he again is in Rouen where he finishes his paintings a few days later.

Matisse returns to Morocco on September 30. Camoin and Madame Matisse join him at Tangiers at the end of October. Camoin writes to Marquet on December 30: "I have just left the hospital at Tangiers where I have just completed a very painful course for diphtheria!... And in Paris, is all well, and the chess and Philidore? Are you still giving Druet good hidings?"[88]

On December 28, Matisse reassures him: "Camoin...is better, and doing the rounds of the houses of ill-repute where he is posing the Jews and Arabs."[89]

1913

From Tangiers in January, Matisse is still asking his friend to join them: "We party every day. Camoin and I can hardly stand up...When do you arrive?"[90] Marquet will not come, he is at work in his studio and all the calls of his friends will be in vain. Matisse comes back to France in February and goes to Ajaccio with his wife. Camoin returns a month or two later.

Druet sends several paintings to New York for the exhibition of modern art that will be held afterwards at Chicago and Boston, from February to May.

From March 31 to April 12 Marquet has a one-man show at the Druet Gallery, including 47 paintings, recent works from Villennes, Paris, Conflans, Honfleur, Rouen, Tangiers and Collioure, as well as figure studies and nudes from the preceding winters. Many reviews appear in the press, in particular in *Le Figaro*, *Gil Blas*, *La Chronique des arts*, *Les Arts et les artistes* and *Comoedia*. On May 30, the Naval Ministry authorizes the painter to follow, from June 1, the naval maneuvers on board the flagship, *Le Vergniaud*. He is also allowed to make sketches and studies at the arsenal at Toulon.[91] On June 6, Camoin writes to him at Toulon: "Impossible to leave Cassis, here I am again in a real mess."[92] Once again he is with Verdilhan. Etienne Terrus addresses a card to the Hôtel du Port: he complains of the heat of his studio at Elne, and mentions that from time to time he sends cards to Mlle. Yvonne."[93]

At the beginning of July, Marquet is at La-Varenne-Saint-Hilaire for a few days. On July 10, Camoin writes to him at the Hôtel du Chalet Bellevue: "We are having games of bowls with old Manguin and the crew...you should really come and bring Ernestine to make the party complete."[94]

From this time on, in all the Marquet correspondence exchanged back and forth with his friends, there are allusions to Yvonne-Ernestine, his model, who follows his movements. At the end of July, Marquet decides to leave for Morocco via Marseilles, to go and see his friends. On August 8 he sends a card to Camoin from the Hôtel Villa de France in Tangiers, where he is "already having a pretty good time."[95]

Elie Faure commissions a little drawing for his *Dostoïevsky*, and Marquet is late replying.

Imbert, editor at the *Studio* of St. Petersburg, wants to dedicate a chapter to Marquet in his book on the origins of French contemporary art, and on August 17 asks him for a short biography, photos of his paintings and his portrait.[96]

On August 20, Etienne Terrus tells the Marquets that: "the fire is burning in the cubist camp at Céret. The women are fighting amongst themselves and the men are doing likewise.

There have been words between the wives of Picasso and Pichot, and between Picasso and a poet."[97]

Marquet, accompanied by a group of friends, goes off to visit the south of Morocco. He sends Manguin a card from Marrakech, and, after multiple adventures, returns to Tangiers where at last he begins to work: "All the friends have gone, I am alone and will try to profit from this by working a little," he writes to Camoin on September 27.[98]

On October 2 he announces to Elie Faure his return to France.[99]

1914

At the beginning of the year, Vollard asks Marquet to illustrate a luxury edition of *Bubu de Montparnasse*. The artist, having bad memories of the time when Charles-Louis Philippe had asked him the same thing, refuses.

The collection of the *Peau de l'Ours* – an association created in 1904 by André Level which bought works of art which were then held in common ownership by the participants[100] – is put up for auction on March 2, 1914. This collection had been put together by a group of young collectors, people who had neither sufficient time nor money to build their own private collection. Marquet is represented in it by two paintings, *Notre-Dame* and *Flamanville*, as well as by a pastel. He thanks André Level for the check that he is given after the sale on April 21.[101]

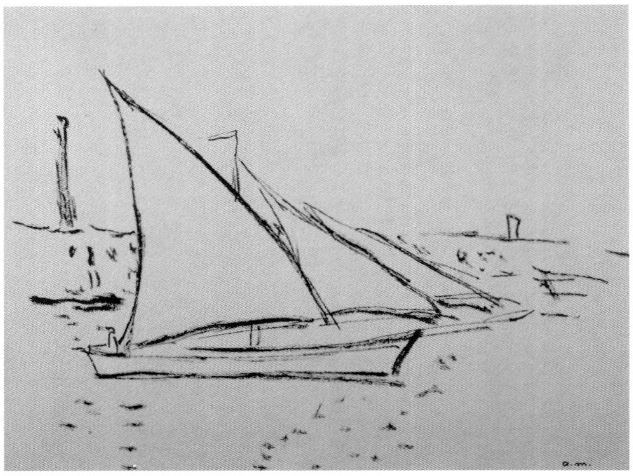

Voiliers à Marseille, 1916 (#60)

March sees the *Exposition internationale* at Lyon in which the artist is represented by five canvases, and in April follows the exhibition of the *Troisième Groupe* (Third Group) at Druet's.

In April 1914 the costumed ball at Van Dongen's studio in the rue Rochereau takes place. Matisse, dressed as a Pope, removes his robe to show himself in a wrestler's leotard on which are inscribed the most frightful names. Of course Marquet accompanied him.[102]

May sees departure for Holland. In June he is installed at the Hôtel Victoria in Rotterdam. In 1968, Madame Marquet explained: "Marquet having failed to capture the spirit of Hamburg left in search of that which had thrilled him."[103] He works for a month in Rotterdam and is back in Paris in July.

It is the time of the general mobilization. Marquet and Matisse fail the medical: Camoin, Montfort and Jean Puy leave, along with numerous comrades.

At the end of August the two friends, as they can be of no use to their country, leave for Collioure to work. They correspond with Camoin stationed with the 115th territorial near Dijon.

Staying at the Hôtel de la Gare, Marquet works at the port, painting the animation on the beach, and its fishing boats.

At the end of October, with Juan Gris and Eugène Terrus, he goes to Céret to visit Manolo the sculptor. Back in Paris in November, he gets back to work. From 19, quai Saint-Michel, where he once again has taken an apartment, now on the fourth floor, Matisse writes to Camoin: "Marquet is continuing his painting of fish of last year."[104] To this day, this work remains lost.

The two friends walk the boulevards with Van Dongen but find Paris sad, as Marquet recounts to Camoin in December: "Paris is still not very gay, the *cafés* are closed at eight each night and nearly no lights in the street."[105]

Henri Manguin takes refuge in Switzerland with his family and manages to find lodging in Lausanne with the help of Paul Vallotton.[106]

1915

Marquet and Matisse send letters and parcels to Camoin, in the army. They also help the other painters and comrades who have left for battle.

On May 3, Jean Puy, with his very characteristic humor, writes to Marquet: "At night at the feet of peeled hills, as my gargle stews, I write to you sitting on these old buttocks of an almost forty year-old territorial, in luck to become a feeble *macrolite* if the bullets of the *boches* don't come and put a term to my generous life."[107]

In June, Camoin complains of the heat at the same time as thanking Marquet for his packages and his support with regards to Druet.

After probably passing several weeks in July with his family in Teich, Marquet returns to the banks of the Marne in August and September. From there he writes to Elie Faure, a doctor in the army.[108] At La Varenne he returns to the motifs of 1913 and goes to work in the company of Yvonne and the "Schmitz brats." On December 4 he receives a letter from Camoin, a surgeon-major's cyclist since Matisse had sent him his bicycle.[109] On November 22 Matisse confides in Camoin that he "does not despair of getting Marquet to Marseilles." He has not seen his friend for fifteen days, since staying at Issy-les-Moulineaux.[110]

On December 6, he tells Camoin of their arrival in Marseilles "nearly a week ago." They are not bored, and walk on the rue Bouterie. Elie Faure, on leave, comes to join them.[111]

Matisse leaves Marseilles not long after, but Marquet stays on at the Hôtel Beauvau. He gets caught up with George Besson who is accompanied by the "Jourdain tribe," warms himself in the sun and has "no desire to return."[112] He writes to Albert André: "All is well, a little tired by this life of a debauchee that I am led into by those topers Besson, Apy and Mathieu."[113]

Matisse, who has stopped for a while at Arcachon, compliments Marquet: "What a lovely country this Arcachon Basin, you never even told me you sly old devil (I say that as a joke as I know you like it a lot, without mentioning it too much) its just like the Japan of the prints."[114]

1916

In January, Marquet is still in Marseilles, having fun and working little.

Elie Faure has not been able to see him while passing through and Marquet writes to him on January 15 that he is sorry not to have dropped by, but that he is generally at the Hôtel Beauvais or the Hôtel Méridien.[115] On January 25, Elie Faure tells him of the death of Druet whom he personally didn't like: "Druet is dead. I wasn't very close to him and took no trouble hiding it from you, but it is possible that you will feel some loss, as after all he had confidence in you at a moment when materially you needed someone to have confidence in you."[116]

Marquet returns to Paris a few days later and he works. In March, he receives a rather honest and discouraged letter from Jean Puy who is returning from the front lines.

On March 1 the *Triennial du Jeu de Paume* opens, four works by the artist are included.

Camoin, in the camouflage unit of the 13th artillery regiment, comes home on leave in June to Paris, where he finds all his old friends, before leaving for Amiens.

In the spring, Marquet gets to know Walther Halvorsen, a Norwegian collector and dealer, who comes to visit the studio. That year, several sales take place that benefit charities. Each time, Marquet offers one of his paintings.

Bernheim-Jeune exhibits the *Group C* in June. Three paintings by the artist are included.

In July he leaves for Marseilles: he works in the studio of the painter Louis Frégier, then he installs himself in the studio of Eugène Montfort, quai de la Rive Neuve, a studio he rents until the end of the war. In Marseilles, his sketchbook in hand, in the street, in the port, or from the window of his studio, he sketches and paints the picturesque swarm on the *quais*, and the coming and going of boats.

The summer is very hot, but in August thunderstorms cool the atmosphere down and he "feels a little more disposed to work."[117] He invites his friends to visit during their leave.

In October and November, there is an exhibition *Maîtres Français* (French masters) at Wintherthur where the painter is represented by six paintings belonging to Swiss collectors. At the end of the year, Matisse tells him that he is off to the Côte d'Azur. Marquet comes back to work in Paris.

1917

A letter of January 9 addressed to Dr. Elie Faure announces that the painter "returned more than a month ago to the fogs of the quai Saint-Michel." After the sunshine of Marseilles, he works in the cold, on the boulevards, but he will return to Marseilles in the spring.[118]

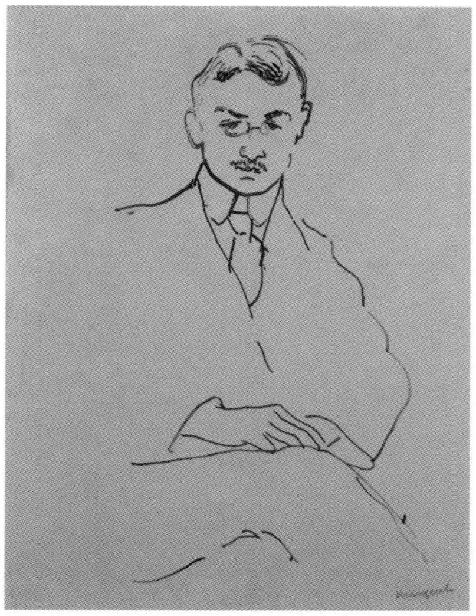

Portrait de George Besson, 1917 (#63)

On January 19, Madame Marval confides in the collector Alfred Rome, that Marquet is at present doing good business and feels like her the development of the soul of a collector."[119]

In February, the artist writes to George Besson who is in the Jura at Saint-Claude: "I'm still in Paris, held back by a few paintings that I want to finish and by the fear of dying of cold in the Midi, where even if there are cinemas, you can't find picture galleries in which to warm up for a couple of hours every day. More coal, *cochon de Sembat*."[120]

In March, Marquet is in Barcelona where he takes walks and enjoys himself. He invites Matisse to join him: on April 11, he sends him a card from the Balearic Isles.[121]

In April the exhibition/sale of works to profit the *Fraternité des artistes* (brotherhood of artists) takes place at the galerie Georges Petit. Claude Monet buys a *Port de Naples* (Port of Naples) and invites Marquet and Matisse to come to lunch with him at Giverny. He tells them of the times of trains to Mantes, where his car will await them.[122]

In July, Marval, Matisse and Marquet go to Chenonceaux, at the invitation of the owner of the *château*, Georges Menier. On July 14, Menier writes to Marquet: "OK for next Sunday; I will send the car to get you at Amboise at 11.30am. Very happy that you are pleased to come and get to know this beautiful corner of Touraine."[123] Marquet brings back a sketch from his short stay.

The artist rents a house at Samois-sur-Seine for two months so as to work. Louis Jou comes with him for a few days during his leave. Yvonne keeps him company and plays the role of mistress of the house. In October he returns to Marseilles again for a stay of several months.

The war does not impede the galleries from organizing numerous exhibitions in Paris, and Marquet exhibits regularly with his dealers, Druet and Bernheim-Jeune.

In December, George Besson becomes Marquet's "son." He tells this story: in the rue Bouterie one day, with Matisse, they were accosted "by a short-skirted woman" who decreed that Marquet was his (Besson's) father despite their only seven years age difference.[124]

1918

In January, Marquet is still in Marseilles, painting. A letter from André Rouveyre dated January 12 evokes their meeting: "I was very happy indeed to see you in such form; living as peacefully as you did when we were young."[125] On January 17, Camoin writes to Matisse who has joined Marquet: "Have you found an atelier at Marseilles?...How I regret not being able to join you...Who knows, perhaps on my next leave in February I will come and spend two or three days, especially if you are there also as well as Marquet."[126] Camoin arrives too late to join his friends at Marseilles. Matisse has left for Nice where Marquet joins him in March for a few days, before returning to Paris. They make numerous excursions in the region and visit Renoir at les Collettes. In a crammed train, the return to the capital is hardly agreeable. In Paris, the crack of bombs and guns and the continual visits to the cellar during alerts convince Marquet to leave the quai Saint-Michel in April.

Walther Halvorsen organizes an exhibition of French painters in Sweden and Norway and comes to Paris to make his choice. Paintings by Marquet are included along with works by Matisse, Bonnard, Braque, Dufy, Friesz, Manguin, and numerous well-known artists.

In Marseilles in May, the artist continues to work on his port paintings. Matisse writes to Georges Besson on May 9: "Marquet is back in Marseilles, he made a little trip to Paris and is again in Marseilles from where he sent me a card a few days back signed by Ernestine. He intends to set himself up at l'Estaque to work. I will see him on the way back."[127] Eugène Montfort asks Marquet to illustrate his little book *Le Brigadier Triboulère*.

In the calm of l'Estaque, which today is a part of Marseilles, the summer passes in work and receiving visits from friends. Marquet, staying at the Hôtel de Château-Fallet with Yvonne-Ernestine, at last is able to announce to Matisse the return of good weather on June 16.[128]

On July 10, Matisse tells him of goings-on on in Paris, on the street: "The Goths came back the day after my return and I also spent several days in the cellar. We even had two alerts in one night, and three bombs near the house...Three bombs fell in the Seine the night before, at the quai Saint-Michel and quai de la Tournelle. The explosion shattered all the windows on the *quai*. Nearly all the panes at your house are broken."[129]

The painter Baignières, at Nîmes, stationed with the 179th artillery regiment, asks Marquet to come and visit him on his bicycle, but the month of August passes and "like sister Anna" he does not see him arrive.[130] On October 11, he is still hoping that Marquet will stop at Nîmes on his way back.[131]

In November the war ends and Marquet celebrates the victory in Paris with his comrades.

1919

In Paris in January Marquet thanks George Besson for his present of cigarette holders, and sends him best wishes for the year.[132]

On January 25, suffering from flu, he calls the doctor Elie Faure to his rescue: "I would be very happy if it were possible for you to give me something to get me out of this as soon as possible."[133] He is advised to go and seek out the sun. Marquet joins Matisse at Nice, at the Hôtel de la Méditerranée et de la Côte d'Azur, where Matisse has been since the autumn of 1918. At 25, Promenade des Anglais, this comfortable hotel, demolished in 1929, allows him some weeks of convalescence with his friend. On April 18, he writes to Elie Faure: "I arrived in Nice rather tired, but not in such bad shape, and from then on I've got better and better...the weather is superb, it's already summer," and on the 21st he is more precise: "Though my general health continues to improve, I have a touch of diarrhea, having got rather tired out on longish walks after already having decided to explore the cinemas of Nice at night."[134]

Matisse and Marquet pay a visit to Renoir and pose with him for photographs. At the end of April, Marquet goes to Marseilles for the move from the studio at quai de Rive Neuve, due to the niggardly behavior of Montfort, who wants to drag him to court for a late rent payment of 50 francs. A bout of shingles which have paralyzed the right side of the artist's face complicate the move. He consigns his things to the care of the Hôtel de la Méditerranée, quai des Belges.

In May, Marquet exhibits at *La Triennale* (the triennial) two of his canvases of Marseilles. During this time, he is resting and gaining strength at the Hôtel de La Réserve, on the Corniche at Marseilles. There, on May 17, he receives news from Jean Puy. Camoin comes and stays with him for a few days, and Besson is soon to arrive. He keeps up his health bulletin for Elie Faure.

On May 22, he informs Faure that his health is not too bad, that he has been able to do a bit of painting, that he is thinking of coming back to Paris in two or three weeks, and that he would be able to go swimming as the weather is superb. In June he tells him of his return, and on the 30th, in Paris, he asks him to dinner. On July 7, he tells Faure of his imminent departure, and on the 18th writes to him from Herblay, at the Hôtel Camus, where he works throughout the summer.[135]

Gösta Olson, a gallery-owner from Stockholm, recalls Marquet, as he was when they met

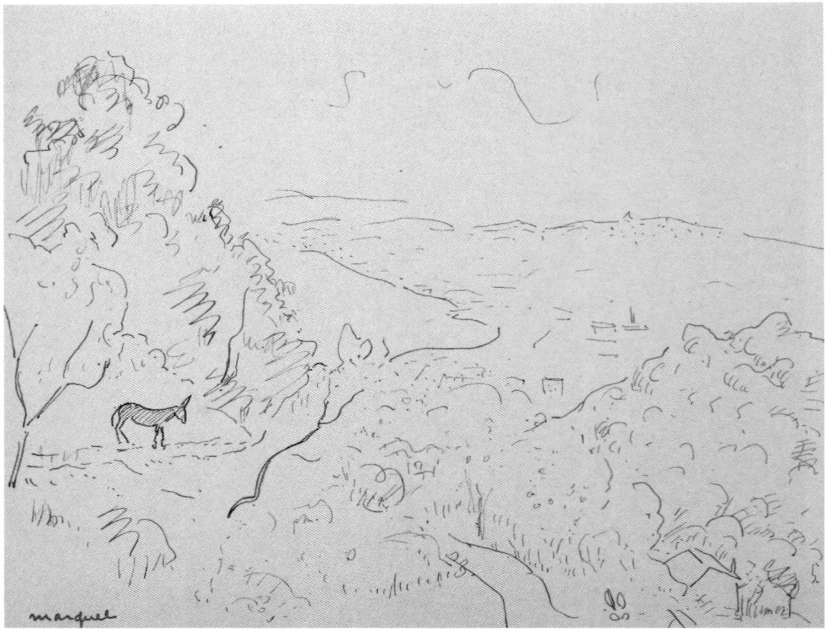

Alger, 1921 (#66)

in the summer of 1919: "He was still single and was really one of a kind. He had a slight limp but he did a lot of physical training and sport. Every morning he had an appointment with a boxer...who came to give him lessons."[136]

From Herblay in August Yvonne and Marquet send a postcard to Albert André and his wife, before returning to Marseilles to finish the move.

In September he writes to George Besson: "My old son, I have left the Hôtel de la Réserve and have installed myself at the Hôtel de la Méditerranée on the Vieux-Port. I am going to work there a few days before going back to Paris. Am loaded down with a ton of parcels."[137]

In November, Marquet shows a *Nu* at the *Salon d'Automne*. Throughout the last months of 1919,[138] he shows the desire to leave for Algiers.

1920

The year 1920 marks a turning point in Marquet's life and work. Suffering every winter in Paris from persistent bouts of flu, his friend Elie Faure advises him to head for the sun during this season. "Leave?" Marcelle Marquet writes later. "Marquet could see no objection, but where to? He had worked at Menton, at Saint-Tropez, at Agay, at Collioure, at Marseilles. Strange to say, he was looking for a country that he did not know. Morocco, he had seen very quickly. Why not Algeria?"[139]

In January, carrying letters of introduction, he took ship for Algiers from Marseilles. On the 26th, he sends a card to Elie Faure to tell him that "the weather is marvelous in Algiers," and that he "thinks he will work there."[140]

One of the letters of introduction is addressed to a young French woman living in Algiers, Marcelle Martinet, whom he is later to marry. She shows him the town, drags him "along little paths" that she loves, "which, crossing ravines and meadows, wound around and overhung Algiers."[141]

One February 27, Marquet writes a long letter to Matisse telling him of the excursions on his trip and boosting the beauties of the Casbah.[142] So as to paint he checks in at the Royal Hôtel, which overlooks the port. From his terrace, he is able to paint and admire the magnificent panorama of the bay. During his stay in Algiers, he receives letters from friends. Jean Puy exclaims: "What a lucky dog you are, sitting on top of palm trees gorging yourself on dates, coconuts and fried locusts...while a few whiskered monkeys come and make faces at you and try and steal your eye-glasses."[143]

George Besson asks him for all sorts of details on his life, which will be included in his book published a few months later.[144]

In Algiers Marquet meets several collectors, including Louis Meley, who owns a magnificent property on the outskirts of town and who regularly invites artists to the Villa Abd el Tif at the weekend. There, the painter gets close to Jean Launois, a resident at the villa, who accompanies him on his trips across the Sahara. A certain Adèle, who has just disembarked at Algiers and who does not want to let go of him,[145] seems to be one of the reasons for his first departure into the desert, where he hopes that she will not follow him.

On May 3, Louis Meley arranges their goodbye meeting at the Royal Hôtel for the 6th.[146] At the end of the month, Marquet is in Paris.

In May the 12th *Exposition internationale* takes place in Venice, including two of his paintings, and from May 25 to June 4 there is an exhibition of the *3ème groupe* at Druet's.

In June, he exhibits three paintings at Crès', and takes part in the exhibition *Jeune peinture française* (Young French Painting) at the galerie Manzi-Joyant. Invited by Signac to come and discover the area, he sets himself up for the summer in La Rochelle where he works from August to October.

On August 12, Matisse writes to Georges Besson: "Our dear Albert is at La Rochelle, I have just heard. I was thinking of going to see him at Bougival where he is supposed to be spending the summer."[147]

Marquet stays at the Hôtellerie du Pays d'Ouest, 6 Quai Duperre. Besson comes to spend two days with him and thanks him on September 11: "I have not forgotten the two exquisite days at La Rochelle."[148] The card shows their friend Baignières painted by Evenepoël under the title *Portrait Rouge* (Red Portrait), now at the musée de Brussels.

The artist corresponds with Marcelle Martinet over the summer.

Camoin, since his marriage at the beginning of the year, elicits no sign of life to his friends.

On his return to Paris, around October 25 – the date given by a card from Marquet to Elie Faure[149] – the artist is preparing his one-man show at the galerie Druet, which will take place from November 22 to December 3.

1921

In January Marquet leaves for Algiers where he travels and works; he writes to his friends, Matisse and Besson in particular, and until March at the Royal Hôtel receives numerous callers interested in his painting. He leaves with Jean Launois and Marcelle Martinet for the Sahara, for an odyssey across the desert by bus. On the 26th, he sends a card to Matisse and gives him his address: *poste restante* at Laghouat,[150] where he is to stay several weeks, seduced by the beauty of the landscape and the kindness of the inhabitants. On May 14, he thanks Elie Faure for sending two books and tells him of his forthcoming return to Paris after a magnificent voyage in the south of Algeria.[151] During this second voyage in the Sahara, Marcelle Martinet, who speaks a little Arabic, helps Marquet and Launois to feel at home in Laghouat: "One endeavors to get lodgings elsewhere than the mediocre and banal hotel, in a welcoming house, surrounding a patio, four empty rooms that our generous hosts found furniture for in less than an hour."[152] At the end of a few weeks in the oasis, they go to see the Mzab and take the bus for Ghardaia. They return through the desert in the direction of Algiers prior to going back to France.

In Saint-Tropez for the summer, Camoin writes to Matisse: "In Paris I had a few games of chess and one of billiards with Marquet, who seems to have got rid of his bird."[153] Camoin and his friend were passionate chess players and interminable games took up whole evenings.

A few interesting exhibitions took place during the year. From April 23 to May 31, the *33ème exposition de beaux-arts* (33rd fine art exhibition) in Rouen: from May 3 to 21, 60 *Nus* (sixty nudes) at Bernheim-Jeune's: From June 11 to August 15, *Art Français en Rhénanie* (French art in the Rhineland), at Wiesbaden and at Strasbourg.

Marquet no doubt went the year before to Sables-d'Olonne and to La Chaume. On August 2, he writes to Elie Faure: "It's even prettier than La Rochelle. I am delighted to have come here and I am working a lot."[154]

He rents a room at 6, quai du Maréchal Joffre, in a little boarding house. From his windows he can gaze at the beach and jetties, seen in a few paintings. That which interests him the most, is the movement of the boats in the port of La Chaume, the fishermens' little houses, and the coming and goings of the fishing boats between the jetties.

Jean Launois is originally from Sables-d'Olonne and it is he, without doubt, who convinced his friend Marquet to go there for the summer. He meets the painter André Fraye, and the sailor and painter Paul-Emile Pajot, from whom he buys several watercolors of boats. Jean Huguet dedicates a book to Pajot and recounts the meetings of the two men.[155]

Walther Halvorsen comes to spend a few weeks with Marquet and watches him work.

In his new Ford, Marquet goes back to Paris. During the year he had passed his driving test and has obtained a license. He sets himself to driving, and makes a trip that takes him from Paris to Bordeaux then to Arcachon. Marcelle Marquet writes in 1968: "From that moment, he made all his trips in France, Spain, North Africa and Italy driving his open tourer. He feared neither wind, sun, nor rain. He delighted at being in the countryside."[156]

In September, the artist shows his paintings to Elie Faure. At the *Salon d'Automne*, which takes place from November 1 to December 20, Marquet will be represented by *Le Port de La Rochelle* and *Le Port d'Alger*.

Charles Fegdal, in the *Revue contemporaine* (Contemporary review) of November publishes an article on Sables-d'Olonne and the artists who met up there during the summer of 1921.[157]

1922

In the beginning of the year, Marquet receives his mail in Algiers at the Maison Venot, boulevard de France. With Marcelle Martinet and Jean Launois, they head south, for a trip on camels'-back. He writes to George Besson: "Your father's backside is aching like hell due to the long camel rides. It's just the beginning. In a few days we're off by the same means of conveyance for a long trip in the Sahara...send me news, *poste restante* at Touggourt, I'll be happy."[158]

From Touggourt to Nefta, the progress is tiring and very uncomfortable. Launois "Has difficulty with it," writes Marcelle Marquet.[159] They stray in the desert gardens: Marcelle Marquet and the painter find it more difficult to separate at the end of the trip.

Marquet tells George Besson that he will be in Marseilles for the first days of June.[160]

Numerous exhibitions take place in 1922, in which Marquet is represented by a few paintings: at Venice, Pittsburgh, Brussels, Ghent, and in Paris at Bernheim-Jeune's, Druet's, and at the *Salon d'Automne*.

A series of canvases of Notre-Dame de Paris are executed from the hotel on the rue du Petit-Pont, that lead one to suppose that the artist paints in the capital for a large portion of the summer.

In December an article signed Tabarant in *Le Bulletin de la vie artistique* (The artistic life bulletin) shows that in a collection as important as that of Kojiro Matsukata, Marquet is well represented.

1923

On February 10 in Algiers, Marquet marries Marcelle Martinet. He hoped to have his friend George Besson at the wedding but his hopes are in vain: "I waited as all the boats arrived to see if you were there with your top hat. No son, no top hat, your lady-friend was in despair and the whole party was very sad. To set me right after these disappointments, I am leaving in the Ford for Tunis."[161] He stays there a couple of days, before reaching Carthage. From his hotel, the artist looks out on the gulf: "Ruins in a noble landscape but the sea is a bit far, the hotel isolated...no foreground, hardly enough for three or four paintings."[162]

They continue their journey and arrive at Sidi Bou Said where they discover "white houses, blue woodwork, cactuses, agaves, an unfurling of wild flowers...dominating a lively sea."[163] Delighted, they decide to stay for a while. They stay six months interrupted by a short visit to Paris in June. They come back to spend the summer in this little town where they are warmly received and where they will live happily all summer. Albert paints and Marcelle writes. "If we had not left after six months, we would have ended staying there all our lives."[164] Dating from this stay in Tunisia, Marquet exhibits every year at the *Salon des artistes tunisiens* (Salon of Tunisian artists) and he keeps up contacts with the artists of the country.

They will return to Paris "between September 22 and 25," passing by Marseilles, as Marquet tells Camoin,[165] but the return trip is prolonged, as he tells Henri Matisse that he is "headed for Paris" as late as November 12.[166]

The stay in Paris is short. He exhibits at Druet's a series of paintings of North Africa in December. He writes to his friends, in particular to Elie Faure and Manguin: "When are you coming? My exhibition opens December 3. You should be there to help me install, there are more than sixty paintings."[167] There is a good review in *Comoedia* on December 11: "Little or no tone of violence. No brutality...The painter seems to have shed the harshness of his early years so as to enhance the subtle and nuanced softness of these recent views which he has chosen...He has gained in delicacy that which he has toned down in vigor."

1924

Albert and Marcelle Marquet leave Paris in January headed for Algiers, broken by a few days in Marseilles visiting friends.

In February, Marcelle sends a letter to George Besson at the Villa Miramar, chemin Laperlier. Marquet, a lazy correspondent, leaves his wife to reply to his mail from the early years of their marriage. But he himself writes to a few close friends, principally Matisse. Marcelle Marquet befriends the wives of Camoin, Besson and Albert André, giving her free reign for her passion for writing. Author of stories, she also writes poems.

Marquet will work a lot from their villa, and reacquaints himself with family life, among the French Algerian community.

After several months in Algiers they drive back in their car, crossing Spain.

From March 10 to April 10, at the Hôtel de la Curiosité et des Beaux-Arts, in Paris, the first collectors' exhibition to benefit the *Société des amis du Luxembourg* (Society of the friends of Luxembourg) is held. Marquet is well represented in the collections of Aubry, Pacquement, Trystram, Menier, Ziegler, Goujon and Kapferer.

Japan opens its doors to contemporary French art in May with an exhibition at Tokyo and Osaka.

A postcard from Belle-Ile-en-Mer, addressed to Camoin and signed by Marcelle Marquet, Jean Puy and Grenouillette ("little frog," Manguin's model).[168] Puy, who knows the Ile very well, no doubt succeeded in attracting Marquet to Brittany where he stays a few days; from there he heads off across France with Puy, Manguin and Manguin's family. They continue on to La Rochelle where Manguin decides to stay and work for a while. Marquet, who has already worked at La Rochelle, continues on towards the southwest with Jean Puy. At the mercy of breakdowns, they stop often to repair the car.

At the end of June, they are in Bordeaux, which Marquet has never revisited to paint since his childhood. The town is for him a bearer of bad memories of his school years.[169] Manguin comes to join them and the artists continue their trip towards Bayonne and the Pyrenees as far as Sète. The charm of the town and the port holds Marquet for several weeks, while Manguin carries on. Installed on the balcony of his room at the Grand Hôtel, by the side of the canal, the artist undertakes a series of paintings. He also paints from the quay, facing the jetty.

At the end of August, they return to Paris, stopping at his whim.

At the *Salon d'Automne* he shows a *Port de Sète*, and *Port de Bordeaux*.

On November 6 the sale of Maurice Leclanché's collection takes place. He was an intelligent collector of the principal painters of the contemporary French school.[170]

1925

From Algiers, where he is in January, tired of all the same landscapes, Marquet leaves on the advice of his wife and his friends for Bougie, in Kabylie. With Marcelle he checks in to the Hôtel d'Orient for two months. Later, Marcelle evokes the town in these terms: "Forgotten port, often empty but so well framed, so Marquet said: a landscape made for Poussin, hundred year-old trees, enormous carobs...fruit-trees...calm and fury following each other."[171] There, inspired by the magnificent landscape, he paints the gulf, the port and its warehouses, the town and its flowering trees.

Charles Fegdal, with whom the painter has had ties since La Chaume, gives a lecture on February 4 on "a few artists' studios." On February 8, *L'Ame Gauloise* (the Soul of Gaul) reproduces a few extracts.[172] Deciding to make a book out of it, Fegdal writes to Marquet who replies from Bougie on March 17: he sends him his picture, and says he will be in Paris at the end of April.[173]

After a return trip full of detours, touristy stops and visits to friends, the car brings Marquet back to Paris where in May he exhibits with the *3ème groupe*, at the galerie Druet.

Walther Havorsen proposes to the artist and his wife that they should visit his country, Norway. He rents them a villa at Hesnès, accompanies them throughout the summer, and serves as guide and interpreter. They visit first Oslo and then Hesnès, where Marquet finds heat surprising for a Nordic country. This troubles him, so he works from the house. Surrounded by noisy friends, he goes fishing, bathes, takes walks, as well as "a cruise to the Finnish frontier on the glacial ocean." They go from port to port, from fjord to island, on calm waters. From Norway, they congratulate Matisse for his *legion d'honneur* (legion of honor).[174]

In September, they return to Paris. On the 21st they announce their arrival to Matisse "to attend the Matisse-Friesz banquet."[175]

In November the galerie Bernheim-Jeune exhibits 17 works by Marquet belonging partly to Druet and partly to the artist. In this exhibition he presents the results of his work in Norway.

The contract between Marquet, Druet and Bernheim-Jeune is renewed for two years on November 20. It is agreed that the artist will attempt to sell two-thirds of his production to Druet's, and one-third to Bernheim-Jeune. Exhibitions will be held principally at the galerie Druet, where Bernheim can exhibit his works alongside those belonging to Druet.

The comrades, dispersed during the summer, are together again in Paris fairly regularly. Manguin will occupy Marquet's studio at Marseilles for a while.

1926

"Every year we returned to Algiers, changing hotels and houses. Marquet knew that I was attached to my country and that things to paint were not lacking," writes Marcelle Marquet.[176]

From Algiers, Marquet leaves for Tunisia in search of the light, which he finds so unusual. He installs them at La Goulette, at the entrance to the port of Tunis, at 62, avenue de Carthage. The house where they are to live for a few weeks is on the beach. It permits the artist to paint the sea in all its aspects according to the rhythm of the passage of sailing boats and fishing-smacks. Unfortunately the house is infested with fleas, the cause of serious trouble."[177]

On March 28, Louis Jou writes: "Dear old Marquet. Despite all the delightful charms of this beguiling Goulette, I am stuck at the Quai aux Fleurs for another month...I'll await you on May 24 at les Baux to go to Saintes-Maries-de-la-Mer. It's a deal. I have assurances that the Suarès' will also be there. It should be fun."[178]

They return via les Baux and then to Paris at the end of May.

Marquet exhibits a very beautiful selection of paintings at the *Salon d'hiver* (winter salon) at Algiers; there, his work is surrounded by paintings by Flandrin, Asselijn and several less well-known painters.[179] In Paris, at the *Salon des Trente ans d'art indépendant* (salon of thirty years of independent art), Marquet shows six paintings. For the centenary of Gustave Moreau, an exhibition brings his students back together in April, at the Galerie Georges Petit. Druet's purchases from the artist are presented in the *Exposition du 3ème groupe*, from May 17 to 28.

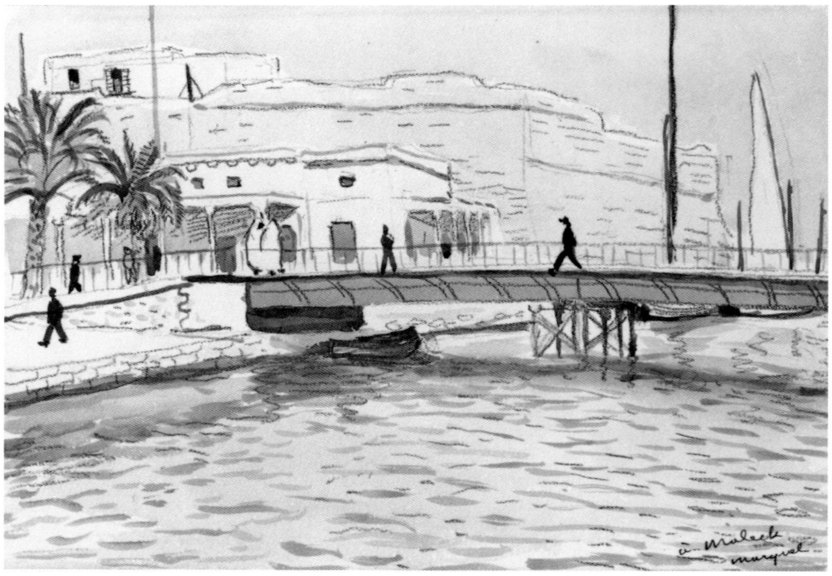

La Goulette, Tunis, 1926 (#45)

In June he is artist of honor at the *XVème exposition internationale de Venise* (15th Venice international) where 15 of his works are exhibited. His works are also shown in New York, Tokyo, Munich, Geneva, Stockholm, Brussels and Pittsburgh.

In the month of July, Marquet is in Hendaye, after very likely spending a short time with his family near Bordeaux. He stays longer than planned on the banks of the Bidassoa where he is in his element. First he stays at Hendaye-la-Plage at the villa Amaryllis; then he moves to the rue des Grenadiers near the port, to the villa A Aguerremendi. He stays there until December.

At the end of July, the artist tells Camoin, at Endounne near Marseilles, of his present address and informs him that the Buick "climbs all the hills."[180] To Matisse he writes from Fontarabie in Spain, a small town on the bay facing Hendaye.

On December 25 he tells Camoin of his return, and they begin again their games of chess and billiards."[181]

1927

In Algiers, from the first days of the year, the painter executes a series of views of the Place du Gouvernement from the Hôtel de la Régence. There are only few paintings from this series in the purchases made in May by the Druet Gallery.

On February 15, Manguin asks Marquet: "When do you think you'll leave Paris?"; he is in Toulon, and Camoin who has also been there, has not stopped to see him.[182] In March (the 22nd?), a postcard from Marcelle to the painter Mainssieux and his lady-friend Zohra Boudemine – a model who poses for numerous artists, including Marquet – relates that they will leave Marseilles on the 29th, bound for the Near East.[183]

Several cards from Marquet to Manguin in the collection of Jean-Pierre Manguin are posted from Constantinople and Jerusalem in April.

In June, Marquet and his wife leave for Normandy. Signac has glowingly described the Vieux-Port area to them, and they settle in a little boarding house near the river. George Besson and Camoin both pay them a visit. On July 16, Madame Marquet tells Madame Camoin that that they will stay at Vieux-Port until the end of the month and ask them to bring "raincoats and heavy shoes."[184] It rains a lot that year in Normandy, and despite the charm of the region, they leave for Rouen hoping to find the sun. Marquet had worked in this city in 1912. For a change of scenery, he goes as far as Canteleu where they discover an *auberge* looking out over

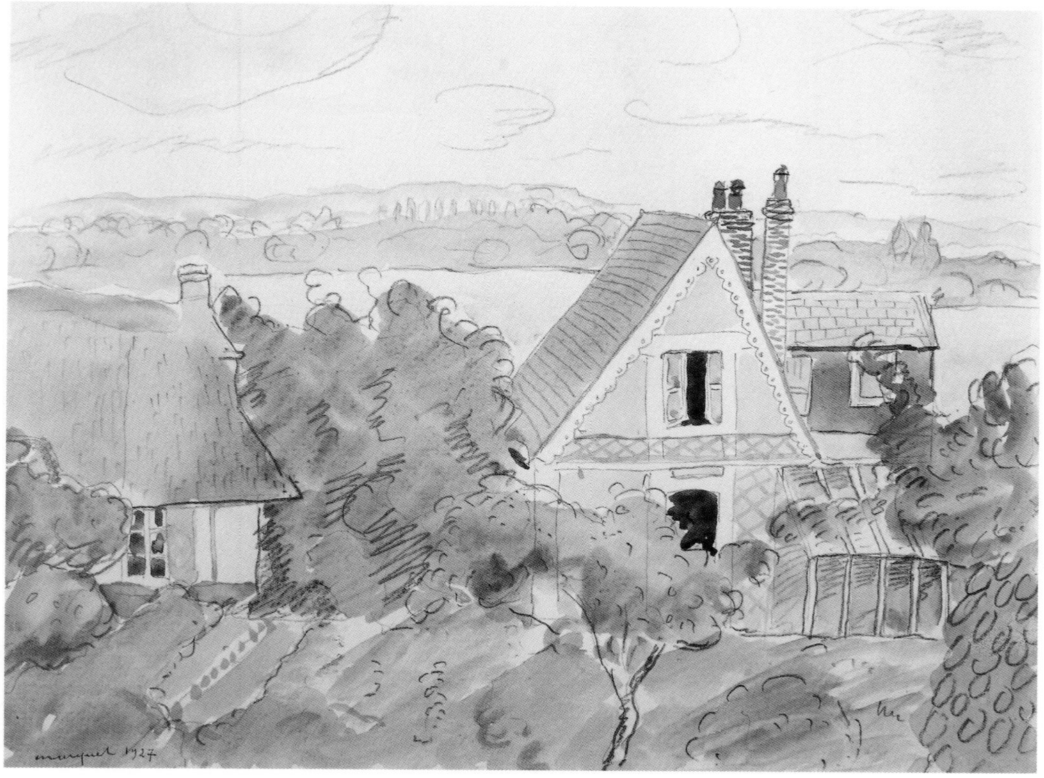

Saint-Jean-de-Luz, 1927 (#46)

the town, the Hôtel des Chasseurs, where they are given the owners' room. From his window, Marquet can study the whole of Rouen spread out beneath him.[185] He paints a series of practically identical views, which are distinguished by their various atmospheric effects. In September, tired of rain, they leave for Saint-Jean-de-Luz and the sun, making a tourist circuit via the vacation places of their friends. Marquet tells Camoin that he is covering the whole of Brittany, where "the weather is superb."[186] They reach Saint-Jean in October. Postcards are sent to George Besson[187] and Camoin[188] to give them their address – Villa Benjamin on the quai de l'Infante – and to invite them to come. "At last, the sun."

The artist plans on staying a month or two. He returns to Paris from this trip at the end of the year with numerous canvases.

1928

In January, the Galerie Giroux in Brussels opens an important exhibition of Marquet's work, recorded in the Druet archives.

On January 3, Lola Camoin writes from Orange: she is waiting impatiently for the arrival of the Marquets in Marseilles.[189] Invited to the opening of the *Exposition d'art français* in Cairo, the Marquets leave Paris after January 24, the date on which they get their visa for Egypt.[190]

In Cairo they go for donkey rides with Jules Guiffrey, curator of the museé du Louvre, and Georges Duthuit, the son-in-law of Matisse. An avalanche of invitations frightens Marquet off, and he takes refuge in Assouan where he is unknown. The Nile and its feluccas seduce him, and he works on several paintings. On March 13, Madame Marquet writes to Madame Camoin: "The heat is beginning to make itself felt" and tells her that they are going off down the Nile on a houseboat. In the end of March they are once again in Cairo, and by mid-April in Algiers.[191]

On April 22, Louis Jou writes to his friend in Algiers. He has just finished his second book and hopes to see him on his return in May. "...I'm counting on being there towards the end of the month, so as to deal you a thrashing (at chess).[192] Marquet returns to Paris for the opening of his one man show which is held at the galerie Druet, from April 30 to May 11. A good notice signed Denoinville in the *Journal des Arts* of May 19, "Being a painter, is in addition to the love that a real artist has for nature...to possess the innate gift of art. It is the case up to a certain point with Mr. Albert Marquet, a pantheist painter *par excellence* (who) is less of an imaginative than a very silent contemplator."[193]

Brittany, which he has visited but little, attracts Marquet. He spends the summer at Audierne, at the Hôtel de France. On the terrace, or on the paths plummeting down to the port, the artist works. He receives visits from the painters of the region; by chance he meets Max Jacob at the Pointe du Raz. It may be in 1927 or 1928 that he fails to meet up with Jean Puy and writes to him: "What a calamity! You came to Benodet and we were no longer there. I mark this day with a black stone. Now I'm back in Paris, alas!"[194]

Paul Signac writes to George Besson on September 7: "We have finished with a circuit of the rocks and the painters of Brittany...met up with Puy at Belle-Ile, Marquet at Audierne, and Asselin at Concarneau, the first two at work, and the third in a bistro!"[195]

Back in Paris, Marquet participates in the jubilee of the *Salon d'Automne*, with a *Hambourg* and two paintings of Audierne.

He reacquaints himself with portraiture when painting Maria Lani, the young woman who mystifies fashionable Paris passing herself off as a celebrated German actress.

1929

The winter exhibitions of 1928–1929 follow their course in Paris: at the galerie Druet a group exhibition, *Denis, Flandrin, Dufrenoy, Marquet, etc*, and at the salle de la Renaissance, *Oeuvres des XIXème et XXème siècles* (nineteenth and twentieth century works). Abroad, Toledo (Ohio), Oslo, Copenhagen, Budapest and Prague exhibit works by Marquet.

At Algiers, the stay develops into an excursion in the Sahara. At Laghouat, Albert and Marcelle Marquet are accompanied by Jean Launois and his wife, as well as the painter, Maurice Bouviolle. Jean Launois was married in 1927 to Aimée Lévy, niece of the writer Suarès, a friend of Marquet's.

At Laghouat, the painter's photo is taken with his friends on the patio of the Moorish villa already described in 1921. He paints a few pictures, as well as numerous watercolors and drawings. A postcard illustrated by Marquet is sent to George Besson: "greetings from Laghouat, it's raining, it's cold, will be back in Paris soon." And Marcelle adds: "Wonderful weather, we'll write from Algiers."[196]

In April, two documents retrieved from the archives relate that on April 5 the artist orders a parcel of canvases and colors from the shop *A l'académie de peinture* (at the academy of painting), rue du Dragon, and another parcel on April 11, from *Morin et Janet*, rue Lepic.[197]

In Paris in April the *Exposition du 3ème groupe* is held at Druet's.

In Poissy for the summer, they live at the villa Marie-Charlotte on the Ile de Migneaux: "His garden went right down to the Seine. To his jetty was tied a boat on which he passed the greater part of his days."[198]

On August 3 he receives a postcard from Louis Jou, in Venice: "Where are you, old boy, for my part I'm watching the beautiful Venetian women go by...So many little boats here, you would have what you wanted, I assure you."[199]

Marquet works for two months on his island, but he takes pleasure in showing to his wife a region that he knows well and whose charm he appreciates. That year he also works on the illustrations for the book *Moussa le petit noir*, published by Marcelle Marquet under her pseudonym, Marcelle Marty.

In the *Cahiers d'aujourd'hui* series published by Editions Crès, the director George Besson dedicates to his friend a book abundantly illustrated with reproductions of his works.

From October 7 to 18, a joint exhibition at Druet's with Manguin, Mayol, etc. From November 3 to December 22, at the *Salon d'Automne*, he shows two works.

In December, at the Georges Petit Gallery, he shows fifteen paintings. "At George Petit's, which under the lead of Bernheim-Jeune has taken a more active modernist orientation," reads *Le Journal des Arts*, "a lovely and convincing exhibition of works by Marquet! A painter who synthesizes nature in one of the most intelligent ways and who is one of our best contemporary landscapists, with a broad vision free of all conventional theory."[200]

1930

On the road as of February, Marquet signals his passing on the 1st to Camoin through the intermediary of Marcelle Marquet. He is at Carcassonne and on Sunday will be in Barcelona: "When will you arrive?"[201]

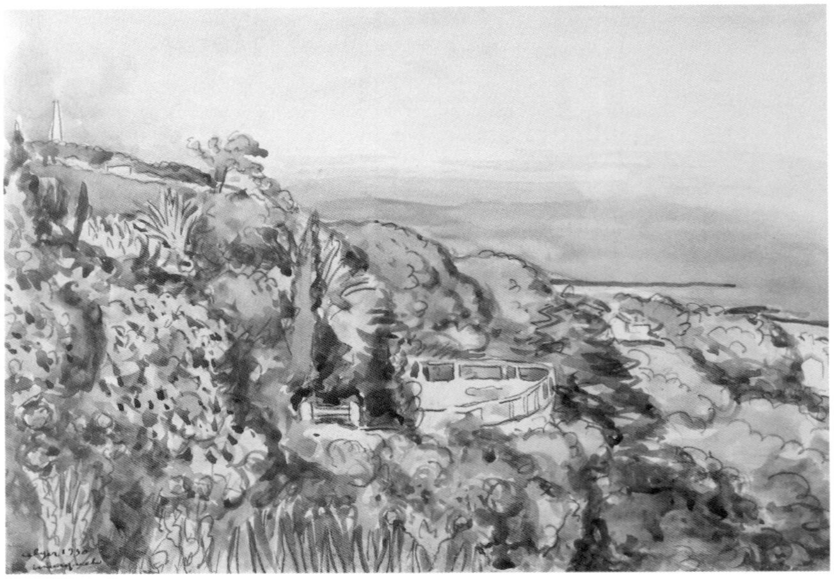

Alger, 1930 (#48)

In Barcelona the Marquets are rejoined by the Camoins who will accompany them across Spain, passing via Madrid, Seville and Granada. Marquet writes to his friends Matisse and Manguin. A photo of Marquet as a bullfighter is published in the journal *Vient de paraître*, in April. This trip was organized hastily. Marquet, encouraged "by a Catalan painter living in Montmartre," is received "in Barcelona by artists of the region who were happy to know brothers-in-art who had the luck to live in Paris...The Camoins who were with them seemed happy with the trip..."[202] It's a tourist trip as far as Algeciras. They visit monuments, and pass their evenings in *cafés* admiring the flamenco dancers. Though he does not paint, Marquet draws and his sketchbooks fill up. The Camoins take their leave at Cadiz and Marquet decides to stop at Algeciras to work a little. The canal that passes alongside the hotel, and its boat traffic, inspire him to delicate watercolors.

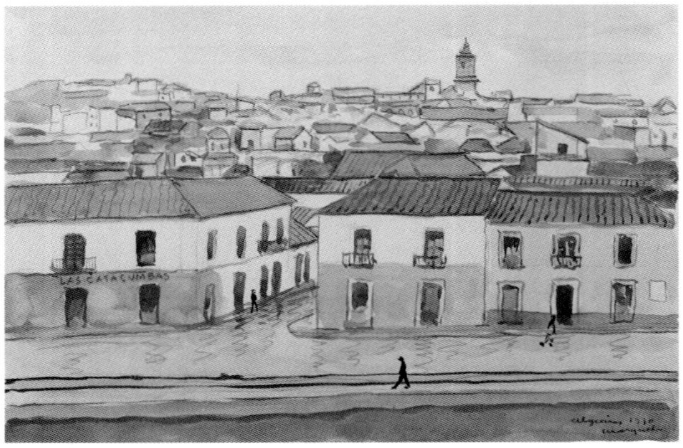

Algesiras, 1930 (#47)

In March, in Gibraltar, he writes to Camoin who is back in France, at Mazargue. Then from Tétouan, on the 25th, Marcelle writes to Lola Camoin, "Tétouan is magnificent, we are leaving after dinner for Tangiers." From Tangiers, they go through "Fez, then Tlemcen, Oran and Algiers."[203]

From March 29th, Marquet's passport carries the stamp of the *Commissariat à la sûreté régionale* (Regional Security Commissariat), at Oujda.

Francis Jourdain tells him there is a building site at the corner of the rue Dauphine and the quai des Grands Augustins. Marquet, who in his youth had worked from the window of a little hotel on this site, is very tempted by the purchase of an apartment in the new building, and decides to "take the plunge." He worries that his means are sufficient, and he delegates his wife, who is in charge of his affairs, to take care of the purchase.[204]

In Paris, in May, the Henri Canonne sale took place, and in June, that of Sauphar. These important collectors and connoisseurs possessed works by Marquet. From this year onwards, Georges Gramont gets interested in the artist, and begins to acquire his works.

In May and July at the Petit Palais is held the important exhibition, *Centenaire de la conquête de l'Algerie;*" Marquet is represented by two works.

At Boulogne-sur-Mer for the summer, the Marquets stay at the villa Pige-Vents, boulevard Sainte-Beuve. Marcelle Marquet writes: "It deserved its name. As soon as you forgot to close a window, doors were slamming everywhere."[205] From his balcony, the artist gazes down at the sea and the jetty. He is able to paint tempests, and boats entering and leaving the harbor. From a room booked at the port, he varies his subjects and profits from the activity on the quays. The Camoins come to spend part of the summer with them.

Marcelle receives a card from her friends André Gide, and Billy and Sam Quinchon, from Saint-Florent, in Corsica, on which they can be seen posing with a donkey.[206]

1931

The previous year in Spain Marquet met numerous artists. In January, the Catalan painter Creixans sends him his best wishes from Cordova, and writes: "When going to the places where we wandered together I stop and I think of you."[207]

On February 26, he also receives a card from the diplomat Marcel Ray with whom he will often travel, particularly in 1933.[208]

Creixans introduces to Marquet the ceramicist Artigas who will work with him a lot during the course of the year. He bonds also with the sculptor Pedro Gargallo, a friend of Artigas.

The apartment purchased by the artist on the corner of the rue Dauphine is on the fifth floor. The painter is able to admire from the windows of the apartment a superb view of the Pont-Neuf, l'Ile de la Cité and Notre-Dame. With Artigas, in the ceramicist's studio at Charenton, Marquet works on the designs for the tiles of the bathroom, a hard and completely new type of work for the artist, who is going to paint the tiles reproducing the paintings of his travels. This unique work is hidden and saved from the covetous Germans during the Second World War.

Exhibitions pile up in Paris, in the provinces, and abroad. In March, Camoin and Marquet have a joint show in Rouen.

The *Ecole de Paris* exhibition takes place in Prague.

In June, Marcelle Marquet is reunited with her brother Robert, and his children. They rent a house at Triel-sur-Seine. The artist works on the banks of the river. The garden of the house stretches all the way down to the water, where fishermen and moored sailboats liven the banks.

Marquet already knew Triel having passed through several times during his visits to Poissy and Villennes. The house is very lively during the summer. Artigas is received as a friend, as well as Pedro Gargallo and his family. Bonnard comes to see them as a neighbor. Several writer friends of Marquet, for example the poet Paul Fort, have houses at Triel or its surroundings.

At the end of August the move from 19, quai Saint-Michel takes place. In the new apartment, much bigger than the old one, the

Marquets host, with their casual kindness, all their close friends, in particular Camoin, Manguin, Besson, Dufy, Luce, Valtat and Jourdain. Matisse distanced himself somewhat from the little group, as his many activities and a mounting success make him rather less available.

A similar collecting spirit burns within Signac, Marquet, Camoin, Matisse and Manguin.

In the autumn there is a slight misunderstanding that disrupts the cordiality a little, relating to a painting wanted by Signac that Marquet, due to financial worries, is obliged to offer to a more generous collector. Marcelle Marquet explains their situation to George Besson who served as intermediary: "Albert fears there has been a misunderstanding between himself and Signac...You know that we have a hard year to get through due to our move, in other words a lot of bills...Reality does not allow us to miss the opportunity of a sale...Make a note of telling Signac how upset Marquet is and how he hopes that another painting might tempt him."[209]

1932

On January 5, Marquet is nominated associate of the *Section de peinture* (painting section) by the *classe des Beaux-Arts de Bruxelles* (Brussels Fine Arts Class).[210]

Charles-Auguste Girard organizes an exhibition called *Le Dessin vivant* (Living drawing). He becomes, after Druet and Bernheim-Jeune, one of the dealers who fight for Marquet's paintings.

As every year, Algiers welcomes Marquet and his wife for a few weeks. While there, Marquet works from El Biar. They live in a villa, Dar el Aurida, on rue Delcassé.

In Paris, he paints from his windows.

With the arrival of summer, Camoin and Marquet are invited to Brittany, to Ploumanach, with the Eiffel family. Little work is done, but Marquet brings back several watercolors from his stay in his friend's house.

In September, another trip to Spain, and from every stop Marcelle writes to Madame Camoin. They visit Compostella, stop at Vigo, Ondorroa and Santander, where the artist is able to work, and at the end of the month arrive at Oporto, the "terminus." They return via Castille, Pamplona and le col de Roncevaux. They are in Paris "around October 4th."[211]

At the *Salon d'Automne*, Marquet shows a painting of *La Samaritaine* (the department store) that is highly admired by Gabriel Cognacq, the owner of that store: "Yesterday I visited the *Salon d'Automne*, you are really its king! Apart from anything else, it's a wonderful advert for *La Samaritaine*: how great to have a client like you."[212]

On November 14, Paul Fort dedicates a poem to his friend the "Master Albert Marquet," which is entitled *La Plainte de l'arche de Noé*.

1933

At the end of March, Marcel Ray and his wife Suzanne persuade the Marquets to go with them on a long voyage in Eastern Europe where Marcel has to take up his duties once more. The cruise in the Mediterranean tempts Marquet. They go via Greece, disembark at Athens where they visit the museums, then go to Volo. At Constantinople they stay several days, enough time for watercolors and excursions. Eventually they arrive at Galatz, on the banks of the Danube in Rumania, where Ray is to work. Left to themselves, Marquet and his wife decide to leave as the place does not appeal to them. The wife of a high Rumanian official puts a boat at their disposal, and the artist finds himself once again in the midst of river traffic, which seduces him immediately. The river takes them as far as its mouth, and at Sulina they discover the delta. A car takes them to Vulkov, "a green Venice," where they stay with locals. Back in Galatz, Marquet, won over by the river, decides to go to Vienna by going up the Danube. The long voyage gives him the chance to fill several sketchbooks with drawings and watercolors.[213] Several of these images are later published by Marcelle Marquet in 1954, in *Le Danube. Voyage de Printemps*.

In April, there is a one-man show of the artist's work at Bernheim-Jeune, and at Druet's the exhibition *Fleurs et Fruits*, as well as the *Exposition du 3ème groupe*.

In the summer, again in the company of Marcel and Suzanne Ray, Marquet and his wife stay at Les Sables-d'Olonne, on the embankment. From his window, the artist paints a series of canvases from the embankment and the beach skirted by the jetty. Madame Marquet's family joins them. That summer Lola Camoin is expecting. The forthcoming child is to be the godchild of Marcelle Marquet. Born in October, the baby is a girl, Anne-Marie.

They return to Paris for an exhibition, *Marines*, at Katia Granoff's. After comes the *Salon d'Automne*.

Throughout the year, important shows are happening abroad: in Buenos Aires, New York, Amsterdam, Chicago, Madrid, Bucharest, Pittsburgh, and at the inauguration of the museum at Springfield.

1934

The Algiers trip in January is remarkable for snow. With Robert Martinet and his family, they go skiing in the hills at Chréa, the winter sports resort closest to Algiers.

George Besson who is preparing a new book, asks Marcelle Marquet for a few details on their bathroom, and in her reply she says: "We think we will be back in a few weeks. We will have seen Algiers in the snow – the hardest winter I've seen there. From 4 to 6° – The Atlas mountains are white right to their base. Albert has worked very hard. They wanted him to do a show here but he preferred to put it off until later. Algiers is the only town where exhibitions are profitable."[214]

On March 25, from Morocco, they tell Camoin of their return,[215] but their visit lasts into May, judging by the cards sent by the artist to Manguin (collection Jean-Paul Manguin).

At the *Salon des Indépendants*, the two paintings by Marquet were hung beside those of his friends, and on February 23, Manguin wrote to Raoul de Mathan: "We are all reunited in the same gallery, this rejuvenates us all deucedly![216]

In June an exhibition of forty-eight works and a series of watercolors at the Druet Gallery, the theme of which is as much Paris as Spain, Rumania, les Sables-d'Olonne, Constantinople and Algiers, from that year's trip.

Charles Devau writes in *Beaux-Arts*: "If it is true that in most of the works one finds the same style, then in each of these new nuances form the soul of the painting."[217]

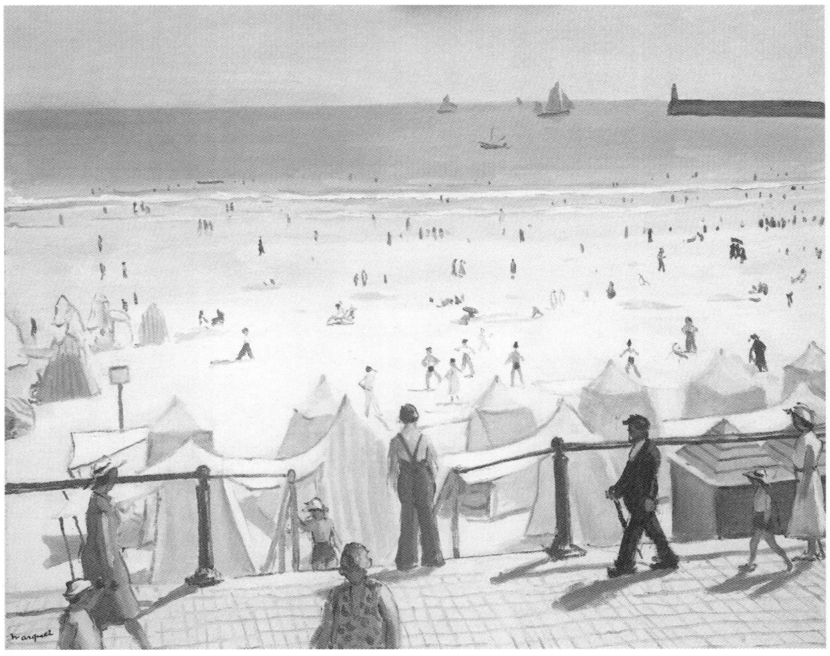

Plage des Sables-d'Olonne, 1933 (#31)

In the summer, according to Marcelle, "tempted by the appeal of a poster, we set off for the USSR. Boarding a Soviet ship at Dunkirk, disembarking at Leningrad, we crossed Russia, we stopped at Moscow, Kharkov, Rostov, and Tiflis, to pick up in Batoum an Italian passenger boat that took us on a tour of the Mediterranean before bringing us back to Marseilles."[218] A letter from L. Kriborskaïa, their guide in Leningrad, dated 1959, is addressed to Marcelle Marquet and tells of her memories of the trip: "I remember a beautiful day when I accompanied you to Peterhof. Mr. Marquet did not want to avail himself of the services of Intourist for a car. I can still see you, full of adventurous gaiety, on the platform of a tramway car, then on the train for the suburbs and in the bus like all the soviet passengers."[219] In Russia, Marquet did no work.

The Marquets write to Camoin and the Eiffels who are staying in Switzerland: "We are traveling like royalty." They return on September 20.[220] Only just returned, forty-eight hours later they leave for Le Havre.

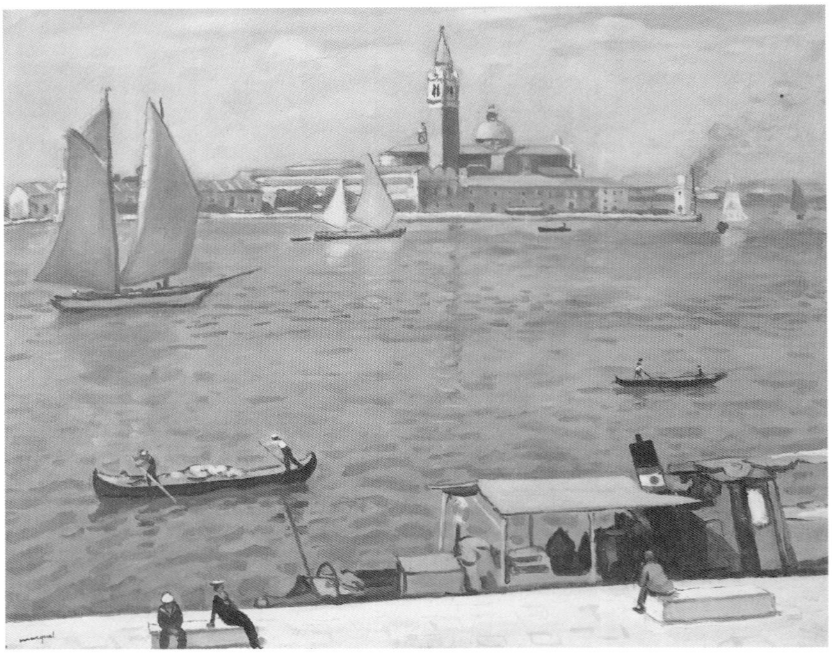

Venise. La voile jaune, 1936 (#34)

Madame Druet writes to them in September: "I remind you that M.O. Senn could give your husband facilities for work in the port...I would be happy to hear you tell of your impressions (of Russia)."[221]

At Le Havre they stay at the Hôtel Continental and for three weeks Marquet paints the port, and the pilots' bay. They leave via Dieppe.

At the end of November the galerie des Beaux-Arts opens the exhibition *Les Fauves*, in the studio of Gustave Moreau, where Marquet shows twelve paintings.

1935

On January 5 Marcel Ray replies to a letter of Marcelle Marquet: "If when it comes down to it you go to Rabat do not forget that I am on excellent terms with the Resident, General Ponsot and his *chef de Cabinet* Sicot."[222]

At the beginning of this year Marquet searches yet again for a place to go and work.

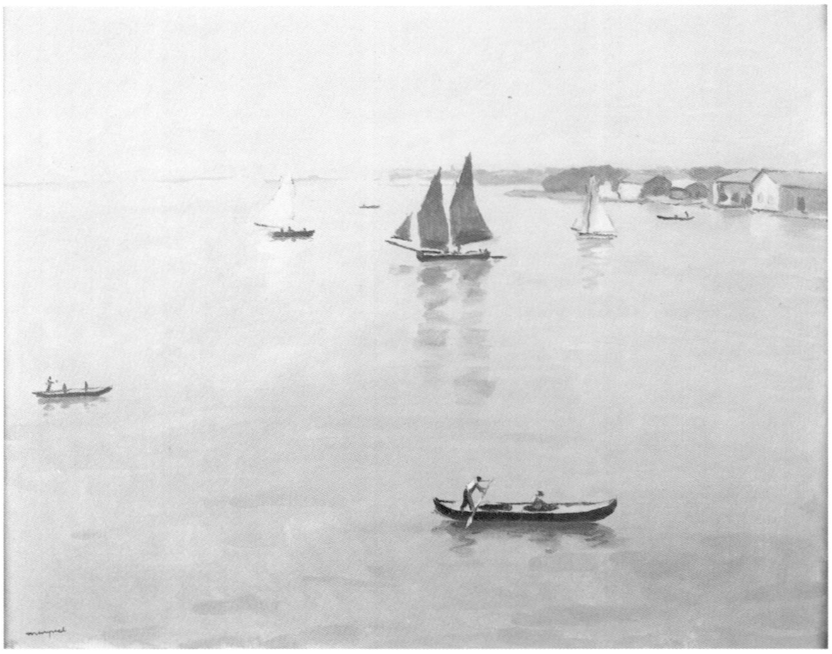

La lagune à Venise, 1936 (#35)

He corresponds with Matisse about an exhibition at the Petit Palais planned for December, but Matisse replies from Nice: "I am unable to profit from your offer which has revived in me deliciously the feelings of our old and deep friendship...I have taken up work again a few days ago...I wish you and your wife a pleasant journey...a long vacation and some sensible skiing progress...Aren't you going to Morocco to do some snow effects?"[223]

The Marquets thus leave for Algiers to ski, and they then go to Rabat, as they tell George Besson at the end of February or the beginning of March.[224] At the hotel in Rabat for a few days, they then move to a house in the Oudaïas district lent to them by the *Beaux-Arts*.

On April 19, Camoin writes to Matisse: "I have had news of Marquet from Rex Ingram the film director who has returned from Rabat: Marquet has rented a studio in Rabat from a painter whose name Ingram cannot remember and he will probably work there the entire season."[225]

According to his habit, the artist works in several studios and spends his time between the Oudaïas and the studio mentioned by Camoin. At the end of the visit they go to Marrakech.

Back in France in May, the Marquets go off to Nice to visit Matisse.

In Paris, the painter completes the organization of his one-man show that will take place from June 13 to July 6 at the Tooth Gallery in London.

Wanting to revisit the land of his childhood, for two weeks at the end of July he rents the villa Robinson in Pyla. The correspondence continues with Matisse, better than ever since the beginning of the year, and the friends seem happy to have found each other again. At Pyla, surrounded with family, Marquet works a lot.

During these months of mixed holiday and work, an exhibition is organized for the end of the year for the galerie Vallotton in Lausanne and then for Basle. From September 14 to 28 he exhibits watercolors and some canvases that will then be taken up by the galerie Aktuaryus in Zurich. Vallotton awaits their visits in October. Marquet gets back to Paris at the beginning of October, and on the 7th Marcelle Marquet writes to him that they "will not go to Switzerland for the moment but rather later in the winter when there is snow on the mountains."[226] They leave for Lausanne at the end of the year.

1936

Marquet and his wife arrive in Lausanne at the end of December, 1935: "We will arrive in Lausanne Wednesday or Thursday (the 29th or 30th). Be kind enough to tell us which hotel has the view..."[227] They are received by the Vallottons, who set them up at the Hôtel Belvedere. Paul Vallotton dies on January 23, and the artist's stay is disrupted by this loss. He is also on edge due to persistent bad weather.

In the hotel, Marquet executes a series of views of snowy roofs, and mountains in the mist and snow. While they are there, Aktuaryus exhibits Marquet's work in Strasbourg, and then in Zurich where a few paintings and watercolors shown by Paul Vallotton the year before are shown.

After Lausanne, Marquet heads for the mountains. He is not used to such driving, and he finds it hard. First they stay a few days at Crans-sur-Serre before heading on for Davos. When he eventually arrives, after a difficult ascent, a room with a terrace at the Hôtel Esplanade gives him the reward of a distant view of the town and the mountains that surround it. During this stay, Marcelle Marquet continues to correspond with dealers and museums so as to organize the presentation of her husband's work in different Swiss towns, for that same year and those following. A shrewd businesswoman, she relieves Marquet of the worries of organization and sales, giving him more time to paint. After a stay of around ten days, and a series of paintings, on February 25 Marcelle Marquet tells the Vallottons: "we are leaving Davos tomorrow... Zurich (Hôtel Central)...We will go to Algiers... we will be back in Paris around March 15."[228]

In March of 1936 or 1937, an exhibition entitled *Marquet and Camoin* is held at the Mignon-Massart Gallery.

From May 6 to 16, the Vallotton Gallery at Lausanne holds an exhibition of his work, comprising of paintings from Crans, Montreux and Lausanne.

Arriving in Paris in March, Marquet learns that he is the "chief exhibitor at the French section of the Venice Biennale."

Venice is no stranger to the artist who had visited it during his stays in 1908 and 1909. He does not feel the need to paint there but "nonetheless (takes) his painting things."[229]

Invited to the Danieli's for the opening, the painter instantly dislikes its (the hotel's) lack of simplicity. At the Biennale they meet Balbina Balbi who is introduced to them by relations. She gets them a room in a lodging-house/hotel that she owns: the Pension Bucintoro, on Riva degli Schiavoni. Marquet cannot resist the desire to paint, and quickly gets to work. On July 3, he sends a card to George Besson: "I am beginning to forgive the poor painters who have done so many daubs in Venice. "*La peinture a l'huile, c'est bien difficile.*"[230]

In July, Marcelle Marquet leaves to join her family for several weeks on the Côte d'Azur, and her husband feels completely abandoned. He writes her a series of tender letters telling her everything he does and sees: "The days are passing very slowly, this month of August will have no end." The heat stops him working during the day, so he has to wait for the sun to become less fierce before getting down to it. "The weather is always brilliant, too good, its quite monotonous and I can't wait to see a bit of gray sky."[231] A few days of cooler weather reward the painter for his waiting but the sun and the heat come back quickly and he is obliged to work "in the morning from 6 to 7.30, and in the evening around 4 or 5." Marcelle returns at the end of August to the huge delight of Marquet, and in September she writes to the Camoins that they are leaving Venice to tour Venetia before heading back for Genoa and the Côte d'Azur, stopping to see them at St. Tropez."[232]

In October they are in Paris. In December, a large exhibition of the paintings made in Venice is held at the Druet Gallery. Some of the works are sold.

1937

In January a Marquet exhibition opens at the galerie Athénée in Geneva.

The artist returns to Switzerland, to stay in Montreux. He paints a series of canvases of the lake, and the mountains seen from his hotel. He also paints a small picture of Geneva. Marcelle Marquet remembers: "Marquet always liked the snow...at Ouchy as at Montreux...the greatness of the scenery after a while seemed to him to lack intimacy."[233] Numerous exhibitions will be held in Switzerland in the future.

After their stay in Algiers, in the summer Marquet rediscovers the banks of the Seine. The painter Luce lives in Rolleboise and it may be him who advised the artist to stay there.

Marquet is offered a house belonging to an old woman. Simple but including a garden of hollyhocks, the house seduces the painter with its windows looking out on the river and the lock. He rents it for two years. He will pay visits to the painters at Rolleboise among whom are Alfred Veillet and Luce. It is to be a calm summer, contrasting greatly with the great agitation of the voyages of the year before.

In November, they return to Paris and receive a visit from Jean Puy, who writes to them on the 26th: "I would like to promise to visit you next Wednesday around 3pm, I have taken it on myself to bring with me Mme. Perless, wife of a banker, who buys painting a little, a very little."[234]

Pictures by Marquet are shown in Paris, at the *Salon des Indépendants* from February 7 to March 8, at the galerie Guy Stein from April 28 to May 22, and at the galerie Druet in May and June. From June to October, at the Petit Palais, the exhibition *Les Maîtres de l'art indépendant* (masters of independent art) is held, where Marquet is represented by thirty-seven paintings from private collections, and in December, the exhibition *Marquet* is held at the galerie de l'Elysée. In the provinces, his work is seen at the *Salon du Sud-Est* (Salon of the southeast) in Lyon, at the *Salon des Indépendants Bordelais* in Bordeaux, and at an exhibition in Mulhouse in November and December.

Abroad, after Geneva, come the exhibitions of the *Cercle Manès* in Prague; the Hahnloser collection at Winthherthur, *Art Français contemporain* at Berlin in June-July, an exhibition in Pittsburgh from October 14 to December 56, and another at the Franska Konst Galeriet in Stockholm in November. In November in St.Tropez the musée Tropelen is inaugurated, thanks to the help of Georges Grammont.

1938

Having done business for several years with the dealer Gösta Olson in Stockholm, Marquet, through his wife, corresponds with Olson from January 12. As the painter has the intention to go to Stockholm in February, he asks Olson for

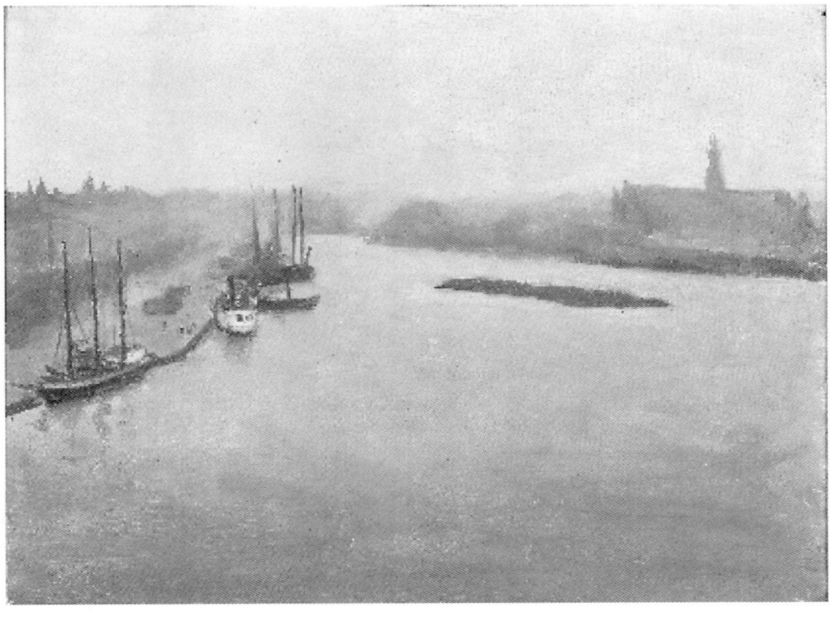

Brume à Stockholm, 1938 (#36)

practical information: well-placed hotel, snow, temperature at this time of year.[235]

A Marquet exhibition is to be held in Amsterdam in February, and this opportunity decides them to undertake the voyage to Sweden, which as yet they do not know.

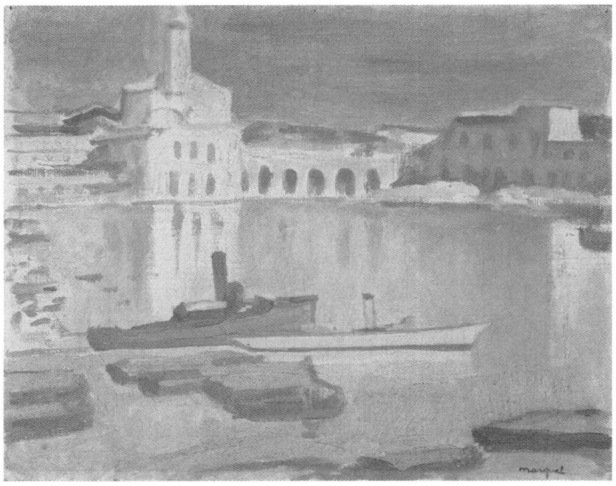

Paysage au remorqueur, 1939 (#38)

After an exhibition in January at Bernheim-Jeune, the artist leaves on February 8 for Amsterdam where he plans staying two or three weeks at the Amstel Hôtel. He works on a few paintings from his window, makes few visits to the gallery where his work is being shown, visits museums, and appreciates the Dutch sky. He finds the locals a little too cold and he establishes few contacts with them.

The hotel strike in Sweden worries them, but nonetheless Olson finds them a hotel that will be pleased to have them.

On February 24, Marcelle tells Olson that they are boarding on the 26th on the Bélé, a Swedish ship that will stop for a brief while at Lübeck. They arrive in Stockholm on March 4, where Gösta Olson awaits them.

A few days later the Anschluss takes place, and the atmosphere becomes heavier. Nevertheless, the following weeks are interesting for Marquet, warmly welcomed by the Swedes. They will stay for two months in Stockholm, months of intense work. At the end of the visit, from April 28 to May 15, an exhibition is organized at the Svenska Franska Konst Galeriet of Gösta Olson. It shows the artist's work during his stay in the town.

After a visit to Copenhagen where the painter wanders the streets, at the beginning of May they return to Paris.

At Méricourt at the beginning of the summer, Marquet works on his views of the Seine. In August, they are in Paris. The painter André Barbier suggests renting them a house at La Frette for the autumn. The house is unfurnished. Unable to take occupancy straight away, they accept the invitation of a friend who lives at Cap Brun near Toulon. The artist paints a few pictures but as the region does not inspire him sufficiently, he heads for the Ile de Porquerolles of which he has heard great things. Enthralled by this charming spot, he executes a series of paintings and decides to come back next year, in the summer, to paint and take a family holiday.

Louis Vauxcelles dedicates an article on September 16 in *Beaux-Arts* to Eugène Blot who has just died. Along with Berthe Weill and Druet, this dealer was one of those who helped the Fauves in their younger days.

In October, Marcelle Marquet, under the pseudonym of Marcelle Marty, goes off to promote her novel *Un Sidi ou la vie est belle* (A gentleman, or life is good).[236]

At the international exhibition at Pittsburgh, which takes place from October 14 to December 14, Marquet wins the "First Honorable Mention" for his painting of the *Pont-Neuf, la nuit* (The Pont-Neuf at Night).

He meets the painter François Desnoyer during the exhibition/sale that Desnoyer is organizing at the *Maison de la Pensée Française* (Center for French Thought). The money raised will serve to bring aid to refugees made homeless by the Germans. Desnoyer later said: "It's that exhibition which yielded for me the priceless friendship of Albert Marquet and his wife, of George Besson, and other personalities in the field of arts and letters."[237]

1939

In Paris from February 2 to 18, at the galerie Rodrigues-Henriques, the artist exhibits forty watercolors and drawings. In Algiers the following month, Marcelle and Albert Marquet live with family. The painter is to execute a series of views from the roofs of the town, seen from the Mustapha area where he is staying.

In the Pierre Bordes hall, from March 25 to April 8, an exhibition of Marquet's work is held. All the works exhibited belong to collectors from Algiers.

A large exhibition takes place at Basle, at the Kunsthalle. Planned at least two years before and delayed, it opens on March 18. Represented are the works of Albert Marquet, Pierre Laprade, George Bouche, Lucien Mainssieux and Gabriel Fournier.

Marquet lends the house at La Frette to the Desnoyers when, at the beginning of the summer, he leaves with his wife for Porquerolles where they will be joined by Robert Martinet and his family. They stay at a ravishing villa by the sea, and the artist, confronted with the subjects he loves, works very hard. Unfortunately the declaration of war pulls them brutally from their state of blissful unconsciousness. The first to leave the island is Robert Martinet, who is mobilized.

Marquet decides to leave immediately for Paris to put his paintings away safely. They rejoin François Desnoyer and his wife at La Frette: "The house was big enough to house us all and the two painters could work together without bothering each other."[238]

During the winter they alternate, four days in Paris, three at La Frette; they do without comfort and in front of the fire receive friends and talk about the war. "On Sunday there were often friends of Marquet's who came to stay for the day: the painters Manguin, Camoin, Celebonovitch, the ceramicist Artigas, the Bessons, the Cachin-Signacs, the Tavernier musicians, and Alice Merkel."[239] The evenings were enlivened by games of dominos, chess, and stories told with remarkable verve and humor by Marcelle.

In his studio in the attic, Marquet paints a series of canvases of the Seine in winter.

Marcelle asks Gösta Olson how long he figures on keeping the paintings he has in storage: she tells him of their precipitous return across France to put their paintings into safety, and tells him: "You would have loved the French people

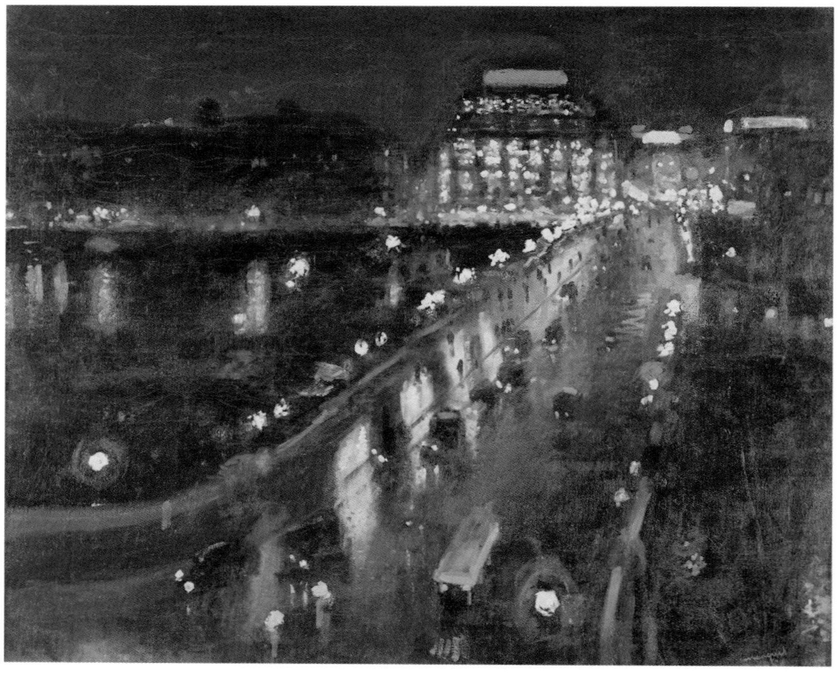

Le Pont Neuf, la nuit, ca. 1935–1939 (#32)

if you had seen them put up with that stifling worry. Even now they are joking. We have seen again the old greatcoats of 1914–1918, the guarded bridges and the crammed trains."[240]

1940

In Algiers at the beginning of the year, Marcelle Marquet corresponds with Lola Camoin and sends them their wishes, saying that they are there for a "month." They live in the house of Marcelle's grandparents, at 16, rue Mercurie.[241]

On their return to France, they spend their time between Paris and La Frette and await events.

From April 23 to May 11 an important exhibition is held at the galerie des Beaux-Arts entitled *Oeuvres de Marquet* (Works by Marquet). On that occasion an article by Maximilien Gauthier appears in the *Beaux-Arts* of May 1.

So as to allow Marquet to move around, Robert Rey, *inspecteur général des beaux-arts* (Inspector General of Fine Arts), gives the artist a *laissez-passer* on May 28.[242]

Marquet has signed the bill of protestation of artists and intellectuals against Nazism. In June the situation becomes dangerous for the painter who decides to go and take refuge in the Midi.

They have to trust their paintings to their friends; luckily their car is working and they have gas coupons, but the exodus of thousands of people slows their progress. They arrive at Céret after a long and difficult trip. With their friend Artigas they are quickly made aware that it is impossible to return. They live at the villa La Flore. They find in the area numerous acquaintances: Pierre Brune, Jean Cassou, and Raoul Dufy. They receive news from Manguin, Camoin and Albert André. At Vernet-les-Bains, at the Hôtel Beau Soleil, they take the cure in August and contemplate going to spend several weeks in Collioure, at the end of the month.[243] The trip is taken in anguish for friends of whom they can get no news, and Marquet paints very little. At Collioure, they take a room at the Hôtel de la Balette; the artist does a few watercolors and paintings to shake himself out of his inaction. On September 2, Marcelle writes to Malek and Albert André: "Here we are in Collioure, where Marquet returns for each catastrophe, he was here in 1914, he is here now and he is painting...the climate of Céret, rather changeable and hard, did not suit me, Collioure is much better for me. Besson writes that you have news of Werth...Old Luce has lost his wife and he is somewhere with the "occupiers." Marcel Ray is keeping note of people he meets in Aix...We are off to Algeria...here there has been no butter for two months. We get by. Oil is rare, but fish and good fruit...We'll stay at Collioure until the end of the month, and we will take ship no doubt with my brother. Write. Did you know that André Lhote and Chagall are in Gordes? Jacques Guenne is in Villeneuve. You are in luck. We only have Maillol, Dufy and Van Leer in this region."[244]

Marquet and his wife leave Collioure for Algeria at the end of September and they arrive in October. Marcelle's father lends them a little apartment at 107, boulevard Bru, where they will stay all winter.

1941

The Germans requisition the house at La Frette. The painter Desnoyer removes from the forces of the occupation the paintings by his friend stored in the studio.

Vlaminck goes and hides a group of his works at Rueil.

The apartment of boulevard Bru is small and Marquet suffers greatly under this hardship. Luckily the window opens onto vast horizons and he paints.

In Nice, Matisse is sick: suffering from constant *malaises*, he leaves for Lyon to have an operation on a congenital malformation of the intestine.[245]

In Algeria Marquet is threatened with prosecution. The good heart of the painter and his wife led them to lodge for a week a young unknown in distress, seemingly a pilot escaped from prison and wanting to rejoin in London the forces of Free France. It transpires that this unknown is in fact an escaped prisoner who posed as a victim of the Germans whereas in fact he was in prison for swindling. The good faith of the painter is quickly proven.[246]

Informed by Jean Puy of the operation undergone by his friend Matisse, Marquet takes up again this correspondence that he will continue until his death. On March 20 he writes: "The countryside at the moment is splendid... I had never yet seen anything so beautiful...Will we be prisoners much longer on the Moorish coast? Time is beginning to pass slowly."[247]

In May he recuperates the "paintings left in the Aveyron and in the Roussillon in a safe or *chez* Pepito." Marcelle's brother does the trip and relates to his sister all the privations their friends are undergoing. Marcelle tells Albert André that (they have) "purchased a property, 'Djenan Sidi Said' a quarter of an hour from Algiers...(they will be there) around June 8 or 10.[248]

In May, at the galerie du Minaret at Algiers, an exhibition of Marquet's works is organized with the help of Robert Martinet. It will allow the artist to pay for his house. Several articles in *L'Echo d'Alger* on May 9, 10 and 15 announce and comment on this exhibition.

On May 22, Matisse writes to his friend: "I'm leaving Lyon tonight for Nice – which I left on January 8 (90 days in the clinic and two months in a hotel with the flu)."[249]

Albert and Marcelle try their best to help their friends in need. They send parcels with all the non-perishable goods that they soon pick in their garden. Robert Martinet, tempted by selling pictures, helps Marquet and his friends to sell their work. He will organize shows with Robert Martin who is director of a gallery in Algiers. The dealer Charles-Auguste Girard comes to the studio and buys numerous paintings, and the connoisseurs of the area continue to acquire.

In a letter dated September to Matisse, the painter announces to his friend that he "has

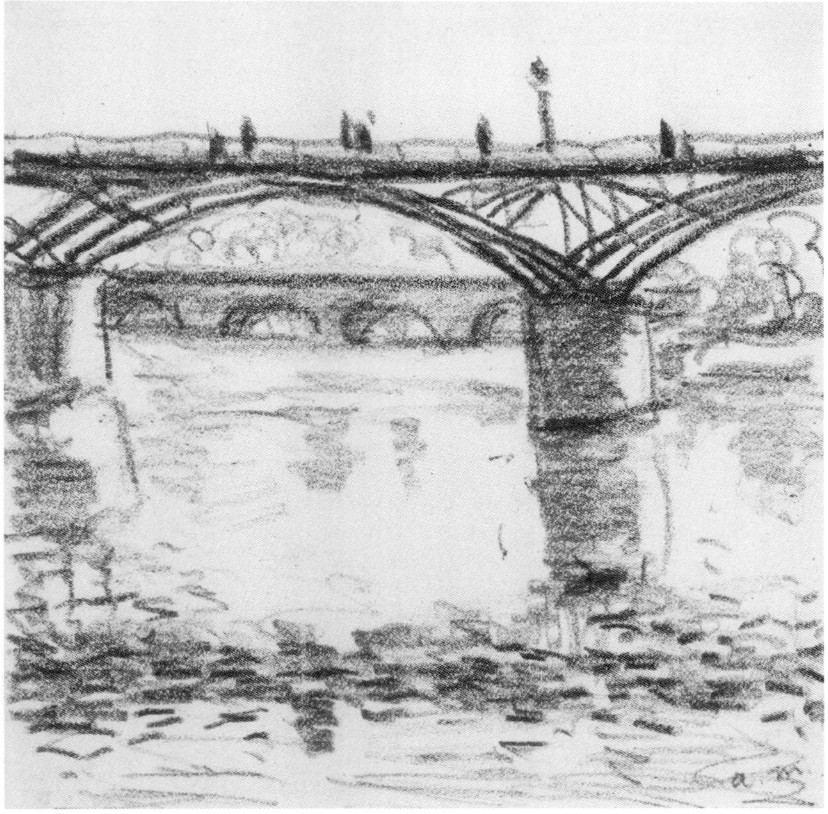

Le Pont des Arts, 1946 (#70)

found an apartment with a magnificent view, at 27 (sic) boulevard Carnot." He has the intention of passing the winter there, as it is easier to heat than their house in the country.[250]

During the autumn, Marquet works in town. Their car having stayed in France, Marcelle helps him to carry supplies and they carry the baskets together on public transport.

On November 22 and 23, Marquet and his wife participate in the cultural days of the *Jeune France* (Young France) group at the Tipasa site.

1942

On January 16, Matisse, from Nice, writes to Marquet: "I've just had a letter from our old friend Puy who is still tormented and perplexed in his thoughts about what painting should be...Did you not know that our fat Derain, big-mouth Vlaminck, Mr. Dunoyer de Segonzac, and the pitiful Friesz, made a study trip to Germany and came back very satisfied. They are spineless!"[251] The trip is organized by the German sculptor Arno Breker. A photograph is published which saddens all the friends of these painters.

On March 3, Matisse thanks his friends for the oranges, and Marquet describes to him the enchantment of the Algerian spring and tells him about raising rabbits, chickens and guinea-fowl, all of which they do on their property.[252]

On August 1, Marcelle tells the Bessons of the death of her father, surrounded by his family, which occurred on July 8. She writes stories, rejected by Albin Michel.[253] Matisse, suffering once more, corresponds with his friend and keeps him up to date with what is happening to friends and relatives. He is looked after by a friend of Marquet's: Doctor Gutmann, a Jewish doctor who has managed to change his name and hide.

It is an "abnormally fresh summer in Algiers,"[254] Marquet writes to Matisse on August 15; on the 21st, Marquet writes that he is recovering slowly from the problems caused by his gall-bladder, and that he his once again painting."[255] Marcelle Marquet has to stop making parcels for their friends. They are no longer allowed to send help to people who are not family members.

In September, Marquet tells Matisse that Manguin "is threatened with the amputation of both legs."[256] He prepares his canvases as in the old days, but lacks powder and oil. Matisse replies on September 15 asking him for explications.[257] Marcelle Marquet elaborates a few days later: Manguin is suffering from arteritis.

From the spring of 1942, the Allies are in collaboration with the North African resistance. On October 21 comes the conference of Cherchell and on November 8, an American squadron lands an expeditionary force at Algiers, Oran and Casablanca. New American and British contingents arrive in the days that follow.[258]

Marquet joins in with the merry-making mob, and paints a few paintings of battleships anchored at sea. Unfortunately his apartment at boulevard Carnot is requisitioned and has to stay at "Djenan Sidi Said." From there he watches the bombardment of the town and paints.

Jean Launois disappears from the scene at the end of this year. Marcelle Marquet had to resolve to close the door to him because of his inveterate alcoholism.[259] It is André Hambourg, long-time friend of Launois – who had been able to stay at the Villa Abd-el-Tif in 1933 thanks to Hambourg's help – who discovers his friend dead in his hotel room on November 26.

All the artists of the Villa Abd-el-Tif are requisitioned for *le Génie*, the camouflage section, for the length of the war.[260]

1943

Deprived of his apartment in town, Marquet discovers a friend of his youth, the painter Armand Assus, who lives with his family in an apartment on the Square Bresson. They go painting together often, from the second floor of a nearby hotel, situated on the seafront (probably the Hôtel Terminus). Assus very frequently visits Marquet with his family. At the end of the war, they are together again in Paris.[261]

At Djenan Sidi Said, the artist opens his door wide to numerous visitors, friends, collectors, and travelers who are passing through Algiers or who are refugees and have been recommended to them, such as André Gide, Saint-Exupéry, Henri Bosco, Emmanuel Bove and his wife Louise, and Alice Merkel the musician and wife of André Tavernier, among others. Marquet and his wife take part in all the lectures and festivities organized in town.

At the request of Jean Alazard, director of the Musée national des Beaux-Arts, the painter presents one of his paintings to Général de Gaulle, at the beginning of the month of July.[262]

He encounters fairly often the painter André Hambourg and goes to dine with him.

Matisse has installed himself in Vence in the fall to avoid the bombardments.[263]

George Besson dedicates a special edition of *Le Point* to his friend Marquet: Camoin and Matisse between them write the commentary.[264]

In December, at the Pierre Bordes hall, the exhibition/sale of works offered by the artists of Algeria in support of the national effort for the Résistance takes place, in which exhibition Marquet offers one of his paintings. With Fernez and Assus he is one of the organizers of this event.

1944

The painter Mainssieux, ex-husband of Marcelle Marquet's friend Zohra, writes to Marquet on the subject of a little painting that the painter had given him. Marquet replies on February 22: "Have received your news and regret that I cannot say it is with pleasure as I understand that you are ill...On the subject of the little painting I am very happy to learn that there was no truth in the news I got from a painter friend who assured me he had seen it at a big collector's in Algiers."[265]

At Djenan Sidi Said Marquet continues to paint his garden, his animals, his house, but lassitude is making itself felt, and from the announcement of Victory in May, the artist begins to think along the lines of returning to France. He writes to his friends to get their views, in particular to Matisse whom he believes is still in Nice. On November 6 Matisse sends him a letter saying: "I did reply to you with cards and am astounded that they never got to you...I came to Vence to get away from the bombardments. I have been here for a year and a half ...Deliverance has occurred without damage...In the month of April Madame Matisse and Marguerite were arrested by the Gestapo. Madame Matisse was in Fresnes for three months and was then sentenced to three months in prison which were added to her detention...Marguerite has been in confinement until the month of August in Rennes, and sent to Belfort...she is now back in Paris."[266]

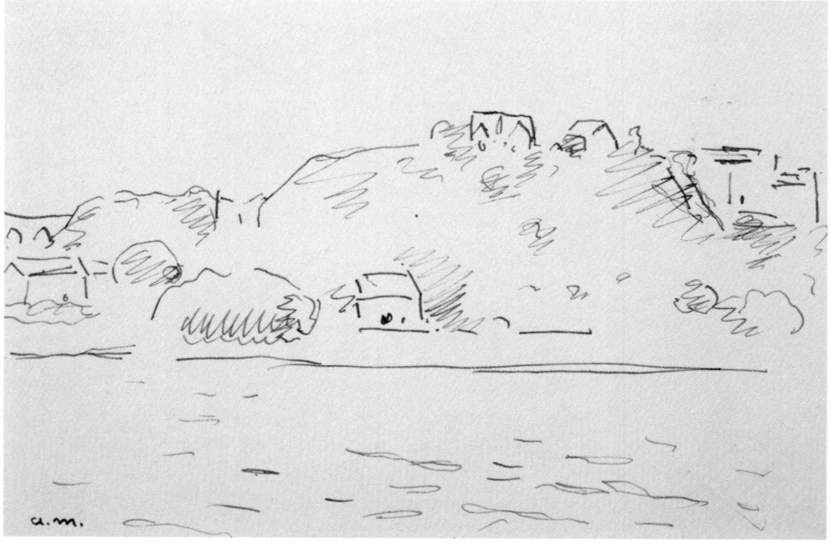

La Frette au bord de l'eau, 1945 (#69)

In his reply, Marquet says that he wants to return to Paris, but that the news he is getting is not encouraging. He is afraid of being cold during the winter.[267]

On January 26, Marcelle replies to Besson: "Yes you are right, in '34 Albert would have thought it "funny" and mostly useless to affiliate with any party, but times have changed...the task of reforming of the world would seem to lie with the communist party. You know Albert well enough to know...that he is not made for the soapbox, public life, and demonstrations. Those types of thing make him particularly unhappy...and as he does not want to deceive anyone, and as he is what he is with no hope of remedy, he will join as long as he is not asked to do things for which he is not made."[270] The painter joins the party.

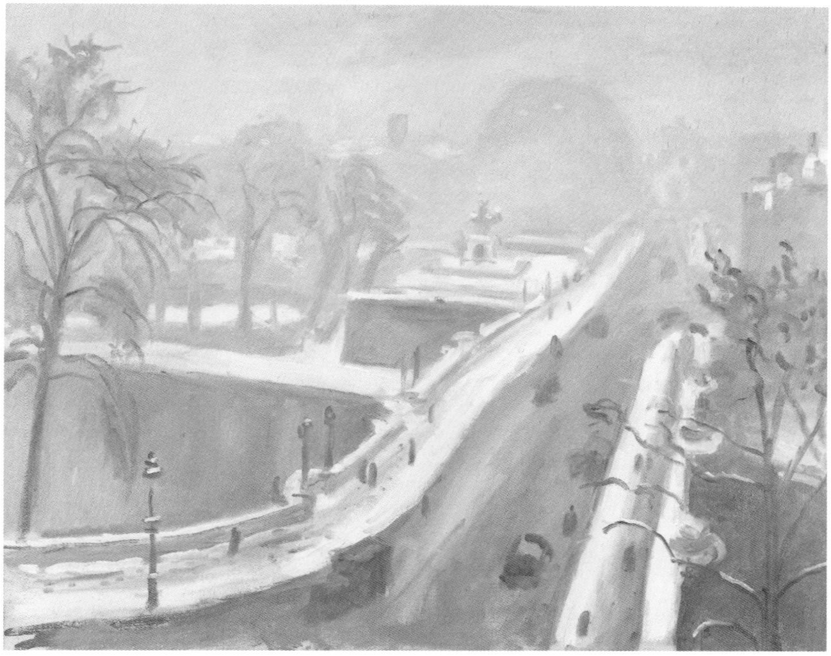

Le Pont Neuf sous la neige, 1947 (#39)

Marcelle receives a letter from the Bessons and replies to them on December 4: "At last some news. You had us worried...we are reveling at the moment in an exceptional autumn, warm and sunny, so good that instead of going back to town we are staying in the country...The Rays are here...André Tavernier and his wife Alice Merkel have a good job at the radio...Matisse is in Vence...from the Albert Andrés a few cards. On his way through, Charles Vildrac gave us news of Francis (Jourdain)...My cousin told us a good story. You know that he was in charge of moving the paintings, drawings and watercolors from our apartment. He had hired a little and discrete studio and had piled everything there. The *boches* found out. They summonsed him and gave him the heavy interrogation for ten days." The cousin denied everything and during the interrogation managed to re-hide the paintings.

The Marquets plan returning in April, as their apartment, occupied by friends of their cousin, has not been requisitioned.[268]

The winter will be spent in Algiers. On December 28, via Mr. Maeght, Matisse gets to them two long letters telling of the death of Maillol and Maurice Denis. Marquet sees Bonnard, Carlos Raymond, Marthe Lebasque and Rouveyre. Camoin writes from Paris, as does Puy; he speaks of Vlaminck, Friesz and Gris.[269]

1945

On December 5, 1944, Charles Walch asks George Besson to persuade Marquet to join the communist party.

On January 30 a large artistic gala is organized by Combat (a clandestine resistance movement of which Albert Camus was a part) in the Pierre-Bordes hall in Algiers. Albert Marquet sends a painting, which is auctioned off in aid of social works and the combatants of Combat.[271]

Marquet tells Matisse of his return "in April or May" to France. In April he starts to get ready, but is inconsolable at the thought of leaving his garden. They have plane tickets for the end of the month."[272]

On May 8, they are in Paris. The painter gives an interview to the journalist André Warnod of *Arts*, an article that is to appear on May 25 on the front page.

From Paris, Marquet continues to send news to Matisse who is still in Vence, but the post is not reliable. Therefore one letter, illustrated and written at the end of April, does not leave Algeria until May 3. Matisse sometimes thinks that his friend has forgotten him. On June 11 he tells Marquet of his arrival in Paris towards the end of the month.[273]

In Paris, Marquet works hard, not painting, but giving himself to colored lithography: "Another sensational development, they came to ask me to be a candidate for the *Institut*...I fell down on my backside, but I replied with our old war-cry, shit to the *Institut*."[274] The offer was made by Mr. David Weill.

The summer passes in the house at La Frette that Marquet had rediscovered with joy. On Sundays, with friends, old customs reassert themselves. Camoin is to be one of the most assiduous visitors.

Paintings arrive from Algiers, escorted by Marcelle's brother. A few missing cases will only be found after a second trip to Marseilles: "Robert has had to return to Marseilles and he fished out the two cases in a dock of unclaimed items even though they had the addresses painted in black, as high as your hand. One case was open and all the papers separating the paintings to stop them sticking together were missing...we are only missing now the case with linen, clothes, shoes, provisions, typewriter and my papers."[275]

The winter is spent between Paris and La Frette where heating has been installed for them.

Exhibitions have begun again for the artist, and he shows his work at various exhibitions. In February an exhibition of drawings at the galerie Couleur du Temps, then at the *Salon de la Marine*, at the *Salon d'Automne*, and at the galerie Charpentier, amongst others.

1946

In January, Matisse sends to Marquet a parcel of oranges, and is thanked by Marquet who also announces their departure for Algeria at the end of the month.[276]

Matisse replies on January 3: "How I understand your sighing for the sky of Algiers...I cannot stand Paris, there are too many people...it is nonetheless good to have come to Paris so as to realize how solitude, which can weigh a little heavy after a while, is good."[277]

On January 15, Marquet receives from the ministry a commission: "Mr. Albert Marquet...is asked to go to Biskra (Algeria) so as to paint the portrait of Si Bou Aziz Ben Gana, Cheikh el Arab, which is commissioned from him by the State."[278] We do not know if the artist carried out the commission.

Homage to Marquet is rendered by the mairie du VIème (town hall of the sixth arrondissement) and by the committee for mutual aid to artists and intellectuals. Numerous artists are present, including Camoin, Asselin, Leon Werth and Francis Jourdain.[279]

At the end of February, Marcelle writes to the Bessons from Algiers: "Good and rapid trip. Quite a long stop at Marignane, to eat at the buffet of the aerodrome. Telegraph your arrival to my brother, 30, avenue Dujonchay. We will await you."[280] To Lola Camoin on February 1 she writes: "We have just arrived at the end of a period of catastrophic rain in which two of our terraces have collapsed. Apart from that all is well...We are living on boulevard Carnot with the young household of Jean-Claude Arlette... they are preparing exams, but we will be in the country soon..."[281] She asks the Bessons a few days later, "Have you packed?"[282] In March the Bessons tell the Marquets that they cannot come.

Her brother has organized an exhibition at the galerie Colin, which opens on January 18, and sells all the Marquets and all the Camoins. Albert André has less luck.

On April 15, the artist participates in a sale, organized in Paris, at the galerie Charpentier, on the initiative of the *Association nationale des artistes prisonniers de guerre* (national association of artist prisoners of war). His painting earns 105,000 ff. On June 21, he replies to the call of the O.P.E.J. to help Jewish orphans and victims of deportation. The sale takes place at the galerie des Beaux-Arts on June 28. The exhibitions abroad start up again in great quantity: at Lausanne, Brussels, Rome, Liège, Zurich, Wiesbaden and Berlin, Stockholm, Lisbon and Oslo.

The summer starts well at La Frette and in Paris. The friends Desnoyer and Marquet, with a group of colleagues – Lurçat, Goerg, Osouf, Couturier and Germaine Richier – are invited by the *syndicat d'intitiative* (tourist office) of the canton of Grisons in Switzerland. From August 7 to 16 they are there, sketchbooks in hand, on a trip of friendship. They visit the studios of Swiss artists, promenade in the towns and villages, and Marcelle says: "What a pleasant trip! We enjoyed it without imagining that it would be Marquet's last. He drew...he promised to return."[283]

In autumn at La Frette, the sweetness of the banks of the Seine and the countryside are helpful to the declining health of the artist. In November, they return to Paris, and on December 20 Camoin writes to Matisse, "I am waiting for old Marquet who is coming with his wife and his sister-in-law to dinner with us... Shame that you will not be here."[284]

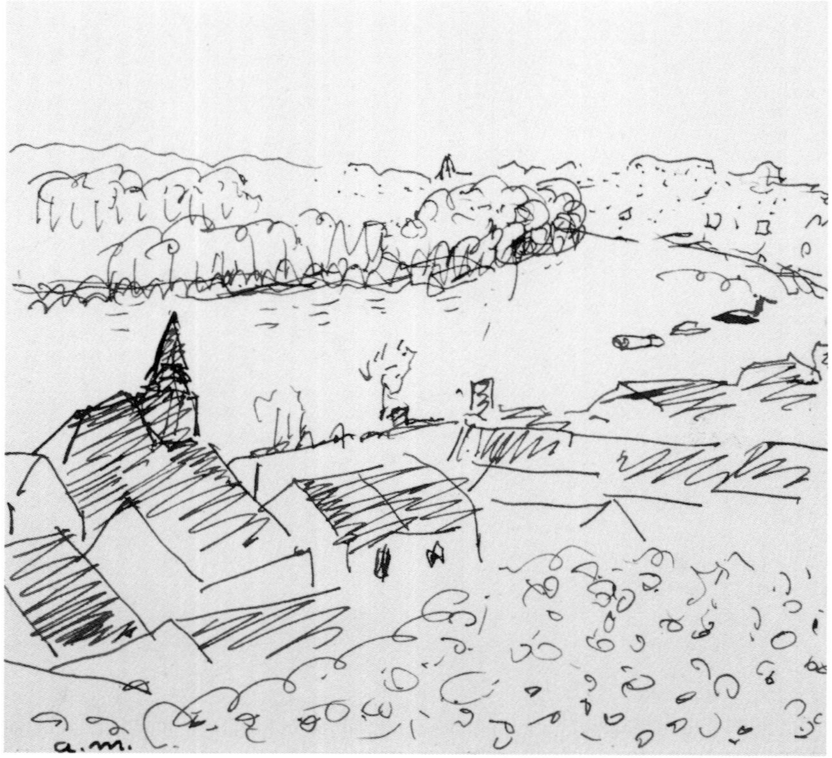

La Frette vue d'en haut, 1945 (#68)

1947

After an operation on his gall bladder on January 14, Marquet starts painting again, two days after returning home on the 31st. He paints a series of snow on the Pont-Neuf, destined to be his last eight paintings.

The *Journal* of Aimée Launois, at the musée de Bordeaux, is a precious witness to the artist's last months. On January 27, she writes: "They operated on Marquet, I understood from Marcelle's voice on the telephone that it was serious and how devastated she was. The operation went well...His illness stirs up many sad memories for me...he was a witness at our wedding. Jean loved him." On February 10 she tells of household life after the operation: "I went to see the Marquets. I hesitated even to 'phone, as it's a perpetual zoo over there. Everyone is worried about Marquet's health. And now that he is on his feet, all his friends want to see him...so much brouhaha around a man who has just had a cancer operation."[285] As the months pass, the cancer grows, and the oedema makes him suffer terribly.

In April he finds the strength to correspond with Matisse. On his return to Vence, Matisse sends him some parcels of fruit.

Marquet no longer feels the urge to paint, he does some engraving, but that also tires him very quickly.

On June 2, Matisse asks him for news, in a lighthearted manner, without mentioning the real cause of his condition, and he also speaks of his own past problems: "I tell you of my past and present misfortunes in the hope of giving you a little patience in the trial that you are presently undergoing. I hope to get back to Paris at the end of July."[286]

Marquet passes away on June 14, in the morning. On the 16th, accompanied by his family and numerous friends, he is buried in the cemetery at La Frette, in a lot chosen by Marcelle, at the top of a little hill overlooking the Seine and the countryside he loved so much.

1 Municipal archives, Bordeaux, France
2 Marcelle Marquet, *Marquet* (Paris: Robert Laffont, 1951) 20–21
3 Letter to George Besson, 1920. A. André – G. Besson archives, France
4 Archives of the Gustave Moreau Museum, Paris
5 C. Roger-Marx, *Marquet* in *Gazette des Beaux-Arts* (March, 1939) 175–193
6 J.-A Cartier, *Gustave Moreau*, in *Gazette des Beaux-Arts* (May/June, 1963), 347–357
7 Archives of the Musée des Beaux-Art, Bordeaux, France
8 Archives of the Gustave Moreau Museum, Paris
9 Archives of the Wildenstein Institute, Paris
10 Ibid
11 Ibid
12 P. Schneider, *Matisse* (Paris: Flammarion, 1948), 725
13 Letter from Camoin to Manguin, January 18, 1900. Archives of the Wildenstein Institute, Paris
14 G. Coquiot, *Les Salons: Les Indépendants* in *Gil Blas* (1901), 2
15 *Petites expositions. Expositions de divers artists chez Hessèle*, in *La Chronique des arts et de la curiosité* (March 2, 1901), 67
16 J.-P. Crespelle, *Les Fauves* (Neufchâtel: Ides et Calendes, 1962), 339–341
17 B. Weill, *Pan dans l'oeil* (Paris: Librairie Lipschutz, 1933), 74
18 Letter of August 23, 1902, Wildenstein Archives, Paris.
19 Archives of the Wildenstein Institute, Paris
20 Ibid
21 Letters of July 7 and August 10, 1903. Jean-Pierre Manguin collection, France
22 Archives of the Wildenstein Institute, Paris
23 J.-P. Crespelle, *Les Fauves*, 340–341
24 Letter from Raoul Dufy to George Besson, January 7, 1948. A. André – G. Besson archives, France
25 Letter from Marquet to Matisse, July/August 1904. Matisse Heirs archives, Paris
26 Archives of the Wildenstein Institute, Paris
27 Matisse Heirs archives, Paris
28 Archives of the Wildenstein Institute, Paris
29 Letter from Frantz Jourdain to Marquet of May 2, 1905. Archives of the Wildenstein Institute, Paris

30 *La Chronique des arts et de la curiosité* (April 1, 1905), 99
31 Archives of the Wildenstein Institute, Paris
32 Ibid
33 Matisse Heirs archives, Paris
34 L. Manguin and C. Manguin, *Henri Manguin. Catalogue de l'oeuvre peint* (Neufchâtel: Ides et Calendes, 1980), biographical notes
35 Camoin Archives, Paris
36 Claudine Grammont, *Correspondance entre Charles Camoin et Henri Matisse*, (Lausanne: *La Bibliothèque des Arts, "Pergamine"* collection, 1997), 18
37 Letter from Marquet to Matisse, July 15 1905. Matisse Heirs archives, Paris
38 Letters from Marquet to Camoin and Camoin to Marquet, August 1905. Camoin and Wildenstein Institute Archives.
39 Archives of the Wildenstein Institute, Paris
40 Letter from Vlaminck to Marquet, January 20, 1906. Archives of the Wildenstein Institute, Paris
41 Letter from Camoin to Marquet, January/February 1906. Archives of the Wildenstein Institute, Paris
42 Sale, Paris, Druot, December 12, 1985, #131
43 Letter from Marquet to Matisse, June 1906. Matisse Heirs archives, Paris
44 Archives of the Wildenstein Institute, Paris
45 Matisse Heirs archives, Paris
46 Ibid
47 Archives of the Wildenstein Institute, Paris
48 Jean-Pierre Manguin collection, France
49 Postcards of January 3 and 5, 1907. Archives of the Wildenstein Institute, Paris
50 Fondation Custodia (Coll. F. Lugt), Institut Néerlandais, Paris, inv. N. 9358 a-h
51 Archives of the Wildenstein Institute, Paris
52 Marcelle Marquet, *Marquet*, 139
53 Camoin archives, Paris
54 Ibid
55 Letter from Tyge Moller to Marquet of May 12, 1908. Archives of the Wildenstein Institute, Paris
56 Letter from Eugène Montfort to Marquet (no date), Archives of the Wildenstein Institute, Paris
57 Camoin archives, Paris
58 Postcard of August 25, 1908. Archives of the Wildenstein Institute, Paris, Paris
59 Collection Jean-Pierre Manguin, France
60 Matisse Heirs archives, Paris
61 Archives of the Wildenstein Institute, Paris
62 Ibid
63 Camoin archives, Paris
64 Archives of the History of Art. The Getty Center for the History of Art and Humanities, Los Angeles, CA
65 Matisse Heirs archives, Paris
66 Letter from Marquet to Matisse of April 11, 1910. Matisse Heirs archives, Paris
67 Archives of the Wildenstein Institute, Paris
68 Ibid
69 Camoin archives, Paris
70 Archives of the Wildenstein Institute, Paris
71 Matisse Heirs archives, Paris
72 Archives of the Wildenstein Institute, Paris
73 Camoin archives, Paris
74 Archives of the Wildenstein Institute, Paris
75 Jean-Pierre Manguin collection, France
76 Ibid
77 Archives of the Wildenstein Institute, Paris
78 Matisse Heirs archives, Paris
79 Camoin archives, Paris
80 Matisse Heirs archives, Paris
81 R. Jean, *Petites expositions* in *La Chronique des arts et de la curiosité* (January 6, 1912), 2
82 Matisse Heirs archives, Paris
83 Letter from Marquet to Vallotton of March 7, 1912. Vallotton archives, Lausanne, Switzerland.
84 Matisse Heirs archives, Paris
85 Camoin archives, Paris
86 Jean-Pierre Manguin collection, France
87 Archives of the Wildenstein Institute, Paris
88 Ibid
89 Ibid
90 Ibid
91 Letter from the *Minstère de la Marine* to Marquet, in *L'Art et la Mer* (#12, 1976), 46
92 Archives of the Wildenstein Institute, Paris
93 Ibid
94 Ibid
95 Camoin archives, Paris
96 Archives of the Wildenstein Institute, Paris
97 Ibid
98 Camoin archives, Paris
99 Elie Faure archives, Paris
100 J.-P. Crespelle, *Les Fauves*, no page given
101 G. Habasque, *Quand on vendait la peau de l'ours* in *L'Oeil* (March, 1965), 17–21
102 Sale, Paris, Druout, March 30 1990, #114
103 Marcelle Marquet, *Marquet. Voyages* (Lausanne: La Bibliothèque des Arts, 1968), 12
104 Claudine Grammont, *Correspondance entre Charles Camoin et Henri Matisse*, 67
105 Camoin archives, Paris
106 M. Ducrey, G. Ducrey, *La galerie Paul Vallotton* (Lausanne: 1988), 32
107 Archives of the Wildenstein Institute, Paris
108 (July 1915) Elie Faure archives, Paris
109 Archives of the Wildenstein Institute, Paris
110 Camoin archives, Paris
111 Claudine Grammont, *Correspondance entre Charles Camoin et Henri Matisse*, 67
112 Matisse Heirs archives, Paris
113 Letter from Marquet and Besson to Albert André. A. André – G. Besson archives, France
114 Archives of the Wildenstein Institute, Paris
115 Elie Faure archives, Paris
116 Archives of the Wildenstein Institute, Paris
117 Letter from Marquet to Matisse of August 18, 1916. Matisse Heirs archives, Paris
118 Elie Faure archives, Paris
119 Letter posted by François Roussier
120 Letter of February 2, 1917. A. André – G. Besson archives, France
121 Letters from Marquet to Matisse of February 2 and April 11, 1917. Matisse Heirs archives, Paris
122 D. Wildenstein, *Monet* (Paris: Wildenstein, 1991), v. V, 214, letter #3040
123 Archives of the Wildenstein Institute, Paris
124 Preface by George Besson, *Marquet et ses amis* (Chartres: 1961)
125 Archives of the Wildenstein Institute, Paris
126 Claudine Grammont, *Correspondance entre Charles Camoin et Henri Matisse*, 108
127 A. André – G. Besson archives, France
128 Matisse Heirs archives, Paris
129 Archives of the Wildenstein Institute, Paris
130 Letters from Baignières to Marquet of August 13 and 23, 1918. Archives of the Wildenstein Institute, Paris
131 Archives of the Wildenstein Institute, Paris
132 A. André – G. Besson archives, France
133 Elie Faure archives, Paris
134 Ibid
135 Ibid
136 Gösta Olson, *Från Ling till Picasso* (Stockholm: Albert Bonniers Förlag, 1965)
137 A. André – G. Besson archives, France
138 Letters from Marquet to Matisse (n.d) (film of 1919)
139 Marcelle Marquet, *Marquet. Voyages*, 16
140 Elie Faure archives, Paris
141 Marcelle Marquet, *Marquet*, 60
142 Matisse Heirs archives, Paris
143 Archives of the Wildenstein Institute, Paris
144 George Besson, *Marquet* (Paris: G. Crès et. Cie, 1920)
145 Letter from Marquet to Matisse (n.d), Matisse Heirs archives, Paris
146 Archives of the Wildenstein Institute, Paris
147 A. André – G. Besson archives, France
148 Archives of the Wildenstein Institute, Paris
149 Elie Faure archives, Paris
150 Matisse Heirs archives, Paris
151 Elie Faure archives, Paris
152 Marcelle Marquet, *Marquet*, 61
153 Claudine Grammont, *Correspondance entre Charles Camoin et Henri Matisse*, 108
154 Elie Faure archives, Paris
155 J. Huguet, *Paul-Emile Pajot marin pêcheur* (Paris: Andrew Bonnet, 1975)
156 Marcelle Marquet, *Marquet. Voyages*, 16
157 C. Fegdal, *Art* in *La Revue Contemporaine* (November 1921), 860–862
158 A. André – G. Besson archives, France
159 Marcelle Marquet, *Marquet*, 74
160 A. André – G. Besson archives, France
161 Ibid
162 Marcelle Marquet, *Marquet. Voyages*, 20
163 See note 159
164 Marcelle Marquet, *Marquet*, 76–82
165 Camoin archives, Paris
166 Matisse Heirs archives, Paris
167 Jean-Pierre Manguin collection, France
168 Camoin archives, Paris
169 Marcelle Marquet, *Marquet. Voyages* (no page given)
170 S. de Ricci, *Les ventes* in *Beaux-Arts* (December 1, 1924)
171 Marcelle Marquet, *Marquet. Voyages*, 24
172 C. Fegdal. *Une Conference. L'Atelier de Marquet* in *L'Ame Gauloise* (February 8, 1925)
173 Fegdal family collection, Paris
174 Marcelle Marquet, *Marquet*, 91–92
175 Matisse Heirs archives, Paris
176 Marcelle Marquet, *Marquet. Voyages*, 26
177 Ibid, 25
178 Archives of the Wildenstein Institute, Paris
179 J. A., *Les Expositions. Salons algériens*, in *Beaux-Arts* (March 1, 1926)
180 Camoin archives, Paris
181 Ibid
182 Archives of the Wildenstein Institute, Paris
183 Archives of the Musée Mainssieux, Voiron, France.
184 Camoin archives, Paris
185 Marcelle Marquet, *Marquet. Voyages*, 28
186 Camoin archives, Paris
187 A. André – G. Besson archives, France
188 Camoin archives, Paris
189 Archives of the Wildenstein Institute, Paris
190 Marquet's passport, Musée des Beaux-Art, Bordeaux, France
191 Camoin archives, Paris
192 Archives of the Wildenstein Institute, Paris
193 G. Denoinville, *Sensations d'arts* in *Le Journal des Arts* (May 19, 1928), 2
194 Archives of the Wildenstein Institute, Paris
195 A. André – G. Besson archives, France
196 Ibid
197 Archives of the Wildenstein Institute, Paris
198 Marcelle Marquet, *Marquet. Voyages*, 34
199 Archives of the Wildenstein Institute, Paris
200 *Sensations d'arts* in *Le Journal des Arts* (December 14, 1929)
201 Camoin archives, Paris
202 Marcelle Marquet, *Marquet. Voyages*, 34
203 Camoin archives, Paris
204 F. Jourdain, *Marquet* (Paris. Editions du Cercle d'Art, 1959), 120
205 Camoin archives, Paris
206 Archives of the Wildenstein Institute, Paris
207 Ibid
208 Ibid
209 A. André – G. Besson archives, France
210 Archives of the Musée des Beaux-Arts de Bordeaux, France
211 Camoin archives, Paris
212 Archives of the Wildenstein Institute, Paris
213 Marcelle Marquet, *Marquet. Voyages*, 38–40
214 A. André – G. Besson archives, France
215 Camoin archives, Paris
216 Raoul de Mathan archives, Paris

217 C. Devau, *A Paris – Albert Marquet* in *Beaux-Arts* (June 8, 1934), 8
218 Marcelle Marquet, *Marquet*, 125–127
219 Archives of the Musée des Beaux-Arts de Bordeaux, France
220 Archives of the Wildenstein Institute, Paris
221 Ibid
222 Ibid
223 Ibid
224 A. André – G. Besson archives, France
225 Claudine Grammont, *Correspondance entre Charles Camoin et Henri Matisse*, 136
226 Archives of the Vallotton Gallery, Lausanne, Switzerland
227 Ibid
228 Archives of the Vallotton Gallery, Lausanne, Switzerland
229 Marcelle Marquet, *Marquet. Voyages*, 50
230 A. André – G. Besson archives, France (editor's note: This phrase may actually be taken from a children's song, the completed refrain of which goes:
"La peinture à l'huile
C'est bien difficile
Mais c'est bien plus beau
Que la peinture à l'eau")
231 Archives of the Wildenstein Institute, Paris
232 Camoin archives, Paris
233 Marcelle Marquet, *Marquet. Voyages*, 50
234 Archives of the Wildenstein Institute, Paris
235 Marcelle Marquet, *Marquet. Voyages*, 50
236 J.L., *Les lettres. Entretien avec Marcelle Marty*, in *Beaux-Arts* (December 16, 1938), 1
237 S. Desnoyer, *Desnoyer et ses amis* (Montfermeil: Jacques Renaud, Editions Recherche et expression, 1977), 94
238 Marcelle Marquet, *Marquet. Voyages*, 58
239 S. Desnoyer, *Desnoyer et ses amis*, 94
240 Archives of the Svensk-Franska Konstgalleriet – Galerie Bonnier, Geneva, Switzerland
241 Camoin archives, Paris
242 Archives of the Musée des Beaux-Arts de Bordeaux, France
243 A. André – G. Besson archives, France
244 Ibid
245 Claudine Grammont, *Correspondance entre Charles Camoin et Henri Matisse*, 136
246 A. André – G. Besson archives, France
247 Matisse Heirs archives, Paris
248 A. André – G. Besson archives, France
249 Archives of the Wildenstein Institute, Paris
250 Matisse Heirs archives, Paris
251 Archives of the Wildenstein Institute, Paris
252 Matisse Heirs archives, Paris
253 A. André – G. Besson archives, France
254 Matisse Heirs archives, Paris
255 Archives of the Wildenstein Institute, Paris
256 Matisse Heirs archives, Paris
257 Archives of the Wildenstein Institute, Paris
258 *L'Echo d'Alger*, (November 8 to 18, 1942)
259 Claudine Grammont, *Correspondance entre Charles Camoin et Henri Matisse*, 187–188
260 According to André Hambourg
261 Information supplied by André Assus, the painter's son
262 *L'Echo d'Alger*, (July 3, 1943), 1
263 Archives of the Wildenstein Institute, Paris
264 G. Besson, *Marquet. Dessins* in *Le Point* (December 1943)
265 Archives of the Musée Mainssieux, Voiron, France.
266 Archives of the Wildenstein Institute, Paris
267 Matisse Heirs archives, Paris
268 A. André – G. Besson archives, France
269 Archives of the Wildenstein Institute, Paris
270 A. André – G. Besson archives, France
271 *L'Echo d'Alger*, (January 30, 1945), 2
272 Matisse Heirs archives, Paris
273 Archives of the Wildenstein Institute, Paris
274 Matisse Heirs archives, Paris
275 A. André – G. Besson archives, France
276 Matisse Heirs archives, Paris
277 Archives of the Wildenstein Institute, Paris
278 Archives of the Musée des Beaux-Arts de Bordeaux, France
279 *Hommage à Albert Marquet* in *Arts* (January 18, 1946)
280 A. André – G. Besson archives, France
281 Camoin archives, Paris
282 A. André – G. Besson archives, France
283 S. Desnoyer, *Desnoyer et ses amis*, 140
284 Claudine Grammont, *Correspondance entre Charles Camoin et Henri Matisse*, 219
285 Archives of the Musée des Beaux-Arts de Bordeaux, France
286 Matisse Heirs archives, Paris

Photography Credits

A. Loubry, Musée de Roubaix

Ch. Vignaud, Musées de Poitiers

Charles Choffet, Musée des Beaux-Arts et d'Archéologie de Besançon

Daniel Le Nevé, Musée d'art moderne de Troyes

Jacques Faujour, Photo Cnac/Mnam Dist.RMN, Collection Centre Georges Pompidou, Musée national d'art moderne, Paris.

Jean-Claude Planchet, Photo Cnac/Mnam Dist.RMN, Collection Centre Georges Pompidou, Musée national d'art moderne, Paris.

Lysiane Gauthier, Musée des Beaux-Arts de Bordeaux

Philippe Migeat, Photo Cnac/Mnam Dist.RMN, Collection Centre Georges Pompidou, Musée national d'art moderne, Paris.

P.S. Azema, Musée de l'Annonciade, Saint-Tropez

L. Aubert, Musée du Château de Montbéliard

Frédéric Jaulmes, Musée Fabre, Montpellier

Acknowledgement of lenders

This exhibition was made possible through the kind cooperation of the following:

Bagnols-sur-Cèze, Musée Albert-André
Alain Girard, conservateur départemental en chef des musées du Gard

Besançon, Musée des Beaux-Arts et d'Archéologie
Marie-Hélène Lavallée, conservateur en chef du Patrimoine, directeur des musées de Besançon
Françoise Soulier-François, conservateur

Bordeaux, Musée des Beaux-Arts
Francis Ribemont, conservateur en chef, directeur des musées de Bordeaux
Dominique Cante, conservateur

Les Sables-d'Olonne, Musée de l'Abbaye Sainte-Croix
Benoît Decron, conservateur

Montbéliard, Musée du Château
Bernard Fauchille, conservateur

Poitiers, Musée Sainte-Croix
Philippe Bata, conservateur

Roubaix, Musée d'art et d'industrie
Bruno Gaudichon, conservateur en chef

Saint-Tropez, Musée de l'Annonciade
Jean-Paul Monery, conservateur

Troyes, Musée d'art moderne
Philippe Chabert, conservateur en chef

Koffi Annan, Secrétaire Général de l'Organisation des Nations Unies, New-York
Jean-David Levitte, Ambassadeur de France, Mission Permanente de la France auprès des Nations Unies
Jean-Charles Bou, Secrétaire Général de la Mission Permanente de la France auprès des Nations Unies

Denis Conus, chef du service de l'administration et de la conservation des résidences présidentielles
Laurence Reculet

Claude Martin, Ambassadeur de France en Allemagne
Laurent Lebé, intendant de l'ambassade de France en Allemagne

Jean-Georges Lavit, conservateur en chef du Patrimoine, Directeur de la Mission du Patrimoine du Ministère des Affaires Etrangères

Patrick Roger, services du Premier Ministre

Michèle Paret et Nicole Castais, documentalistes au Wildenstein Institute, chargées du catalogue raisonné Albert Marquet
Elisabeth Spain, documentaliste au Wildenstein Institute